AMERICA

AND THE

WORLD

ZBIGNIEW BRZEZINSKI

AMERICA

AND THE

WORLD

NEW AMERICA
FOUNDATION

BRENT
SCOWCROFT

CONVERSATIONS

on the FUTURE

of AMERICAN

FOREIGN POLICY

BASIC
BOOKS

A MEMBER OF THE PERSEUS BOOKS GROUP

NEW YORK

DESIGN BY JANE RAESE
Text set in 12-point Adobe Caslon

Cataloging-in-Publication Data is available from the Library of Congress
ISBN 978-0-465-01501-6

1 3 5 7 9 10 8 6 4 2

CONTENTS

INTRODUCTION

THIS BOOK IS AN INVITATION to join a conversation with two of the wisest observers of American foreign policy, Zbigniew Brzezinski and Brent Scowcroft. Over many mornings and afternoons in the spring of 2008, they sat down together to talk through our country's current problems—and to look for solutions. The result is an intellectual journey, led by two of the nation's best guides, into the world of choices the next president will confront.

As readers turn the pages of this book, they should imagine themselves sitting around a big conference table in an office building overlooking Pennsylvania Avenue. A few blocks up the street is the White House, where these two men managed the nation's statecraft in their years as national security advisor. They arrive for each session immaculately dressed, as if heading for the Oval Office to brief the president. We start each conversation with a big cup of coffee or maybe a diet soda—and sometimes a jolt of sugar from some cookies or cake brought from home—and then we turn on the tape recorder.

I invite you to listen in as two of America's most clear-sighted practitioners of foreign policy think about the future.

The starting point for these conversations was their belief that the world is changing in fundamental ways, and that our traditional models for understanding America's role don't work very well. Both men believe the United States is in some difficulty abroad because it hasn't yet adapted to these new realities. Both question conventional wisdom and received ideas—and try to view the world with fresh eyes. Both are fundamentally optimistic about America's future, as you will see, but only if the country can rise to the challenge of dealing with the world as it now is, not as we wish it to be.

This book was an experiment to see if a prominent Democrat and a prominent Republican—speaking only for themselves and not for or against either party—could find common ground for a new start in foreign policy. Brzezinski and Scowcroft had special standing for this exercise, since each was a prescient early skeptic about the war in Iraq. They understood before most other foreign policy analysts the dangers and difficulties the United States would face if it toppled Saddam Hussein, and they courageously decided to speak out publicly with their concerns. For that reason alone, we should listen carefully to what they have to say now. Although they differ on some particulars—especially the speed with which America can safely withdraw from Iraq—I found that in each session, they were converging toward a shared framework.

I came to the pleasurable task of moderating these conversations as a journalist who has been writing about foreign policy issues for more than thirty years. The effort to find common ground is one I believe in. In my columns for the *Washington Post*, I try to write from the center of the debate: I listen to what people have to say, I provoke them when that's needed, and I try to pose the questions my readers would ask if they were present. That's what I have attempted to do here.

Brzezinski and Scowcroft were the quintessential cold warriors, and they describe in this book some of the secret history that led to the eventual fall of the Berlin Wall and the collapse of Soviet communism. But that world is gone, and you will find no triumphalism or nostalgia here. Instead, the two men worry that a cold war mindset persists among U.S. policymakers—and that it blinds us to the new balance of forces in the world. The theme that keeps returning through these pages is how much the world has changed since that war ended.

Each reader will sum up this conversation in a different way, but here are some common themes that I found as moderator: Brzezinski and Scowcroft start from national interest; they are foreign policy realists in that sense. But they believe the United States must engage a changing world rather than react defensively to it. Their goal is for America to align itself with these forces of change, wherever possible, rather than stand apart from them. Again and again, they speak of the need for flexibility, for openness, for a willingness to talk with friends and enemies alike.

Most of all, Brzezinski and Scowcroft want to restore a confident, forward-leaning America. They think the country has become too frightened in this age of terrorism, too hunkered down behind physical and intellectual walls. Each time they had to sign in with the guards in the lobby to get a security pass before our sessions, they laughed at the absurdity of our bunker mentality.

Their idea of a twenty-first century American superpower is a nation that reaches out to the world—not to preach, but to listen and cooperate and, where necessary, compel. Both men describe a political revolution that's sweeping the world—Brzezinski speaks of a global awakening, while Scowcroft describes a yearning for dignity. They want America on the side of that process of change.

During the decades of America's rise as the dominant global power, there was a tradition of bipartisan foreign policy. It was always a bit of a myth; political battles accompanied every major foreign policy decision of the twentieth century. But there was a tradition of common strategic dialogue—a process that brought together the nation's best minds and drew from them some basic guideposts about America and the world.

That process swept up a brilliant Harvard-trained professor born in Poland with a gift for speaking in perfect sentences and paragraphs, and an equally brilliant Air Force general from Utah who had the knack for expressing complex ideas in clear language. Brzezinski and Scowcroft accomplished great things during their time in the White House; after they left, they continued to travel and debate and, most of all, to think and observe.

This book brings the two men together for an extended discussion on the eve of the 2008 presidential election. Perhaps it can reanimate the tradition of strategic thinking that Zbig and Brent represent—and encourage a continuing bipartisan conversation about America's problems and how to solve them creatively.

David Ignatius

AMERICA

AND THE

WORLD

ONE

HOW WE GOT HERE

DAVID IGNATIUS: Let me begin by quoting something General George Marshall said: "Don't fight the problem." By that I've always thought he meant "understand the problem," describe it clearly to yourself, and then solve it. But don't fight what it is. So let me ask each of you to begin by describing the problem—the situation in which the United States finds itself as a new president is about to take office, the difficulties we have in a world that's changing, the nature of those changes. Zbig, give me your sense of the problem of the world today, what it looks like— and then we'll talk about what to do.

ZBIGNIEW BRZEZINSKI: I was struck the other day that the president, in his State of the Union message, said the war on terror is the defining ideological challenge of the century. And I said to myself, "Isn't that a little arrogant?" This is the year 2008, and here we are being told what the defining ideological challenge of the century is.

Suppose in 1908 we were asked to define the ideological challenge of the twentieth century. Would many people say right wing and left wing, red and brown totalitarianism? Or in 1808, the challenge of the nineteenth century, how many people would say on the eve of the Congress of Vienna, a conservative triumph, that the nineteenth century would be dominated by nationalist passions in Germany, France, Italy, Poland, and throughout much of Europe?

It's not going to be the war on terror that defines the ideological challenge of our century. It's something more elusive. I think it involves three grand changes.

One is what I call the global political awakening. For the first time, all of humanity is politically active. That's a very, very dramatic change. Second, there's a shift in the center of global power from the Atlantic world to the Far East. Not the collapse of the Atlantic world, but the loss of the domination it's had for five hundred years. And the third is the surfacing of common global problems that we have to address, lest we all suffer grievously. I mean climate and environment, but also poverty and injustice. These define the kind of challenges to which America will have to respond, and its survival and its place in the world will depend on the degree to which it responds well.

IGNATIUS: Zbig, just to complete that thought, what in our ability to deal with those changes today has broken?

BRZEZINSKI: If I had to reduce it to one factor, I would say it is the loss of American confidence. My experience as an adult has been wrapped up in a big global struggle, the cold war. But we waged it with confidence. What I find dismaying these days is this culture of fear that one encounters everywhere.

It's wrapped up with the shock of 9/11, clearly. The fact that the whole country watched it on television shook American confidence. And sad to say, I think fear has also been propagated. That has not been helpful. The kind of issues we have to address are not going to be addressed well if the country is driven by fear.

IGNATIUS: Brent, how would you lead off in assessing the nature of our problem? What's broken in our ability to respond?

BRENT SCOWCROFT: I look at the world in much the same way Zbig does. But let me start from a more historical background. I think the end of the cold war marked a historical discontinuity in the world environment.

The cold war was an intense concentration on a single problem. It mobilized us. It mobilized our friends and allies against a single bloc. It affected our thought processes. It affected our institutions, everything we did. I don't know if there's ever been a time we were more concentrated.

And suddenly, historically in the blink of an eye, that world came to an end, and it was replaced by a world without the existential threat of the cold war. If we made a mistake, we might blow up the planet—that was gone. Instead there were one hundred pinprick problems. Instead of looking through one end of the telescope, at Moscow, we were looking through the other end at this myriad of little problems. And we were dealing with them with thought processes and institutions geared for that one end of the telescope.

IGNATIUS: What was it like to sit in the White House in a world where the great fear was nuclear annihilation? You've sat, each of you, as national security advisor in a unique place. What did it feel like, in the bad moments sitting in that chair, when the world was on the knife edge? Brent?

SCOWCROFT: There was the ever-present thought that if either side made a serious mistake, it could be catastrophic for humanity. Did we spend all our waking moments thinking about that? No. But it was a combination of that and a struggle to understand what the Soviets were up to, and what was their capability of, for example, a technological development that could suddenly make us vulnerable, and change this standoff to an asymmetry.

To me that pervaded everything. When we looked at conflicts, whether it was Korea, Vietnam, all the little pinpricks, it was, "How can we show the Soviets that they can't get away with anything, without running foolish risks of getting involved in a situation neither of us could back out of?"

IGNATIUS: It sounds like there was a fear that any vulnerability anywhere might become a general vulnerability everywhere. That was part of the cold war mentality that we've carried on, perhaps, to our new circumstances. Zbig, what did it feel like for you to be in the cockpit?

BRZEZINSKI: Well, one of my jobs was to coordinate the president's response in the event of a nuclear attack. I assume Brent that was your job too, right? I'm not revealing any secrets, but it was something like this:

We would have initial warning of an attack within one minute of a large-scale launch by the Soviet Union. Roughly by the second minute we'd have a pretty good notion of the scale and the likely targets. By the third minute, we would know more or less when to anticipate impact and so forth. Also by the third minute, the president would be alerted that we have this information. Between the third and seventh minutes, the president then decides how to respond.

It begins to get complicated immediately. If it's an all-out attack, the response is presumably easier. You just react in total. But suppose it's a more selective attack. There are choices to be made. The president is supposed to weigh the options. How will he react? There's an element of uncertainty here. In any case, the process is to be completed roughly by the seventh minute. By which time—I assume this was roughly the same with you guys, right?

SCOWCROFT: So far, uh-huh.

BRZEZINSKI: By the seventh minute, the order to execute had to be transmitted and whatever was decided had to be carried out. This is not entirely theoretical because we once had a small snafu, in the course of which I was woken up at night and told that the strategic command was alerted. It turned out to be an exercise that got somehow or other misconstrued as the real thing that very early on was caught. No big deal.

Roughly by the twenty-eighth minute, there's impact. That is to say, you and your family are dead. Washington's gone. A lot of our military assets are destroyed. But presumably, the president has in the meantime made the decision how to respond. We're already firing back. Six hours later, one hundred fifty million Americans and Soviets are dead.

That is the reality we lived with. And we did everything we could to make it as stable, as subject to rational control, as possible. To be nonprovocative but also to be very alert and determined so that no one on the other side could think they could pull it off and survive.

It's very different now. I think Brent has described it very well— one hundred pinpricks. The new reality is a kind of dispersed turbulence. And that requires, I think, a different mindset, a more sophisticated understanding of the complexity of global change. We need a stewardship based on an intelligent society that understands its responsibilities and is not terrorized into rash decisions demagogically justified, which can isolate us in the world and make us very vulnerable.

▶ ▶ ▶

IGNATIUS: Brent, when the cold war was over, all of a sudden for those of us who had lived through it—it's gone! It was understandable for a time that foreign policy became an optional enterprise because it didn't really matter anymore. And that led to a lot of drift—

SCOWCROFT: And the wake-up call was 9/11.

IGNATIUS: Let me ask you to remember the day the world changed, when the world you'd grown up with and that you and your generation had mastered became a different world. I'm going to say that was the day the Berlin Wall came down, and we realized that the Soviet empire was cracking, probably beyond repair. Brent, you were in the White House. Describe what you can of that day when this long, deadly struggle began to end.

SCOWCROFT: Well, at the time, I would not have said the collapse of the Wall was that day. To me that day was when Jim Baker and Eduard Shevardnadze stood up together and denounced the Iraqi invasion of Kuwait. That, to me, is when the cold war truly ended. Were the Soviets badly wounded at the fall of the Wall? Was the empire crumbling? Yes.

But looking ahead at the time, it wasn't that clear what the outcome would be. Gorbachev was trying to put together a confederation to replace the old Soviet Union. He was trying to revise the structure, not destroy it. So it was still murky there. Did we feel good? Of course. But at that time, when the Wall came down, what

6

the president felt, and I felt, was "don't gloat." If it is the end of the cold war, let's not do World War I over again—victors, vanquished. Instead, everybody wins. We win; the Soviet Union wins. The president, when the Wall was first breached in Berlin, called the press into his office. And Lesley Stahl said, Mr. President, you don't seem very elated. I would think you would want to be dancing on the Wall. And he said, well, I'm not that kind of a person. What he was really saying was, I don't want to gloat. Because the reaction in Moscow may destroy what we're trying to do.

IGNATIUS: That's very sensible. But honestly now, didn't you want to dance on the Wall? Zbig, what are your memories of the end of the cold war? You spent your whole life fighting it.

BRZEZINSKI: Well, first of all, I think President Bush and Brent handled it in a really intelligent and sophisticated way. That was truly masterful. To me, the moment of greatest fulfillment was not the fall of the Wall. Most of my mature life was spent on strategizing how to undermine the Soviet bloc. And I had a whole theory of how to do it, a concept which goes back to the 1960s. My thesis was that we could undermine the partition of Europe by peaceful engagement that penetrates the Soviet bloc and undermines it so that it fragments. The collapse of the Wall was the fulfillment of that expectation.

But the culminating moment for me, of really deep personal satisfaction, came on December 25th, 1991, when the red flag was lowered over the Kremlin and the Soviet Union fell apart. At that moment I knew that something even more important than the loss of the Soviet bloc had taken place, namely that the last large territorial empire was now fragmenting, probably forever.

That was when Gorbachev was forced to resign by Yeltsin, helped by President Kravchuk of Ukraine, independent for only about three weeks. And President Shushkevich of Byelorussia [Belarus], a very tiny, weak little portion of the former Soviet Union, agreed together to dismantle the Soviet Union.

SCOWCROFT: That was a very poignant moment. Because on Christmas day in 1991, Gorbachev called President Bush and said, this is my last phone call. The flag is coming down over the Kremlin, the Soviet flag. I'm resigning my office. The Soviet Union is now history. And my first thought was Yeltsin won.

BRZEZINSKI: Yeah, that's right. That comes back to me now. Yeltsin phoned Bush, then he phoned Gorbachev and told him he had already spoken to Bush. And Gorbachev got very angry. "You spoke first to Bush rather than to me?"

SCOWCROFT: Zbig makes another point about the end of the Soviet Union. The end of the cold war also was the final end of World War I. World War I resulted in a whole series of consequences, among which were communism and fascism, those social movements to reorder society that racked the world. It also marked the end of the world's great empires. Two of them collapsed at the end of World War I: the Ottoman Empire and the Austro-Hungarian. And the last to go was the Soviet. This current axis of turmoil running from the Balkans up through central Asia is also the territory of the last of the world's empires.

IGNATIUS: Well, let's talk about how we progressed from that moment. You mentioned that red flag coming down and the "Empire of Evil" ending. How did we get from there to where we are now, from that moment of ultimate triumph to a moment in which Americans feel very vulnerable? There's a sense of the eclipse of

American power, of a world of difficulty. In that period after the cold war ended, what were the missed opportunities?

BRZEZINSKI: Well, there were missed opportunities and some misconceived actions. The missed opportunities may have involved not taking advantage of the strikingly successful U.S. operation to push Saddam Hussein out of Kuwait, in order to push the Israeli-Palestinian peace treaty.

President Bush, at that time, really stood astride the world in a way that was unprecedented historically. Brent knows more about this than I do. I suspect President Bush expected to be reelected and probably would have tackled that subject later. He did confront Shamir, thereby giving a signal that the United States would be very clear-cut in the definition of its objectives. But politics intervened, and there wasn't an opportunity.

The other missed opportunity pertains to the Clinton years and the post-Soviet space. I'm not sure that we could have sucked the new Russian Federation into a more constructive relationship with the West, and there were limits of what we could do because we had unfinished business also to take care of. Which, in a way, collided with objectives such as stabilizing central Europe, leaving it a no-man's-space between the EU and NATO, and the new Russia.

But we could have perhaps done more to create some sort of shared institutions in which the Russians would feel more a part of the major European adventure that is so important globally today. But all of that pales in comparison to the fatal misjudgment in how we reacted to 9/11.

IGNATIUS: We'll get to 9/11 in a moment. I don't want to rush us there. I do want to ask you, Zbig, because you have a history of being a hard-liner toward the Soviet Union, whether you think we took advantage of Russian weakness in the 1990s in a way that's ended up hurting us.

BRZEZINSKI: Well, I'm not saying what else we could have done. We couldn't have stopped the Baltic states' efforts to regain independence. We couldn't have prevented the Czechs and the Poles and the Hungarians from wanting to be part of the Western world. If we had kept them out, they would today be a no-man's-land, probably the object of serious frictions with the Russians.

Look at problems that the Georgians and the Ukrainians, and even the Estonians have had with the Russians lately. Creating stability and clarity in that part of Europe was, I think, the first strategic objective of the West. Whether that could have been accompanied by some superstructure that would entice the Russians to have a greater sense of participation in the West is a question to which I don't have an answer.

IGNATIUS: Certainly Russians remember that time as a great national humiliation. They talk about Boris Yeltsin as a shameful symbol of their country's pathetic, drunken, feeble state at the time. Brent, Zbig said something that fascinated me in asking what President George H. W. Bush would have done had he had a second term as president. That's something I haven't pondered. Just talk a little bit about that.

SCOWCROFT: Well—yes. Let me say a word first about the Baltic states in the last days of the Soviet Union. That was probably the most sensitive issue between us and the Soviet Union as Eastern Europe started to break away. They were a part of the Soviet Union and yet we had never recognized their incorporation into the Soviet Union, so it was emotional on both sides.

We had strong Baltic lobbies in the United States urging us to declare the independence of the Baltic states. And there were uprisings there and other turmoil. It was very, very delicate. What we succeeded in doing was, rather than force the Soviet Union out of the Baltics, we got them in a position where they themselves recognized the independence of the Baltic states. Now, in the sweep of history, it doesn't matter. But we spent a lot of time on that particular problem.

But as to your general question, we would have followed up the First Gulf War with a move to the Palestinian peace process. One of the things we wanted to demonstrate to the Arab world was that we were prepared to extend our aid to the Arabs in times of stress just as we were to the Israelis. And that unprovoked aggression would meet with our response.

When Saddam kept saying, let's have a general peace process, we said, no, not now. You get out of Kuwait first. And we promised the Arabs that we would turn to the peace process after Kuwait. We ended up with the Conference of Madrid, which was step one. Had the president been reelected that would've been a primary goal of his foreign policy.

IGNATIUS: Would you have gone back to the problem of Saddam in Iraq?

SCOWCROFT: You mean then?

IGNATIUS: I mean would you have allowed Saddam to remain in power? Was that unfinished business that you would've gone back to in a second term?

SCOWCROFT: No, no. That was not unfinished business. We early on decided it was not up to us to drive him from power. And, as you know, in much of foreign policy you never have a complete success.

What we did, though, is leave an Iraq with a Saddam who was still there, with still the same ambitions, but without the capability to achieve them. His army had been crippled, and the sanctions kept him from rebuilding it. He was not a threat at the time of the Second Gulf War. He was still a nasty piece of work, there's no question about that, but he was not a threat in a strategic sense. I think our policy was a success, and I would not do differently in hindsight.

IGNATIUS: Without asking you, Brent, to specifically criticize the current President Bush, I would ask you to explain why you or the first President Bush decided it did not make sense for the United States to go on to Baghdad in 1991, and take Saddam down. Why did you not do that?

SCOWCROFT: There were three reasons. First of all, our coalition, which was significantly Arab, would have split up. The Arabs were not about to march into Iraqi territory.

Secondly, we had a UN mandate to liberate Kuwait. One of the things we were trying to do in all of our actions at this time was to set up patterns of behavior for a post–cold war world to deal with these cases of aggression. If the UN could now operate the Security Council as its framers had designed it, to deal with cases of aggression, then we wanted to make sure we didn't say, "Well, yeah, the Security Council, fine—but we'll go a little farther on our own." That would've destroyed the world we were trying to build.

But finally, and most fundamentally, we knew how to do what we were planning to do. We knew exactly how to get Saddam out of Kuwait. We knew how much force it would take and how to use it. We could've gone to Baghdad almost unopposed. But it would've changed the whole character of the conflict into one where we were occupiers in a hostile land. Our troops would've been subjected to guerilla activity. And we had no strategy for getting out. And that was a situation which I thought would be a disaster to get into.

IGNATIUS: What was your own advice to the president at that time?

SCOWCROFT: Stop. Once we had driven him out of Kuwait—stop.

▶ ▶ ▶

IGNATIUS: So let's stand back and look at how we got to where we are now, in 2008. We had this enormous success of the red flag coming down, triumph in the First Gulf War, and a world that everyone described as a world of one superpower, of unchallenged American military power and authority.

What did that breed in the world of Washington and the minds of policy makers? In what way did it engender attitudes that led us to our present difficulty? Brent, do you think it created a kind of arrogance, an assumption that we could easily have our way?

SCOWCROFT: Yes, I think it did. I think the first thought was this enormous sense of relief—foreign policy didn't matter much anymore. Secondly, we looked around and, compared to anyone else in the world, we were the only superpower. Not since at least the Roman Empire had anyone had this much disparity in power. That was pretty heady stuff.

Of course, what we forgot is we weren't very used to running the world. For most of our history, we sat behind our two oceans, secure, deciding whether we wanted to participate, and if so, how. It was a choice. The Europeans set the framework for strategy, and we decided who to join. Now all of a sudden they're all gone, and we're out there. So yes, we have this power, but we were not used to exercising it on behalf of the world community.

And on top of it all, we were still mired in the thinking of the cold war, and all of our institutions were designed for the cold war.

IGNATIUS: How were we mired? What was that mind-set?

SCOWCROFT: Besides the end of the cold war, the end of World War I, and the end of empires, there were new forces at work. Zbig alluded to them earlier. Our unparalleled power, changes in the nature of war, and most importantly, globalization. One of the things globalization meant, as Zbig alluded to, was the politicization of the world's people.

For most of mankind's past, the average person knew what was going on in his own village and maybe the next village, but not much farther—and he didn't care much. He was not personally involved in battles of empire. Now, almost everyone is aware of most everything that happens in the world. Reaction is inevitable—sometimes strong. That's a new dimension that we haven't begun to understand how to deal with, and the war on terror is only one of its manifestations.

These things were already going on. They didn't start with the end of the cold war. But they were masked by the cold war.

And when the cold war ended, all of a sudden, here they are. I think for a time, we were confused, befuddled. We didn't know what was going on and we didn't think it mattered much. So there was no great urge to develop a strategy in the nineties, because first of all, it would've been very hard, because all of this stuff was changing. But secondly, we didn't think we really needed one.

IGNATIUS: One thing that was happening in the 1990s that we didn't pay much attention to was the rise of a very tall, savvy, wealthy son of a prominent businessman who was, without our really understanding it, declaring war on us. Let me ask each of you: during the nineties, how much attention did you pay to the name Osama bin Laden? Zbig, do you remember focusing on that at all in the mid-nineties?

BRZEZINSKI: No. And the reasons were quite obvious. He wasn't all that important until he accomplished something terribly important. He was one of a number of plotters, fanatically committed to his notion of righteousness, increasingly alienated from the United States, viewing America as a monster that was challenging the very core of his beliefs.

But I would like to go back to what Brent was saying and add that to me, the nineties represent a nurturing period of a posture of self-indulgence and then of extreme arrogance on the part of the United States. Which, after 9/11, led the United States to embark on a course of actions that have been profoundly self-defeating, and in many respects demoralizing.

This self-indulgence fed a sense that, in fact, history had stopped and that we were at the climax of some sort of historical process.

SCOWCROFT: The end of history.

BRZEZINSKI: The end of history, precisely. And that essentially we could sit back and enjoy this new imperial status that was bestowed on us on December 25th, 1991. The arrogance was the thought that we could now define the rules of the game in an international system that was still somewhat interdependent, in spite of our overwhelming power, and that these new rules would permit us to decide when to start wars, how to start wars, how to preempt wars and prevent them. And which then found application after 9/11. And I think our reactions, sad to say, have made 9/11 into at least a tactical triumph for Osama Bin Laden—which it wouldn't have been but for our reactions.

9/11 was a crime. It was terrible. It was all the more damaging because so many Americans watched it in real time and were part of it and suffered with those who are—

SCOWCROFT: Over and over.

BRZEZINSKI: —suffering. Over and over again.

But I think, here I risk sounding partisan, I think that the way we then reacted pushed us into actions that have embroiled us on a very wide front in that part of the world to which Brent was referring earlier. You can draw it by two intersecting lines, one from west to east going from the Sinai to India and China, and one from north to south, from Russia's southern frontier down to the Indian Ocean. And then if you draw a circle around that, there's about six hundred million people there. It's a very troubled area, full of ethnic, religious, territorial, and social conflicts.

And we have now become deeply engaged in it to the extent that we find ourselves stressed financially. The costs are unbelievable. Our armed forces are strained. Every day we hear more and more reports of the vulnerabilities of our military.

Our legitimacy and our credibility have been badly damaged. And all of that essentially accrues to the importance of what Osama did and the way it was galvanized into a national hysteria in which the country actually endorsed the policies that have produced these negative results. These policies were endorsed. They were also endorsed by most Democrats, including some who in the year 2008 are running for president.

I think that was a dramatic, tragic, and avoidable turning point in our history—which can still be redeemed. And this is what Brent and I are talking about. How to redeem it.

▶ ▶ ▶

IGNATIUS: That's our subject. Brent, why don't you pick up the thread there. If you remember where you were on 9/11, maybe that's a starting point.

SCOWCROFT: I certainly remember where I was on 9/11. I was the chairman of a Department of Defense review called the "End to End Review," which was to look at nuclear weapons and their command and control from their inception in the laboratories through production, through deployment and employment, to dismantlement. On the morning of 9/11, we were going to fly in one of the president's flying command posts out to Offutt Air Force Base. We were sitting at Andrews waiting to take off when the first plane hit the Trade Towers. We thought it was an accident.

We were in the air when the second one hit. And I had a chance to watch our command and control operations in action, with the president in Florida, the vice president in the White House command post. It was not a pretty picture. So I had a sort of reserved seat at 9/11.

IGNATIUS: That's so haunting because there you are thinking about end-to-end use of nuclear weapons when Muslim fighters armed with box cutters have figured out they can fly an airplane loaded with jet fuel into a building and take it down. Let me ask you: 9/11 knocked the American gyroscope sharply off balance. It was a big shock. But they say that a gyroscope will come back to its center point if it's spinning fast enough. You can give a gyroscope quite a whack, but it comes back upright if it's spinning. It seems to me that our gyroscope has wobbled further and further away from that center point rather than coming back. And I wonder if you think that's true—and if so, why?

SCOWCROFT: That's an interesting example. It was knocked off, no question about it. Things like wars don't happen in the United States. We fight them, but we fight them somewhere else. And I think it was a real traumatic shock to the American people.

Now, what I suspect happened was that that shock came together with this great sense of superiority we had developed as the only standing superpower. We said, we have all this power. While we have it, we should use it to remake the world, starting with the Middle East, this very troubled area. And that is basically what led us down this path. It was to take advantage of our power, to realize how things had deteriorated since the end of the cold war. 9/11 was a huge surprise. The world was going bad rapidly. We had to do something. We had the power to do it by ourselves. We didn't have time to consult our friends and allies. We could do it alone.

IGNATIUS: Zbig, what do you think?

BRZEZINSKI: I remember that after 9/11, NATO convened and unanimously voted to invoke Article 5 on our behalf, for the first time ever. And we in effect said, "No, thanks." I've often asked myself, "What would've happened if we had played it differently? If we had, of course, condemned 9/11 the way it should be condemned, and the president did condemn it—and if we had then accepted that act of solidarity by our allies and used it as a point of departure for doing what had to be done in Afghanistan.

We overthrew the Taliban regime, which itself was actually not conspiring against us. It was a vicious, fundamentalist, retrogressive regime but oriented towards itself. But it had this perverse code of honor in that it had to protect those to whom it offered hospitality, namely Al-Qaeda, and therefore became objectively a partner in Al-Qaeda's crime.

So we were justified in overthrowing it and in crippling Al-

Qaeda—although unfortunately we didn't carry this to its logical conclusion. Suppose we had stopped there and stuck to that, suppose we hadn't created this atmosphere of fear and suspicion and, I'm sorry to say, deception regarding Iraq and Saddam.

If, instead, we had persisted in seeking to find some sort of a solution to the Israeli-Palestinian conflict which would eliminate it as a major source of anti-Americanism among the Arabs in the Middle East, perhaps it would not provide such fertile soil for the kind of people Osama Bin Laden sent here to attack us. Suppose we had taken that course together with our allies. I think we would have been infinitely better off.

IGNATIUS: Brent, Zbig used the word *deception* in talking about the way in which the threat from Iraq was painted in the months after 9/11. Do you think that's harsh?

SCOWCROFT: It depends who you're talking about. I think the intelligence community made a mistake—which is deadly for intelligence, but we forget how easy it is to do. The mistake was that they never asked themselves the question: If Saddam didn't have weapons of mass destruction, why was he behaving the way he was? In retrospect it was quite clear. He was afraid of his neighbors, afraid of his own people.

BRZEZINSKI: He was bluffing.

SCOWCROFT: And it made great sense. But we knew that he had chemical weapons. He had used them against the Kurds. We knew he had been trying to develop nuclear weapons. And he was a little farther along, we found in '91, than we thought. So we were worried.

But we never asked ourselves *that* question. So we operated on assumption. All these ambiguous signals we saw, we interpreted in a consistent way, which turned out to be wrong. Did some people know it was wrong? Probably. I don't know. I myself thought that there was no reason to believe he had nuclear weapons in 2002. But I didn't know.

IGNATIUS: You each famously had the courage and foresight to speak out before the Iraq War and warn that it was a mistake. You're very unusual in the foreign policy community in that you were willing to give up your seat at the table of tough-minded national security experts by saying, "This is unwise for the United States." It's very important, as a baseline, for people to understand why you made that judgment when you did, when so many others felt differently. So let me ask each of you to explain why you spoke out, and what your convictions were.

BRZEZINSKI: I have been increasingly worried over the last two decades that we may be drawn into a kind of vortex in that part of the world—and that we will become the solitary player, relying largely on force somehow or other to structure what cannot be structured by force. To try to do it on the cheap, and to end up doing it in the manner that becomes increasingly, prohibitively costly for us.

I did not have a special case to plead on behalf of Saddam. I even said before the invasion that if we could get the entire international community to cooperate in it, I would have no problem with it. Because then we would be in a sense repeating what Brent and his boss did a decade or so earlier.

What I was very concerned about was this notion that we were embarking on the basis of false information or false judgments into an adventure, the end of which is hard to anticipate. Which five years later still imposes on us prohibitive costs, objectively, subjectively, financially, economically, morally. Whatever you can cite. And which has the potential of becoming larger and larger.

I don't know what the future holds. But the situation's awfully volatile. I worry that there might be some incident that engages us with the Iranians, thereby enlarging the front from Iraq to Iran and Afghanistan. I'm afraid we may get sucked into something involving Pakistan, for perhaps very good reasons. That we may have to strike at Al-Qaeda and somehow get involved in Pakistani turmoil.

But I fear that we'll then be alone in that venture. Because our initial response was driven largely by this sense of arrogance, "We can do it on our own." And therefore we brushed off the Europeans and even said to them, "If you're not with us, you're against us"—a strange, Leninist phrase for the president to use. And as a consequence I do feel very strongly that 9/11 is not only a tactical success for Osama but a self-inflicted strategic wound for the United States.

IGNATIUS: Brent, when it came to the question of invading Iraq, you acted very courageously, in the personal sense, because you're so close to the Bush family. When you chose to speak out in your op-ed piece in the *Wall Street Journal*, that was an important event. What was going through your mind at that point? What were your fears about the consequences if we proceeded down this road?

SCOWCROFT: I was mostly worried about what I saw as an increasing rush to decision. I've already talked about nuclear weapons. Even if Saddam had a program, he was a long way from a weapon. We had plenty of time for that. The other was his role with Al-Qaeda and Osama Bin Laden. The accusations that he was supporting them seemed fundamentally counterintuitive to me. Osama

Bin Laden is a religious fanatic. Saddam Hussein was a secularist. The Ba'ath Party, I assumed, was anathema to Bin Laden. So I thought we needed to sort this out, and fundamentally I had the same view that I had in 1991, that going into Iraq was an easy adventure, but once we got there . . . This is a very troubled land that was not about to be turned into a democracy. That we had a huge problem if we went in.

Saddam, in fact, was quite well contained. And we had a big problem following 9/11 in dealing with this greater threat of terrorism. I thought going into Iraq would be fundamentally a diversion from our efforts to deal with terrorism. So my position was basically a plea: "Let's talk about this."

IGNATIUS: Slow down.

SCOWCROFT: Slow down because, you know, war rarely solves problems. War has a momentum of its own. Just the fact of making war creates a new environment, which may be favorable, may be unfavorable. But it's frequently different from what anyone can anticipate. Therefore, one shouldn't engage in it without a careful analysis of the consequences.

IGNATIUS: I wonder if part of the predicament we're now in is that we had just emerged from the world you both described, this cold war where you had to be very careful and we accommodated ourselves to living with and managing the status quo. And we decided after 9/11, in those months between September 11, 2001, and March 2003, that the status quo was killing us. The status quo had led to those airplanes flying into the Twin Towers. And we were going to go to the root and take it apart, starting with the worst of the worst, Saddam Hussein. Do you think it's fair to say that we changed from a status quo power into a transforming power?

SCOWCROFT: I think that's too broad. I think we became a transforming power after we were in Iraq. That's when all the democracy arguments came up. They didn't come up so much beforehand.

But I think different elements of the administration had different goals. The Neocon vision probably comes closest to what you described. The Neocons had the idea that Iraq was an ideal place in which to create both a democracy in the region and a launchpad from which to spread democracy throughout the Middle East. To the extent that the U.S. changed from being a status quo to a transforming power, I think it's rooted in this idea or strategic concept.

That's one element, but only one. There was what might be called a "coalition of attitudes." The Neocon group was central because it had this strategic concept. Then there was, I hypothesize, Rumsfeld and Cheney, who probably would be more accurately described as hard-nosed realists. It does appear as though they bought a lot of the strategic insights of the Neocons, but I honestly don't know why.

And then there was the president, who probably was neither a Neocon nor a hard-nosed realist but who was certainly profoundly shocked, even jolted, by 9/11. And even personally, that first day. As such, I have got to believe that he was very receptive to proposals for responses that were not only strong but also strategic or, if you will, transformative.

He was also very taken by Sharon and his prescriptions for what to do about the Israeli-Palestinian conflict in the aftermath of 9/11. And Sharon adopted Bush's own language about terror and terrorism. It became almost his evocative crime. Then there was the showdown precipitated by the Intifada in which the reaction by Sharon was very assertive, backed by the United States. The Intifada was, in a way, precipitated by Sharon when he went up on the Temple on the Mount—

BRZEZINSKI: And that then became the point of departure for a more explicit strategizing, how to remake the Middle East. And curiously, their strategy became a combination of the use of force and of democratizing slogans, in the notion that we'll somehow or other shake the cards and produce a new set. All of that embarked the United States on the precipitous course in which the military intervention of Iraq was part of a larger design. But a design which was vague conceptually and historically unfounded. It ignored entirely the fact that we were plunging headlong into a region which bitterly resents and remembers colonialism under the British. And we were now viewed as a new colonial intruder.

Our strategy in effect postulated that the only way to have stability in the Middle East is to destabilize it. That is to say, overthrow the existing regimes, create the grounds for democracy, and you will have the flowering of liberty. We know the fruits of that.

We insisted on elections among the Palestinians, which produced a victory for Hamas. We made a belated effort to move Egypt towards democracy, thereby probably increasing the viability of the Muslim Brotherhood there. It may emerge as a central political force in Egypt.

And we haven't achieved stability in the region, which I don't think is susceptible to imperial control by a country that is not prepared to pursue the imperial mission to the extreme at whatever cost. We are a kind of half-willing imperial force. We are willing to be an imperialist with one arm tied behind our back. And that's not going to work.

IGNATIUS: An imperialist until it gets tough.

SCOWCROFT: I think we're speculating. We don't know the answer to these questions. I think there was also a fundamental change in the attitude of the president after 9/11. A sort of religious fervor. But we're speculating on what the motivations were.

IGNATIUS: I would just offer one concluding footnote to this discussion. I was a correspondent covering the Middle East in 1982 when the Israelis tired of this terrible, nettlesome problem with Palestinian terror and decided to go all the way.

SCOWCROFT: To Beirut.

IGNATIUS: To go all the way to Beirut. They invaded Lebanon much as we invaded Iraq, trying to go to the heart of this problem. Finally deal with it. And they went in. They thought they had a clear plan. But it turned out they didn't have any clearer plan of how to get out than we did.

And you could argue that Israel still has not recovered in terms of security, strategically, from that roll of the dice. I find a haunting similarity between Sharon's ability to convince Menachem Begin, a quite careful man, to roll the dice in this way, send Israeli troops into Lebanon, and the way in which Bush's advisors convinced him to roll the dice and go into Iraq.

BRZEZINSKI: And that's related to the points we were talking about earlier. You cannot pursue a successful imperial policy in the postimperial age, in which the masses of the world are politically activated. Imperial policies worked because you could work within traditional societies. You could use relatively little force, which was more advanced, against not very united resistance. And you could manage.

Today, you are dealing with aroused, radicalized, sometimes fanatically driven populations, which resist. That's what the Israelis discovered in Lebanon. That's what we're discovering, painfully, in

Iraq. That's what I fear we may end up discovering elsewhere in that region.

SCOWCROFT: The Israelis have a mantra: They respond to force with disproportionate force. And that worked for a time. It doesn't work anymore.

▶ ▶ ▶

IGNATIUS: Well, then you have to stay on the ground with disproportionate force, which is precisely what we didn't do in Iraq. Let me move to a couple of other broad baseline themes. I'll introduce the first by recalling a name that is familiar to the two of you as one of the intellectual framers of the cold war period, and that's Herman Kahn, the great nuclear strategist at the Rand Corporation. Kahn observed in the 1960s that a bipolar world like the one we had in the cold war with the Soviet Union was fairly stable, and that a multipolar world, where you have many diffuse centers of power, would be fairly stable. But that the transition from the one to the other would not be stable and would be very difficult.

That observation has stayed with me. One thing that we haven't discussed yet is the rise of new poles of power. Most strikingly China, but also India and possibly Russia.

We're really looking at a much more complicated world. And the next president's going to have to consider, with all these different poles of power, how he should think about the power of the United States. So let me ask you to speak about that reality of this new world.

SCOWCROFT: Okay, I think this misses one thing, and that's the change in the world caused by globalization. It's no longer the old balance-of-power world of Herman Kahn or the Henry Kissinger world of multiple balances. It's something different. Globalization is eroding national boundaries everywhere. Importantly in information technology, but also in health and environment. Nations can no longer provide for their citizens what they traditionally used to.

When these forces spill over national borders, it makes weaker states even weaker. They are less able to control their territories, and that leaves them open to drug cartels, terrorists, and so on. They're less able to control and provide for their citizens, thus increasing domestic unrest.

What I'm saying is that the world is changing. And what we need to look at is how can we cooperate to get these problems under control, because we can't solve them by ourselves. I would say that the real force of globalization is akin to industrialization two hundred years ago. Industrialization really made the modern nation state; with these big industries you needed to regulate. You needed to control these new forces. That brought about the modern state.

Now globalization's having the same impact, but in the opposite direction.

It's reducing the ability of the nation state, and so the rise of China or India is not like it would have been one hundred years ago. It's a very different kind of world. I would say that we may have seen the end of interstate warfare as a form of conflict resolution for maybe a generation. Instead there are going to be these messy conflicts where, if the great powers participate, they participate through proxies or maybe even together. Describing the world in terms of poles is going to be less and less descriptive. Not only of the way the world is, but of how we need to behave to accomplish our ends.

IGNATIUS: Zbig, you're one of the founders of the idea of the Trilateral Commission. Of these different—poles, if you will, and how to make them cooperate and collaborate. What's your feeling about it? And we do have a world in which we have, you know, ascendant powers. The China that we'll see through the rest of our lifetimes is going to be a world-changing force. At least most of us think so.

BRZEZINSKI: Well, that's certainly true. We have to face the fact that the global system as it now exists was shaped largely between 1945 and 1950, when there were entirely different power realities. So the first order of business is to adjust the existing global institutions to these new realities, which involve the rise of powers like China, India, Japan, with Indonesia on the horizon. Plus the reality that in the background are these volatile, restless, politically awakened masses that continue to put more and more pressure on the system and lead to the kind of threats that Brent was just talking about: the possibility of diversified conflicts spurting all over the place the way sometimes a forest fire spreads and then leaps over boundaries because of winds.

In that kind of world, the premium will have to be put on effective political management of that complex reality. And that I think is going to be very difficult for a mass democracy like America to effectively pursue, in part because our public is woefully uninformed about the implications of these new realities—kind of parochially ignorant. And our diplomacy and our leadership in recent years have not been inclined to engage in the kind of consensual assumption of responsibility that this new age requires. Look at the hesitations, the zig-zagging on climate control and the global environment. Or on the issues of poverty and inequality. I think we're entering a period in which complexity is going to be the biggest challenge.

IGNATIUS: Brent, do you share that?

SCOWCROFT: Oh, I do very much. And to me, it's a world that cries out for what we don't have: mechanisms to deal with it. And you say, well, international organizations. The UN. But the UN is a very weak instrument. It was built for a very different world. I think if we didn't have a UN already, we could not create one in the world of today.

IGNATIUS: Why? Because people would be too fractious?

SCOWCROFT: Yes.

IGNATIUS: Zbig, do you agree?

BRZEZINSKI: Yes.

SCOWCROFT: And there's a new thing. In the UN right now, for example, there's a sense of the—let's call it the developing world. That the UN is run by and for the benefit of the developed world. And since the developing world controls the budget and personnel, they're going to keep it from changing—as happened two years ago when Kofi Annan tried to reform the UN to make it more effective. (Of course, the United States was a primary culprit, submitting, I think, over seven hundred amendments to his proposal days before it was to be submitted.) Anyway, many of the mechanisms we have are out of date, and it's very hard to create new ones. So we're floundering.

IGNATIUS: I have sat in Tehran at a press conference with President Ahmadinejad and heard him say to an Iranian audience, the United Nations was created by the falling powers. The United States and the Allied Powers of 1945. The United Nations is illegitimate today. We need new organizations that represent the rising powers. Us, China. So that idea is certainly out there in the world.

SCOWCROFT: You can go farther. If you look at all of our institutions, many are outdated. Start with the Defense Department. We're better able to fight World War II than we ever were before. The CIA was built and organized on a single target, the Soviet Union. It's struggling now about how best to cope with a completely different world.

NATO is now in Afghanistan, but NATO was not developed for anything like Afghanistan. And then the UN. So we're still in the hangover of the cold war, dealing with a new world, but using institutions which were not built for this world.

IGNATIUS: We're using cold war institutions to deal with post–cold war problems.

SCOWCROFT: Yes.

▶ ▶ ▶

IGNATIUS: Let's talk a little bit about what post–cold war institutions might be like, starting with something Brent said. In a sense, the Industrial Revolution created a kind of hierarchical, bureaucratized modern system of organization. You could say that the perfection of the nation state with its orderly bureaucracy was a product of the Industrial Revolution.

And so the nation state grew and fought wars through the nineteenth century, fought the catastrophic wars of the twentieth century that led to the creation of these international organizations. But in a sense these organizations were even more hierarchical. They were a pyramiding of nations in a big hierarchical system that had layers and layers and layers. That was the crowning wedding-cake achievement of World War II. And as you say, the UN and other international organizations simply are not keeping track with the problems of the real world.

In what my colleague Tom Friedman calls a flat world, this pyramided hierarchy has been flattened so that anybody can connect with anybody else. Increasingly, I hear thoughtful people saying that we need international mechanisms that partake of the same networking technology and feel: spontaneously formed associations or networks of countries, companies, individuals, NGOs that will quickly focus on a problem. Go to work on it and begin to solve it.

Let me ask each of you about the transition from the very hierarchical and bureaucratic international organizations we have to something different. What would that different thing look like?

BRZEZINSKI: I would say that the notion that what you just described represents our one alternative is a little too simplistic. A great many existing institutions can be adapted and changed. The distribution of authority within them needs to be altered. Whether it's the World Bank or the IMF, that's not impossible to do.

Changing the UN is going to be more difficult, particularly the Security Council. The vested interests of the countries that now have special status obviously are going to paralyze change. But even in the United Nations, I think over time changes will take place. Or alternative shadow institutions will emerge.

For example, the G8 is no longer a functioning institution. It has become a little bit discredited because it was originally meant to be an organ of the leading democracies of the world. But we certainly could have a G14 or G16 of the most important global countries—including Asian countries like Japan, India, and China as well as Brazil, Mexico, South Africa, and so forth. And while that wouldn't have the status of the Security Council, it would nevertheless over time acquire some significance if it started dealing responsibly with, let's say, some of the problems of Darfur or some other regional challenges.

Beyond that, you might have some spontaneously arising institutions in response to some specific problems. But I would be a little bit worried if that became the dominant trend, because I think the consequence would be intensifying global instability. You need some points of constancy in the world, of predictability, of shared commitment. I still think, for example, that a redefined Atlantic Alliance makes sense as a factor of stability in the world, provided it's open-ended and willing to admit others once they're prepared to join.

I don't think we want to respond to complexity with a kind of spontaneous creativity which can easily become chaos. Inherent in the global political awakening, in the decline of the centrality of the cold war world, is a general thrust towards intensifying global chaos.

IGNATIUS: Brent?

SCOWCROFT: I think to go from the hierarchal world to a world of distributed networks, if you will, is too extreme. While distributed networks in the Internet and so on are wonderful, nobody seeks power, and nobody really exercises power. But in the real world, it's not that way. The NGOs, left to their own devices, can respond quickly, but they have great difficulty responding together. If you look at the response to the tsunami in Asia a couple of years ago, where did the best response come from? The U.S. Navy, which was organized, ready, and went in while the NGOs were floundering, trying to figure out what the problem was.

You need some kind of combination. You still need someone with hard power, soft power, whatever it is, to say, "This is the way to go," and to mobilize all these others. At the same time, that power, be it the United States or anybody else, can no longer dictate. I think we're searching for some middle ground. Maybe the

UN is a bad model, but it happens to be the only organization that touches everybody right now. I would seek to reform it rather than start over again.

BRZEZINSKI: To start all over again, one would have to have a cataclysm first.

SCOWCROFT: I'm afraid so.

▶ ▶ ▶

IGNATIUS: Let me offer this to sum up this conversation. You brought us on a journey, which is also the journey of your own careers, through the cold war years, a terrible menace that you each had to live with every day. Habits of prudence in foreign policy were born out of those dangers.

Then we've talked about the period after the end of the cold war when there was a kind of loose triumphalism. We sort of stopped worrying about foreign policy. We didn't make rigorous decisions. We were incautious. And we created, or failed to prevent, a lot of the problems that we encounter today.

So I want to ask you to close by talking a bit more about the nature of American leadership in this very complicated world. First, is American leadership necessary? And second, how does it have to be different from what it's been?

BRZEZINSKI: I think American leadership is necessary—if by leadership we mean, first of all, not dictation, but inspiration. If by leadership we mean an enlightened insight into the meaning of history and our time—a leadership that understands what is truly new about the twenty-first century. What is the potential of that century and what are its new global perils? Then that kind of American leadership—it can be a catalyst. Not for actions directed by the United States, but for actions that the global community—maybe we can call them stakeholders in the global system—is prepared collectively to embrace. That kind of leadership is needed. But for that kind of leadership to emerge in America, we not only need very special people as leaders—and they do come up occasionally—but we need a far more enlightened society than we have.

I think Americans are curiously, paradoxically, simultaneously very well-educated and amazingly ignorant. We are a society that lives within itself. We're not interested in the history of other countries.

Today we have a problem with Iran. How many Americans know anything about Iranian history? Do they know that it is a bifurcated history? There have been two Irans. And those two different periods, pre-Islamic and post-Islamic, dialectically define the tensions and the realities of Iran today. If you want to deal with Iran, you have to understand that. Americans spout about Iran. They know nothing about it.

The *National Geographic* has had studies which show that Americans don't know geography. Quite a few Americans entering college could not locate Great Britain on the map. They couldn't locate Iraq on the map after five years of war. Thirty percent couldn't identify the Pacific Ocean. We don't teach global history, we don't teach global geography. I think most Americans don't have the kind of sophistication that an America that inspires, and thereby leads, will have to have if it is to do what this twenty-first century really will demand of us.

SCOWCROFT: I could easily just say amen. But again, this is a part of who we are and from where we have arisen. For most of our history, we've been secure behind two oceans, with weak neighbors on each side. Americans don't have to learn foreign languages. They can travel as widely as most of them want and never leave the United States. So most Americans instinctively just want to be left alone. I don't think they want to mess with the problems of the world.

BRZEZINSKI: They want to enjoy the good life.

SCOWCROFT: They want to enjoy the good life. And local politics is important. They don't even care much, most of the time, what happens in Washington. That's part of the American make-up.

And our political structure seems more and more to cater to the narrow interests of Americans rather than their broader interests. Other than in time of peril, rarely do our leaders really focus decisively on the international scene—the beginning of the cold war, for example, or when Roosevelt tried to steer us in the right direction in the prelude to World War II, or when Eisenhower reached out to Europe to form NATO. It takes that kind of leadership.

When Americans can be stimulated, I think we're good-hearted. We're not narrow and avaricious. But our political structure doesn't seem to play to that. And as I said before, in the world as it is now, only the United States can exercise enlightened leadership. Not direct people what to do. But say, "Gather round. This is the way the world community needs to go."

BRZEZINSKI: Amen.

SCOWCROFT: We're the only ones who can be the guiding light.

—February 20, 2008

TWO

CRISES OF
OUR OWN MAKING

DAVID IGNATIUS: We meet today to talk about the Middle East on the fifth anniversary of the start of the Iraq War. We've all been reading, over the last few days, accounts of what life is like in Iraq after five years of fighting, and about the continuing anguish for Iraqi people and the American people as they look at what has unfolded.

I want to ask you both to focus on what the new president coming into office in January must contend with as he thinks about Iraq. But as a preface to that, I'd like to take you and our readers back to some seminal things that each of you wrote before the war.

I want to begin with you, Brent. You wrote an article that appeared in the *Wall Street Journal* on August 15, 2002, well before the beginning of the war in March 2003. The headline was "Don't Attack Saddam." And it was one of the most forthright statements—

BRENT SCOWCROFT: I didn't write the headline.

IGNATIUS: We reporters always say that, if somebody doesn't like the headline. But in this case, I would think that the headline is one you'd be happy to take credit for. I'm going to read to you a key paragraph from that article. "The central point," you wrote, "is that any campaign against Iraq, whatever the strategy, costs and risks, is certain to divert us for some indefinite period from our war on terrorism. Worse, there is a virtual consensus in the world against an attack on Iraq at this time. So long as that sentiment persists, it would require the U.S. to pursue a virtual 'go it alone' strategy against Iraq, making any military operations correspondently more difficult and expensive. The most serious cost, however, would be to the war on terrorism. Ignoring that clear sentiment will result in a serious degradation in international cooperation with us against terrorism. And make no mistake, we simply cannot win that war without enthusiastic international cooperation, especially on intelligence."

So now, five years into the war, a new president is about to take office in January 2009. Brent, what advice would you give him as he thinks about this most difficult problem at the very top of his agenda?

SCOWCROFT: A lot has happened since I wrote that piece. At that time the war on terror, to me, was the operation in Afghanistan—which, after all, was where Bin Laden had been able to recoup, rejuvenate, and operate.

I haven't changed my views about that article at all. What *has* changed is that we are now in Iraq, and the war has created new conditions. In the Middle East as a whole, as far east as Pakistan, it has inflamed many of the resentments and hatreds and differences within the region, and brought them all to the boiling point.

Whether it's Shia versus Sunni, whether it's Arab versus Persian, all of these hatreds are on the surface to a degree we haven't seen in a long time. We have a very different region. It's also a region that contains two-thirds of the world's oil reserves.

So we have a huge problem. The region is extremely unstable. Lebanon, Jordan, Egypt, wherever you look, there is potential instability. And Iraq is a source of continued instability because it's where Sunni, Shia, Persian, Arab conflicts are violent right now. My feeling is, we can't get out of Iraq, and I think any new president has to recognize that fact.

IGNATIUS: When you say, "We cannot get out of Iraq," I'm sure you don't mean ever.

SCOWCROFT: No, no, I don't mean ever. But the notion that within sixty days we will begin withdrawing our troops is a wrong frame of mind. What does winning in Iraq mean? What do we need to do there? What we need to do is create a stable Iraq rather than one that foments chaos.

I don't know how long that takes. It could take a long time. It perhaps would not take a long time. We can't get the political system there to do what we want. They don't owe us a favor. They didn't ask us in there. So they're going to pursue their own internal struggles. How that will come out, I don't think any of us can tell. But what we need to do is to work for an Iraq that is a force for stability in the region.

IGNATIUS: Zbig, let me turn to you. I want to take you back as well to the period before the war, to an op-ed piece you wrote in the *Washington Post* that also appeared in August 2002.

The headline on this one—which you didn't write—was "If We Must Fight." In it you said, "War is too serious a business, and too unpredictable in its dynamic consequences, especially in a highly flammable region, to be undertaken because of a personal peeve, demagogically articulated fears, or vague factual assertions."

Then you talked about what you thought the administration should be doing, focusing on the same issue that Brent touched on when he wrote about international support. You said, "The United States should soon begin discussions with its allies as well as other concerned powers, including its Arab friends, regarding possible postwar arrangements for Iraq, including a prolonged collective security presence and plans for international financing of the social rehabilitation of the country.

"Doing so, we reinforce the credibility of the U.S. determination to use force in the event that a nonviolent resolution of the issue proves to be impossible." Back in August 2002, you were raising the issue that received so little attention, which was, "What would this postwar Iraq look like? How would we put it back together if we did fight?"

So with that starting point, let me ask you the same question I asked Brent. A new president takes office at the end of January 2009 and invites you to the Oval Office to give your advice. How would you begin?

ZBIGNIEW BRZEZINSKI: Obviously it would make a lot of difference whether I was talking to a victorious Republican candidate or a victorious Democratic candidate. Not that I would change my views, but I would have to cast the argument differently depending on the kind of promises the candidate had made.

Having said that, I would still argue that a solution to the problem posed by our presence in Iraq, a presence that has been terribly costly to us and very destructive of Iraq, requires recognizing that our presence is part of the problem. Iraq cannot be put together if we continue to be there, hoping that somehow our occupation will eventually yield a stable, self-governing, somehow viable Iraq.

Our presence and the necessities of a quasi-combat situation require us to pursue policies which further fragment Iraq. In that sense, they create a self-perpetuating condition of instability. Addressing that reality, and taking into account the excessive costs and the damages to America's standing in the world produced by the war, the president has to set as his goal the termination of U.S. presence.

And then I would argue, depending on who's president, that it can be done with different degrees of rapidity. I personally don't think we should start withdrawals within sixty days. On the other hand—

IGNATIUS: Explain why you think that would be a mistake.

BRZEZINSKI: Because it's terribly abrupt and doesn't give you time to create a political context for the process. But sixteen months might be long enough.

And then I would say to a Democratic president, "you can say that you're going to withdraw." To a Republican I'd say, "you can say to the Iraqis you want to discuss the possibility of American withdrawal." But either one should engage the Iraqi leaders in serious discussions about our long-range relationship with Iraq and about our shorter-range need to disengage. He should focus Iraqi attention on the fact that the occupation's not going to be indefinite—that at some point they'll have to stand on their own feet, sooner in the case of a Democrat, perhaps later in the case of a Republican.

In addition, once it becomes publicly clear that we are serious about terminating this destructive presence, we should set in motion something the Baker-Hamilton Commission talked about, but which was never developed very fully, namely a simultaneous attempt to create some sort of a regional framework, perhaps through a conference involving all of Iraq's neighbors, regarding the region in the wake of American disengagement. Every single one of Iraq's neighbors has an interest in any subsequent instability in Iraq not spilling over. Once they knew we were serious about ending our combat role, all of them would come. We could then even enlarge the scope of the conference to deal with some of the issues of instability, rehabilitation, and so forth.

I think that would be a viable approach. And I am not convinced that the worst-case scenarios being bandied around regarding the consequences of our disengagement actually will happen. There are indications that some parts of Iraq are already becoming de facto self-governing.

IGNATIUS: But you would grant that what you're proposing does take a risk with the lives of the Iraqis, who look to us to help them put the country back together.

BRZEZINSKI: The Iraqi parliament has voted overwhelmingly in favor of American disengagement. Public opinion polls show that most Iraqis dislike our occupation, though I think about thirty percent would like it not to end too quickly. A larger percentage would like it to be terminated fairly fast.

We have to face the fact that irrespective of what we think of ourselves, we are perceived in the region very differently, and especially by the Iraqis. We are seen as essentially a continuator of British colonialism, and we're now in the post-colonial era. Our presence, based primarily on military force, is simply making it impossible for a genuine, autonomous stability to develop in Iraq.

IGNATIUS: Brent, I wonder if we could agree at the outset on the point that Zbig made, that our presence is part of the problem. You said that we can't just get out. But would you agree with Zbig that at the same time, our presence, long-term, is part of the problem here?

SCOWCROFT: I don't think now it's part of the problem. I think it's part of the solution. Part of the diminution of violence in Iraq right now is because the talk about getting out immediately has been reduced. Remember, for the Iraqis and the Iraqi political structure, chaotic though it is, this is a zero sum game. And as long as they think we are leaving, they're jockeying for their position after we have left. If they think we're going to provide essential stability for a time, they may be more willing to reach out and take some risks that, if they're on their own, they're not about to take.

So to say we're part of the problem—yes, in the sense of occupation. The Iraqis are a proud people. They resent that. It's important to try to convince them by our behavior that we're not occupiers, that we are trying to help them, and that we will help only so long as we are needed.

The other factor in this is Iraq's neighbors. One of the abiding dangers of Iraq is that it could fracture into its constituent parts. To me, that is an incitement to violence in the region.

BRZEZINSKI: Well, we have to anticipate that danger, and American disengagement, if it happens sooner rather than later, mitigates against the danger of Iraq fragmenting. Our presence is contributing to the fragmentation of Iraq.

It is also interesting that the most stable and least violent parts of Iraq are the ones that are already self-governing: the Shia south, the Sunni center where we rely on the tribes, and Kurdistan. The longer we stay, the less likely it is that our departure itself will then permit a reunification of Iraq.

So I would argue that engaging the Iraqis in a serious discussion regarding the date for our departure would focus their attention on what needs to be done. It might even precipitate more serious discussions between the Sunnis and the Shiites. And I don't entirely agree, Brent, that the Iraqis don't think we might be contemplating leaving sooner rather than later. This fall there's going to be a wide-ranging debate in the United States that will include the future of Iraq, and the Democratic candidate will be committed to the idea of getting out. The Democrat might even win. I don't see how the Iraqis could conclude that we are committed to staying a long time.

SCOWCROFT: No, I don't think they have. But as of a year ago, the Democratic candidates were running after each other to propose earlier and earlier dates for complete withdrawal. That has quieted down, and I think—

BRZEZINSKI: But they're both committed now.

SCOWCROFT: But the slight indications in Iraq that we might stay, I think you could argue, has contributed to the recent signs of progress.

BRZEZINSKI: If I could sort of add something. I would also argue that we shouldn't focus entirely on Iraq. The war in Iraq is part of a larger conundrum of problems that we face and they all reinforce each other and create tensions and conflicts and risks that we have to be seriously worried about. That includes the festering Israeli-Palestinian issue, which creates a lot of radical anti-American feelings, and then the uncertainties involving our relationship with Iran. I think any approach to the Iraq issue should take into account the interrelationship of these other issues.

SCOWCROFT: I agree. And that's another argument against the position that our focus ought to be on withdrawal. No one in the region thought it was a good idea for us to go into Iraq. It seems to me they are likely to say, "You went in, you made a mess of it, and now you're leaving it to us to solve."

Take Egypt, for example, which was one of our strongest allies in the First Gulf War and is absolutely absent now. Why? I think partly because they've lost faith in us. They've lost faith in what we're about, and our staying ability. To leave now and leave the region to the parties surrounding Iraq would be another step toward chaos in the region.

BRZEZINSKI: But I don't advocate "leaving" the region and abandoning them to the mercies of the others. I argue that we should engage in a serious discussion with the forces in Iraq, not only those in the green zone but also outside, regarding the termination of our combat role.

There is increasing evidence that the Iraqis can assume a more direct responsibility for combat, and that probably some of the insurgency will die down the moment we begin to disengage—because the insurgency is nationalistically against us. Al-Qaeda is there for its own terrorist purposes, which exploits that insurgency.

But insurgency probably will taper off the moment it becomes clear that we are getting ready to terminate the occupation. If we couple that with a regional effort in which we'll be engaged together with others about creating stability around Iraq, we will in fact be assuming a continued role, no longer so heavily reliant on military power, but an approach designed to rehabilitate, to reestablish, to consolidate, to stabilize, and to reassure. Otherwise, we're doomed to stay there for years and years and years.

IGNATIUS: Brent, how would you respond to that? We celebrate today, painfully, the fifth anniversary of our invasion. Someone reading your words might ask, well, am I going to be looking at a tenth anniversary of American occupation with our forces still there? And why would things be any better with five more years of our presence?

SCOWCROFT: I would respond by saying, "Look, we are there. What we mean to do is to produce an Iraq which is self-governing and stable." I agree that we should have these discussions with Iraq's neighbors. But the discussions should be not about our withdrawal but about what it would take to do it. And contrary to what Zbig says, the surge in fact has produced a reduction of violence. Violence is down significantly.

BRZEZINSKI: It's not contrary to what I was saying. I acknowledge that.

IGNATIUS: Zbig, speak—

BRZEZINSKI: And that's one of the reasons that justifies our disengagement.

IGNATIUS: Speak forthrightly to that, in a way that the Democrats have not always done, and give us your evaluation of the consequences of the troop surge.

BRZEZINSKI: Oh, I think it has helped, no doubt about it. But that's another reason why we can start getting ready to leave. If we're going to wait until the Iraqis are ready to be stable and secular or whatever, we're going to be there indefinitely. At some point we have to acknowledge that we're perpetuating the problem and that our presence is no longer so necessary.

Kurdistan is controlled by the Kurds. The central areas are now increasingly handled by the tribes. And Al-Qaeda is getting isolated precisely because the tribes are disowning them, fighting them. And the south is now bastions of Shiite militias. We're—

SCOWCROFT: Yes, but they're fighting each other.

BRZEZINSKI: Fine, that's their problem.

IGNATIUS: Brent, at the end of the day, surely that's true. That is their problem.

SCOWCROFT: What I would argue is that we should not be negotiating withdrawal, but saying the faster you get this together, the more you work, the quicker we can withdraw. So far we've set benchmarks, and threatened them that we'll get out unless they shape up.

Well, they didn't ask us in. Why shouldn't they want us out? But if we say, "We can get out to the degree that you all get your act together," and turn it around so that we're trying to help them, not threatening them, I think we'd have a better chance.

IGNATIUS: Let me see if I can distill this into a joint Scowcroft-Brzezinski memorandum to the next president. The point of agreement I think I hear is that the next president must engage in a discussion with the Iraqis, with the Iraqi government and people, about the future of Iraq as an independent sovereign state, which almost by definition is a state that doesn't have a big American troop presence.

We shouldn't try to lecture to the Iraqis or threaten them with American withdrawal. As Zbig said, a timetable for a quick beginning to the American departure prejudges that conversation.

And that that should be accompanied by a new and very vigorous effort to do what you both talked about before the war began, which is to draw the region into discussions about its future and the future of Iraq. Is that a formulation that you both would be comfortable with if it was dropped on the president's desk?

BRZEZINSKI: Up to a point, yes. But Brent and I have different perspectives on the ultimate remedy for what is now both an Iraqi and an American problem. My view is the Iraqis will only be triggered into doing what they have to do once they realize that we're not going to be there. The longer they have this disliked but also paralyzing American umbrella over them, the longer they are likely to maintain internally intransigent positions that perpetuate and even worsen the fragmentation in Iraq.

IGNATIUS: This presidential campaign in which the Democratic candidate is calling for American troop withdrawals is going to reinforce the feeling among every sensible Iraqi that we are getting out soon. Why wouldn't that lead them to prepare for a potential violent conflict over the future of Iraq? Isn't the danger that rather than encouraging them to get their act together and reconcile, the prospect of American withdrawal would lead them to prepare for the civil war, the conflagration we all fear most?

BRZEZINSKI: Ultimately there may have to be something like a mini civil war. We can more or less predict where the balance of forces is going to be. It's going to be the Shiites with the Kurds against the Sunnis. And the Sunnis will lose, very badly. Precisely because they know that, I think there's a good chance that after some skirmishing, there will be an internal accommodation, because there is still such a thing as Iraqi nationalism.

I recently saw some polls in which a very large majority overall, more so among the Sunnis, somewhat less so among the Shiites, clearly identified themselves as Iraqis and want a unified Iraqi state.

IGNATIUS: That sounds an awful lot like the eighty percent solution that many in the administration advocated, basically saying, "Hey, we've got the Kurds. We've got the Shiites. The heck with the Sunnis." A lot of us would say that's a big part of how we got into the mess we're in. Why is it a good idea now?

BRZEZINSKI: Because at some point the Iraqis have to stand on their feet. The notion that somehow or another we're going to create a kind of Iraqi unity under the occupation, I think is an illusion.

IGNATIUS: Brent, what do you think?

SCOWCROFT: I could agree with your formulation. I would add one thing. One of the fundamental American interests in this whole thing is an Iraq that does not fracture into its constituent parts.

BRZEZINSKI: I agree with that.

SCOWCROFT: That's a formula for disaster in the region, and I think it's the most likely outcome. The Kurds are not going to join with the Shias. The Kurds will say, "You guys fight it out. We're happy." They're already autonomous to an immense degree and then they will go their own way. Certainly the Shia part is stronger than the Sunni part. But the Sunni part has a lot of Sunni Arab money behind it. A civil war could go on for a long time.

BRZEZINSKI: It could. But that really is the worst-case scenario. It is also possible to argue that if we are leaving, there will be pressures on them to accommodate.

SCOWCROFT: There could be.

BRZEZINSKI: Perhaps. And I would argue that if you think of the cost that we're paying, and you know the cost as well as I do, you warned of it earlier than most people, it's in our interest to try to bring this to a close.

SCOWCROFT: Right. But what I'm saying is, neither of us knows what is the most likely outcome. Overarching all this is the possibility of a general Middle East conflict in which the costs of Iraq would look miniscule.

That's what we need to worry about. And I agree with Zbig: This is not the only issue. We've got a whole bunch of issues in the region that could precipitate that kind of problem. Iraq is one, though, which is of our own making and therefore I think we have overall responsibility for it. We cannot simply say, "You Iraqis have to recognize your responsibilities."

BRZEZINSKI: I think you've made a very fair statement. I would only quarrel with the one aspect of it. I do not think we can solve that problem; we are part of the problem. And therefore, convincing the Iraqis that there is a terminal date for our presence is a contribution to a solution, which ultimately has to be an Iraqi solution and not an American one.

SCOWCROFT: That's the fundamental point of difference. I think simply withdrawing is an impediment to a solution. And Zbig thinks it helps.

BRZEZINSKI: That's right.

SCOWCROFT: That is the basic point on which we differ. And that's the basic point on which our political structure differs.

IGNATIUS: I want to turn to what I think we all would regard as the nightmare scenario, which is that as the next president seeks to reduce the U.S. presence—whether rapidly or gradually—Iraq will be pitched into the kind of violent conflagration that we have feared most, that there will be a bloodbath.

About a year ago I asked the foreign minister of Syria, Walid al-Moallem, what he thought about some of the Democrats' proposals for rapid withdrawal. And he looked at me and said, "But, David, that would be immoral." That stayed with me because it seems to me it's profoundly true. For us to leave that country to that kind of horrible bloodshed, if that's what should occur, would be immoral. I want to ask each of you—who've lived at the center of power in the Situation Room—if we saw killing on a very wide scale, thousands of Iraqis dying in ethnic conflict after we had moved into a withdrawal phase, do you think it would be appropriate to send our troops back in? Zbig, what would you do if you had to give advice on that kind of crisis?

BRZEZINSKI: Well, first of all, that involves postulating the worst-case scenario, which I don't think—

IGNATIUS: Yes, but the failure to do worst-case planning before this war—

BRZEZINSKI: That's true.

IGNATIUS: —is part of the problem.

BRZEZINSKI: But it's not necessarily the most likely scenario. I think we would have time to reverse course if necessary. We are not going to leave all at once. Even under the more rapid notions of disengagement—taking about sixteen months—you have plenty of time to take stock.

IGNATIUS: If you have ten thousand people being killed in a day, as you could—I'm not sure you'd have quite as much time as you suggest.

BRZEZINSKI: But the point is, there would be an opportunity to react, even if belatedly.

The process ought to involve, from the start, extensive discussions with all Iraqi leaders, and not just the ones in the green zone, but also al-Hakim, al-Sistani, and al-Sadr, who has quite an independent military force. During these discussions we would be able to make judgments about what is likely to ensue as we begin to leave on a schedule that will have been discussed and communicated to the Iraqi leaders.

So there is a time for reassessment. Otherwise we are the prisoners of a situation we ourselves created, the potential horrors of which we fear, and we would become immobilized because we're not likely ever to have such clarity that things are so stabilized and the Iraqis are so happy that we can suddenly afford to leave.

So it's a question of contingent judgments, which are going to be affected by whether we are advising a Democratic president or a Republican president. A Republican president will listen more carefully to Brent, probably listen politely to me for a little while, then get mad and tell me that I'm totally wrong. A Democratic president may listen to me a little more, but will be, I think, studiously deferential to Brent because of his early position on the subject.

SCOWCROFT: I will say the contrary. And your scenario, I think, is unlikely, but cannot be ruled out.

BRZEZINSKI: The one about the president?

SCOWCROFT: I think if we left Iraq, our political situation would never permit us going back in to quell a civil war, never.

BRZEZINSKI: Well, if it erupted after we left, sure. The country wouldn't tolerate it.

SCOWCROFT: This country would not tolerate it.

IGNATIUS: One question that the next president is obviously going to struggle with is whether the United States can have, should have, a continuing relationship with Iraq in which we would try to help work with Iraq to achieve these goals of internal stability, regional security, prevent the country from breaking apart, without having the negatives of what is seen here and in Iraq as U.S. military occupation.

I want to ask you whether you think that's possible. The Democratic candidates have said that it may be appropriate to have some residual U.S. force in Iraq that focuses on training the Iraqi military, if the Iraqis ask us to continue that, and that has continuing responsibility for chasing terrorist cells to the extent they continue to be a problem, and to do other things. Once you have that residual force, other issues come up. You need bases, supplies, ways to keep that force going. Zbig, what do you think about our continuing relationship with this new Iraq? How do you envision it?

BRZEZINSKI: That is something that could be discussed. It could be discussed more constructively in the context of a clearly stated

American decision to disengage militarily. In that context, it might be possible to have some arrangements, first of all with the Iraqis themselves, for some sort of more remote American presence somewhere in Iraq. There may be some utility in a continued American presence in Kurdistan, as a way of stabilizing what otherwise could become a very volatile situation between the Kurds and the Turks and the Iranians.

But that's rather different from what the administration is discussing right now, which the administration itself has compared to our presence in South Korea—without taking into account the fact that the South Koreans saw us as defending them, and felt threatened by the North for decades. Most Iraqis don't think we came there at their invitation, and, I sense, don't want us to stay indefinitely with that presence symbolized by this enormous fortress we're building now in the middle of Baghdad, and reinforced by bases around the country.

So, yes, some residual presence, not on a very large scale, subject to negotiations with the Iraqis, perhaps fortified by some arrangement with Kuwait for quick access if need be. Perhaps something with Jordan, though the Jordanians would probably be reluctant. Certainly our presence in the Gulf in any case, which is being strengthened through arrangements with some of the emirates.

IGNATIUS: Brent, what do you think about the shape of our continuing role?

SCOWCROFT: To me, withdrawal to residual areas sounds like a permanent presence, which I don't think we ought to hint at in any respect. There's an Iraqi nationalism that can and should be enhanced through the Iraqi military as the symbol of unity where Shias and Sunnis serve side by side—as they did under Saddam.

There are two tasks that the United States has militarily over the near term. One is to control the level of violence, which the Iraqi army can't do alone right now. We're training them. They're getting better. The other is that the Iraqi army now depends completely on us for logistic and operational support. They have fighting units, but we provide everything for those units: movement, supplies, intelligence, everything. We need to develop the Iraqi army's ability to expand into those areas. I have no idea how long that will take. But that's what we ought to do. At a diminishing level? Absolutely.

I'm against any notion of a permanent presence, even as an independent base for security in the Middle East and Iraq. I think that's bad for all the reasons Zbig said. But I think we can only get out when we think we are leaving an Iraq that can manage itself.

▶ ▶ ▶

IGNATIUS: Let me throw out another question for you. This is not about the new president but about the departing president. On President Bush's last day in the Oval Office, he calls you in, Brent, and says, "I just want to visit with you before I leave this place. You wrote before the war that I shouldn't do it, that it was a mistake to attack Saddam. Now, as I'm preparing to leave, I want to know what you think. Did this work out? Or was it a mistake?" How would you answer that question before President Bush?

SCOWCROFT: I think I would say, "Mr. President, that is a question for the historians. It is irrelevant to the current situation. We are now heavily engaged in Iraq and our concentration needs to be on how we deal with that fact—our presence—in a way that leaves an Iraq that is a stabilizing, not a destabilizing, force in the region."

IGNATIUS: Zbig, if President Bush called you in, even though you've been a consistent critic of this war, he might ask you whether the surge had made conditions somewhat more favorable for an outcome that is in the strategic interests of the United States. How would you answer?

BRZEZINSKI: I would answer by saying I agree that the surge has created somewhat more favorable conditions. Whether that is enduring or not, we do not know. But that we should take advantage of it to strive to terminate our presence in Iraq. Because our presence in Iraq is part of the problem and is no longer the source of the solution. But in addition to that, I would say, depending on the date of that visit, and assuming—

SCOWCROFT: The last day.

BRZEZINSKI: Is it the last day?

SCOWCROFT: So you can't talk about the future.

BRZEZINSKI: Okay, then I would not say, "Mr. President, what about your promise to obtain an Israeli-Palestinian settlement before you leave office?" And if it really is the last day, then I hope I would be able to say, "Thank you very much, Mr. President, for not starting an additional war in Iran."

▶ ▶ ▶

IGNATIUS: When the next president takes office and thinks about what to do in Iraq, a huge overriding concern will be the consequences of that decision for Iran—the rising power in the region, and arguably the nation that has benefited most from America's invasion of Iraq and the overthrow of Saddam Hussein. When I was in Iran in 2006 for several weeks of reporting, what I kept hearing over and over again from Iranians—both from people who supported this hard-line regime and from people who hated the regime and President Ahmadinejad—was something like the following. We are a great and rising country, and this is our moment. We are ascendant, and you Americans are in decline. And we want to be recognized as the great nation we are.

So I would put to you: How should we approach this rising Iran, this country that says, "This is our moment; deal with us"? Brent, what would you think is a framework for this very tricky question of how the United States should engage Iran?

SCOWCROFT: Iranian attitudes are an important aspect of it. One of the things we have to remember is that in the course of dealing with terrorism and then Iraq and Afghanistan we have removed Iran's enemies on both sides. And so that feeling in Iran, "our moment has come," is perhaps not too unnatural. Iran is an important state. We have had sharply differing relationships with it. It was our bastion of regional stability under the Shah. When we replaced the British as the outside power in the region, we counted on the Shah to preserve stability. After he left, and with the seizure of our embassy, we and the Iranians developed a visceral dislike of each other. We've had a very unusual relationship.

It seems to me we've approached Iran emotionally. If we get past the emotions, I think we can deal best with the Iranians, first of all, by talking with them. We have gone from not wanting anybody to talk to them to talking to them ourselves, but only about Iraq, not about the broader regional situation.

The fact is Iran lives in a dangerous region. It is a Shia state in a generally Sunni region. It is a Persian state in a generally Arab region. We need to be willing to engage Iran in strategic discussions that can lead to a framework in the region that will allow Iran to feel secure without needing to acquire nuclear weapons.

IGNATIUS: Zbig, few people in America have lived with the tumult of the Iranian revolution in quite the way that you have. You were national security advisor to President Carter at the time of the revolution. You struggled through the horrific months of the seizure of the U.S. embassy and the hostage crisis. What are your starting points? How do you see the strategic issues?

BRZEZINSKI: Well, my starting point would be somewhat like Brent's concluding point. There is no reason to maintain a policy in which we seek to isolate Iran or we demand that they make fundamental concessions as a price for sitting down at the table with us. That's a self-defeating policy that simply perpetuates the existing difficulty.

IGNATIUS: So you think the Bush administration was wrong to demand a halt to nuclear enrichment by the Iranians as a condition of entering negotiations?

BRZEZINSKI: There are two ways of dealing with that problem. If we want them to halt enrichment as the point of departure for negotiations, then we have to give them something in return, because at least under international law and the Nonproliferation Treaty—the NPT—they have the right to enrich. If they're going to forego that right, then we should be prepared to offer to suspend some of the more painful sanctions we have adopted against them. Then there would be a quid pro quo.

The other way of dealing with the problem is to say we'll negotiate without conditions, which means you continue enriching, but we negotiate until such time as we either break off the negotiations because no progress has been made or perhaps some progress evolves. But what creates this counterproductive stalemate is our insistence that there be preconditions. There should be either no preconditions for anyone, or mutual accommodation in which suspension of enrichment is matched by suspension of sanctions.

I would like to go beyond that, David, to the point you raised about the Iranian perception of its own role in the region. A great deal of that perception is self-delusion. Iran is not all that powerful. It is a country with a tremendous number of domestic problems: a country which has been retarded in its economic development; a country in which a very large proportion of the young people are highly dissatisfied with the fanatical religious leadership; a country where a lot of the young people, particularly the women, look at Turkey or Europe as models for their future and not at the more fundamentalist interpretation of the Koran.

Hence it is a country that may be confronting serious internal problems once the Iranians don't feel that the outside world, and particularly the United States, is subjecting them to a siege. I would argue that it's in our interest to relax, because that will not only permit an official dialogue, it will also stimulate more expressions for change within Iran.

Last but not least, while Iran seems quite strong compared to the Middle Eastern countries, it has some very serious internal ethnic problems. Take one specifically. Roughly one-third to one-fourth of the population is Azeri. The Azeris have been assimilated relatively successfully into the Iranian system. But that is beginning to change because there is now an independent Azerbaijan which is on the cusp of becoming very wealthy and increasingly part of the West, because of the Baku-Ceyhan pipeline, with contacts with the United States and access to Europe, and which has a very intelligent domestic program of using massive oil revenues for national rehabilitation and modernization.

The Azeris in Iran and elsewhere will increasingly be looking north. At some point they'll start wondering, "Shouldn't we be part of Azerbaijan?" Add to that the Baluchis in the east, where some unrest is going on, and some of the residual Arabs on the coast near Iraq, and so there are many vulnerabilities that Iran will confront.

Hence the notion of an assertive, dominant Iran that is somehow or other going to assume an imperial status vis-à-vis the Middle East is a little overdrawn. This doesn't mean we should dismiss the risks. But I think we ought to take into account that this reality is much more complex, and not forget the relatively positive role Iran played in the immediate aftermath of 9/11 and our overthrow of the Taliban where they were extremely helpful to us.

IGNATIUS: You raise what is the greatest temptation in foreign policy, which is sitting on an island conjuring up spells like Prospero in Shakespeare's *Tempest*. What is the possibility that these ethnic tensions in Iran could be exploited by American—

BRZEZINSKI: Well, I don't raise it.

IGNATIUS: —policy in a covert operation?

BRZEZINSKI: I think the possibility does indeed exist. And there's no doubt that there is a body of opinion in the United States—and also in Israel—that looks very carefully at Iran and calculates what might be exploited in order to turn Iran into a destabilized mess. My own view is that it's not in our interest for the Middle East to be destabilized as part of a historic, century-long war with Islamic fundamentalism which perhaps at some point will be called World War IV. Destabilization as a policy can only be applied in extreme circumstances. And it is very dangerous in the region on which so much of the world depends for energy and where destabilization can have unforeseen and extraordinarily destructive consequences.

IGNATIUS: Brent, would you agree that the ethnic card exists with Iran? What would you think about the wisdom of playing it?

SCOWCROFT: I think it would be a mistake. We ought to try to encourage the tendencies in Iran to liberalize. Voting patterns of the Iranian people indicate that they want a more open regime. They don't like this regime. By forcing an appeal to Iranian nationalism, at which Ahmadinejad is a master, we play into his hands. We bring the country together. We ought to engage in discussions, to give flower to the more liberal tendencies in Iran and hope for an evolution of the extremists.

IGNATIUS: Let me pose the darkest view of the future of Iran and America's relations with it. That is that Iran is a revolutionary state, still in the red-hot phase of its revolution. We keep waiting for it to burn itself out but it hasn't happened yet. And like revolutionary France and the post-revolutionary France of Napoleon, it will keep pushing to expand until it's stopped. Napoleon finally was stopped when he overreached and invaded Russia. And Napoleon's defeat in 1812 made possible a series of agreements and peace conferences that finally concluded with the Congress of Vienna in 1815, which stabilized Europe, you could argue, for almost one hundred years.

But Iran hasn't been stopped—quite the opposite. Everywhere it pushes, it seems to have success. In Lebanon, it projects power through Hezbollah. In Palestine, through Hamas. It is increasingly the dominant power in Iraq. This revolutionary Iran keeps pushing, keeps threatening. And if you were in a dark mood you could say to yourself that this process the Iranians insist on continuing will only be stopped when Iran is confronted in what many in the region would say is an inevitable war with the United States.

I'd ask you to think about that historical problem and tell me whether you think Iran will continue to be a revolutionary state and whether at some point we will need to use military force to contain it. Zbig? You're a student of history.

BRZEZINSKI: Well, as I was listening to you, David, I was sort of wondering: Do I recognize France or do I recognize Iran? Because I don't think you can be right on both at the same time. Your analysis of France was, I think, historically accurate. But I didn't see the analogies with Iran. What is Iran doing that is similar to Napoleon's expansion into Spain and Portugal, conquest of Italy, blasting to bits Prussia and Austria, eventually marching to Moscow? Nothing. Where is Iran that is so pushy and effective? In Gaza, and Hezbollah? Let's look a little more closely. How did Iran get into Gaza? In part because of the conditions in Gaza. Hamas is not—

Hamas is supported and financed by the Iranians, but it arose because of conditions in Gaza, not because of Napoleonic-type expansion.

As for Hezbollah, can you imagine Hezbollah existing without the original invasion by Israel? The Lebanese were feckless against the invasion, except for the Shiites, who organized themselves into Hezbollah and started resisting more effectively. And who gained from the last war? It began with Hezbollah brutally rocketing the Israelis, and then the Israelis responding by massively bombing Lebanese civilians, thereby strengthening Hezbollah.

That's not an Iranian conquest. So the analogy with revolutionary Napoleonic France doesn't hold water. Iran has gained additional influence largely because of the war in Iraq. But it is a very vulnerable country, very weak inside, with a population increasingly disaffected, except when we help to unite it with excessive American threats and occasionally almost irrational statements. Last week, the president said explicitly, "Iran has stated it wants a nuclear bomb to kill people." There is not one record of any such statement by the Iranians. It is only statements like these that create cohesion in Iran and make it appealing to its increasingly anti-American neighbors.

Iran's mullah elite is losing touch. It can't deal with the country's growing economic crisis or with the growing alienation of the young, who are increasingly attracted to the West. So I don't see the analogy at all.

IGNATIUS: Brent, am I crazy to think that this is a revolutionary state that wishes us ill?

SCOWCROFT: I'd rather not go back to the French Revolution. There are some similarities, ideologically.

BRZEZINSKI: Not to the French Revolution.

SCOWCROFT: Well—yes, there was spreading democracy to the rest of Europe.

BRZEZINSKI: But that was not intolerant fanaticism.

SCOWCROFT: But I think, first of all, that's one of the reasons the Palestinian peace process is so important. If you can succeed in a peace process, you at least partially defang Hezbollah. And Hamas.

One of the reasons the Arabs are so fearful of this Shia crescent backed by Iran is because they think our policy is to abandon them. Sunnis have always been fearful of the Shia rising up. But in most of the countries, they're a considerable minority. I think Iran, as Zbig says, has neither the capability nor the appeal to lead an uprising. But if there's chaos in the region, which there very well could be, they could certainly profit by it. An Israeli-Palestinian settlement would change the psychology of the region and put Iran back on the defensive.

BRZEZINSKI: Let me add a footnote, which again dramatizes the difference between Iran and France. Napoleonic France was a great military power. Beat the hell out of all the imperial powers for a decade and a half. We can pulverize Iran's military, probably without losing a single man; destroy their alleged nuclear arsenal, their industries, kill thousands of Iranians. There isn't very much they can do militarily to us in Iran. But they can exploit the chaos in the region. And it would be hell for us.

IGNATIUS: They could do a lot of damage—

BRZEZINSKI: Indirectly.

IGNATIUS: In Saudi Arabia, in Kuwait, in the UAE.

BRZEZINSKI: That's right, in the region.

SCOWCROFT: By subversion.

BRZEZINSKI: Yeah, exactly. So their weakness is their strength in a way.

IGNATIUS: All right, you won't buy my analogy to revolutionary France. I'm very sorry to hear that.

BRZEZINSKI: Try another one.

IGNATIUS: But what about an analogy to revolutionary China in the late phase of Maoism? You can make an argument that it was only the fanaticism of the Gang of Four—of Madame Mao, the Red Guards—that burned itself into the consciousness of a generation of Chinese and made possible the rise of Deng Xiaoping and the extremely pragmatic Chinese leadership that followed. Some people look at Iran today and say that oddly enough, it may be the craziness of this Ahmadinejad that will bring the moment that we most want.

BRZEZINSKI: There's something to that. With an important difference, also. There is something to that in the sense that the Cultural Revolution and the Great Leap Forward created such massive suffering that there was receptivity to what Deng Xiaoping wanted to do. In Iran, it's different. I think the Iranian population is getting ready for such a change. But it's also a function of the Internet and the fact that that population is quite well educated, and has a lot of ties with the external world, particularly Turkey. In that sense, a social propensity for the emergence of some post-mullah regime is there, provided we stop undermining it by these repetitive threats, which help the mullahs by linking fanaticism and nationalism.

SCOWCROFT: I'll be heretical. I think the Iranian regime is not a revolutionary regime, that the revolution in Iran is the people's desire for more openness. The conservatives, the mullahs, want to hold things back. Ahmadinejad is a third-level official. The revolution is toward openness, and the conservatives have actually been helped by our policies.

BRZEZINSKI: And the regime really isn't that despotic. I'd much rather live in Iran than in Russia, when it comes to democracy.

IGNATIUS: Well, I'd rather be a journalist in Iran, in the sense that I wouldn't worry about getting killed.

So the next national security advisor sitting in the chair that each of you once sat in comes to you in—let's give him a couple of weeks—February 2009 and says, "Brent, Zbig, I'm about to take off on a secret mission to Tehran. I'm flying in an unmarked Gulfstream jet tonight. I land in Tehran tomorrow to begin a secret dialogue with Iran with the hope of exploring the possibility of engagement, and I want your advice."

What would you say? Would you tell him, "Well, that's a crazy idea, don't do it"? Or if you thought it was a reasonable idea, what do you think ought to be on the agenda? Zbig?

BRZEZINSKI: You know, what I would say to him first of all is, "Yes, go, but don't go secretly. That is a really stupid idea." You only go secretly if you know in advance you have assured common interest. Brent went secretly to China, but he knew in advance that the Chinese had interest in that dialogue. We don't know what would happen if we all of a sudden go secretly to Iran. They agree to receive you, but at some point, they'll decide how to exploit the fact, especially if the talks aren't particularly productive. So go openly. There's nothing wrong in talking.

IGNATIUS: But they might not receive you openly.

BRZEZINSKI: Then don't go. If they don't want to talk, there's no point going.

IGNATIUS: They might want to talk, but not openly.

BRZEZINSKI: Then do it through intermediaries and don't fly into Tehran but somewhere else, to establish if they're really serious about a dialogue. One thing I have learned about the Iranians is they're very skillful but very devious negotiators. And you have to be damn sure that you know where you are at any given moment.

So I would say to a hypothetical successor, if you're going to have discussions at a high level, if you are going to be talking to Iranian leaders representing the president, you have to be sure that they're ready to have a dialogue. And then do it openly. No one expects a miracle from a simple conversation. But I think it would be a very useful beginning.

And then the issues that Brent and I have mentioned could be addressed. How do we negotiate in a serious way about the nuclear issue? How do we deal with regional security, specifically Iraq? What can they do to help us in Afghanistan, where once they were very helpful?

IGNATIUS: Brent, what would your advice be to this hypothetical successor who's hell-bent on getting on this Gulfstream jet?

SCOWCROFT: I don't feel so strongly about secret negotiations. I wouldn't do it in Tehran. I would do it in a neutral area. And I would be sensitive to the internal Iranian situation, where discussion with American officials might be considered treason. The first thing I'd ask him is who are you going to talk with, because Iran has a very confused political situation. It's very hard to know who you're talking with and what that person represents.

BRZEZINSKI: Specifically, it would be pointless if he's going to talk to Ahmadinejad. It ought to be someone higher.

IGNATIUS: Someone who is closer to the supreme leader.

SCOWCROFT: Yes.

BRZEZINSKI: Yes.

IGNATIUS: And your agenda for that conversation would be similar to Zbig's?

SCOWCROFT: Yes. Back in the first Bush administration, we had all kinds of feelers from Iran to begin negotiations. At one point I said, "Okay, we'll do it and we'll meet quietly." And we actually had a meeting set up, I believe in Switzerland, and they backed out. I'm assuming they backed out because they couldn't stand the internal tension that would be created by talking with the Americans.

IGNATIUS: Did you know who your interlocutor would be?

SCOWCROFT: No. This was way before Ahmadinejad, even before Khatami.

BRZEZINSKI: That's the kind of stuff you have to know in advance. This is why the famous mission under Reagan was so counterproductive: It really wasn't clear who the interlocutors were.

SCOWCROFT: I met with the former Iranian ambassador. We had breakfast together, and we talked, and he said a lot of interesting things. And I said, "Who do you work for? I know who you report to. Who do you work for?" And he went through this convoluted discussion about their national security council and how everybody has an equal voice and so forth. But it's a difficult problem in any discussions you have with Iran.

BRZEZINSKI: One has to understand the country one is engaged with, and that's particularly needed in the case of Iran. We've mentioned its proud history and other aspects. But something else needs to be mentioned. If you look at the statistical handbook for countries and compare Iran with Turkey, there are remarkable similarities in level of education, in access of women to education. We have this image of the women being totally suppressed in Iran. That's hardly the case.

SCOWCROFT: No, it's not.

BRZEZINSKI: Iran currently has a woman as vice president. I'm sure not more than one percent of Americans know that. Iranian women are lawyers, doctors, members of parliament. Iran has a political system that, while it's certainly not democratic by any stretch, is considerably more democratic than, let's say, that of Russia. The elections are still contested.

The expectations of Iranians are increasingly derived from their observation of Turkey and of Europe. And a significant number of Iranians travel as tourists, especially to Turkey but sometimes beyond. So we're dealing with a country which, if we handle it intelligently, could become increasingly like Turkey. That would be a contribution to stability in the region. It is in our interest for Muslim countries to be successful, to be modern, to remain culturally Muslim but to define their Islamic commitment in significantly different ways from what the mullahs in Iran or some of their counterparts elsewhere are preaching.

IGNATIUS: There is an argument that, in fact, this big, well-educated, modernizing Iran is our natural ally, if it will moderate its behavior in certain respects.

BRZEZINSKI: And Israel's ally too. Don't forget that Israel and Iran had a very extensive relationship—for decades—then broke up.

SCOWCROFT: As a matter of fact, we had a really tough time with Israel during the Iran-Iraq War because they were sending military equipment to Iran.

BRZEZINSKI: Without our permission.

SCOWCROFT: Aircraft spare parts without our permission. That's right.

BRZEZINSKI: Looking even further ahead, one has to recognize that in some respects, Israel and Iran are natural allies. In a region where my neighbor tends to be my enemy, the neighbor of my neighbor is my friend. That was the case until the overthrow of the Shah. And even to this day, there is a significant Jewish community in Tehran, which operates in reasonably normal circumstances. There are well-to-do Iranian Jews in prominent places. Iran has not—except for Ahmadinejad lately—been driven by the kind of fanatical anti-Semitism one finds in some Arab countries.

IGNATIUS: When I talk with Iranian officials, which I can do easily as a journalist, I hear an interest in precisely the kind of dialogue that each of you has described, in which there is an effort to find shared interests that the two countries could explore. The most obvious example is Iraq. I think that to a larger extent than is realized, there is a faction in Iran that would be extremely interested in this kind of dialogue. I take it that both of you would say to the next administration, "This is something to pursue."

SCOWCROFT: I think that's exactly the right strategic approach to Iran. Now, we do have an issue with their nuclear program. It is an important issue, because I think we stand on the cusp of a great flowering of proliferation if Iran is not contained in its attempt to develop a capability for nuclear weapons. That's a somewhat different issue. I would approach that through the strategic approach rather than as a precondition for that broader dialogue.

IGNATIUS: You wouldn't make movement on a nuclear issue a precondition for the strategic talk.

BRZEZINSKI: That's part of a larger discussion.

IGNATIUS: So the new president takes office in January, turns to the two of you, and says, "I want to send joint emissaries to Iran bearing a message from the new administration showing that we're united in a bipartisan policy. But I'm not sure what to say in my communiqué." Brent, you and Zbig have to write the message you'll be carrying to Tehran. What would it say?

SCOWCROFT: There are a lot of things to consider, like who do you talk to? But it would say two things. First, that we're aware you live in a dangerous region, and we're prepared to discuss a regional security framework in which you and your legitimate interests can feel secure. Second, whether or not you want nuclear weapons, you're proceeding on a course that psychologically destabilizes the whole region. It is dangerous. It will bring about a counterreaction. And let's work on this security framework. You don't need nuclear weapons.

IGNATIUS: Zbig, would you add anything to that?

BRZEZINSKI: I think that is well put. I would just simply add one point. Since you are saying you don't want nuclear weapons and you're not seeking them, help us believe you.

SCOWCROFT: Yes.

BRZEZINSKI: And the only way we can accomplish that is by sitting together and figuring out some mechanism whereby you achieve what you say you want, which is a peaceful nuclear program, and we achieve what we need, which is a real sense of security that it's not going to go any further.

IGNATIUS: Let's talk about the Iranian nuclear issue. There has been a strenuous collective effort by the United States and its allies—including three United Nations Security Council Resolutions—condemning Iran for its continuing enrichment of uranium in violation of the Nonproliferation Treaty. None of this has worked. The Iranians continue to push ahead with their program.

And I think it's widely viewed by our allies as a threat. So let me ask you how the United States should deal with this terrible problem. Brent, what is the right way to think about this?

SCOWCROFT: It hasn't worked partly because there is not solidarity among the Big Six—Perm-Five-plus-Germany. I don't think any of them want Iran to continue with their enrichment program. But because the U.S. is the bad cop, everyone else thinks they can be the good cop. The Russians and the Chinese think, "We don't want them to have nuclear weapons. But the Americans will take care of that. In the meantime, we can go ahead and curry favor with them, trade with them, and obtain their oil." I think we need to be more skillful in putting the burden on everybody. So far the Russians have been careful. They haven't stepped over the line. They're supplying the Bushehr nuclear power plant with uranium fuel. But it's leased uranium, which they'll take back after it's burned. So they've been very careful.

But we have to somehow present to the Iranians an absolutely solid international front. While the NPT does not prevent them from enriching uranium as long as they abide by the IAEA rules, it's not an acceptable thing to do, for Iran or anybody else. But in the grand scheme of things, I think a UN process for the provision of enriched uranium to fuel power plants is the way to go. Iran probably would not stand up to a real united front, which there hasn't been up to now.

IGNATIUS: It's been as united as you can get. We've had three Security Council Resolutions with P5 support. Zbig, is there a different course? We've had unity among the allies with the one we've been following, but it isn't working. Is there an alternative way?

BRZEZINSKI: There is, and we have already discussed it. The United States can't be a spectator egging others on but refusing to engage in the game. We have been saying to the Iranians, "We'll negotiate if you make fundamental concessions to us for joining the game." We have to be willing to negotiate seriously, either without conditions or with mutual accommodation.

We have done a reasonably good job in our painfully difficult negotiations with the North Koreans. But bear in mind the North Korean position. They have been saying. "We want nuclear weapons. We're seeking nuclear weapons. We have nuclear weapons." The Iranian position is fundamentally different: "We're not seeking nuclear weapons. We don't want nuclear weapons. And our religion forbids us from having nuclear weapons."

They may be lying through their teeth, but that is a better position for us than the North Korean position. It enables us to go to the Iranians and say, "We're delighted to hear that you're not building nuclear weapons, that you don't want nuclear weapons, and that your religion forbids you from having nuclear weapons. But we're just a little bit suspicious that you might be lying. So let's sit down and discuss how you can help us become convinced. Let's work out some arrangement that respects your right to a comprehensive nuclear program, that respects your right to enrich, but does it in a fashion that gives us security that you will not divert the enrichment of weapons, because we do remember that there was something a few years back which really smacks to us of a secret weapons program—so we have some reason to be suspicious. No offense meant, but let's be serious." I'm obviously caricaturing the process, but that should be the approach.

Last point: I don't think it helps our negotiating position one bit to be hinting about the use of force. First of all, I think the use of force would produce catastrophic consequences that would vastly increase our problems in the region. Second, I think it just makes it easier for the regime to mobilize Iranian nationalism and create a united front against us, which enables them to dig in their heels.

IGNATIUS: Brent?

SCOWCROFT: This is not just an Iranian problem. It's a nuclear problem. Let's suppose the Iranians convince us that they're peaceful. If they're allowed to enrich uranium, I would suspect that Egypt, Saudi Arabia, and Turkey will all want to do the same thing. And soon you would have a flood of enrichment programs, not all wanting to produce nuclear weapons, but wanting to be just one step away from getting them, just in case. That would not be a better world. So we need to look at Iran as the tipping point. Anything that allows Iran to enrich uranium is a deadly peril to a nonproliferated world.

IGNATIUS: Anything that allows them to enrich at all, even under safeguard of the NPT?

SCOWCROFT: Well, they can allow inspectors in. They still haven't completely mastered the enrichment program. Once they succeed, they can kick the inspectors out if they want to.

BRZEZINSKI: It's more than just having inspectors. I think one can maintain some sort of an international program in which an enrichment facility operates within certain parameters that are related to the whole scale of the national nuclear program.

But I think if we start off by saying, "Under no conditions can you enrich," you create a reaction in which the Iranians say, well, I guess there's nothing to negotiate about because you want to deny us something.

SCOWCROFT: But this is why I say it's not just an Iranian problem.

BRZEZINSKI: No, it isn't. It's an international problem.

SCOWCROFT: One of the things we need to do is to say, "We, the nuclear powers, encourage nuclear power. We want to support nuclear power. And to do that, we are prepared to provide enriched uranium at a price below any cost at which you can produce it nationally. And we will remove it after it's burned. We will give IAEA control of the process so that the United States can't, if we don't like your behavior, cut off supplies."

BRZEZINSKI: And it would have to be applicable to all other countries.

SCOWCROFT: All other countries. That's why I say we need to pursue the Iranian program, but in the context of an international regime that would encourage nuclear power but without the threat of enrichment.

IGNATIUS: The Russians—

BRZEZINSKI: And—and we have to be willing to convey the notion that this is a joint problem that we want to solve jointly with the Iranians, and not a solution that we're determined to impose on them, because that won't work.

SCOWCROFT: That's right, yes.

IGNATIUS: Suppose all these good ideas go for naught, and the Iranians do what we most fear. They move to higher levels of enrichment and resume what the CIA says was a weaponization effort that was put on the shelf in 2003. And suppose they move toward testing a nuclear weapon as North Korea has done.

The question at the end of the day that we all have to struggle with is: Can the United States live with a nuclear armed Iran? Is that a tolerable situation? Other countries that we hoped wouldn't get the bomb, notably Pakistan and North Korea, got it, and we're living with it. Why is Iran different? Should we put it in a different category, as a country whose acquisition of nuclear weapons is intolerable to us?

BRZEZINSKI: Well, first of all, we have lived with North Korea claiming that it has the capacity to produce weapons, and it has actually tested a quasi-weapon as part of its program. We did not bomb North Korea. And we have been able to continue negotiations which may resolve that problem.

So there's a lesson here. If Iran built a nuclear weapon, I think one would have to make a judgment based on a wider assessment of the nature of the regime, its internal cohesion, its stability, its relative rationality. Would such a regime, given Iran's six-thousand-year history, really be likely to abdicate national power by handing over a weapon to some terrorist group? And would it do it at an early stage of its weapon's program, when it is totally vulnerable to a counterattack if it did so?

And why do I have to make a judgment on the basis of some sort of an irrational calculation? One cannot entirely exclude the use of force. But force generally ought to be the last resort in the face of truly predictable and not hypothetical threats. And I would avoid, in the meantime, poisoning the negotiating process by repetitive threats which also encourage others to either signal their willingness to use force or maximize their political pressure on us to use force.

IGNATIUS: But to cut to the heart of the issue—Brent, can we live with an Iranian bomb? Or should we go to war to prevent it?

SCOWCROFT: I think the consequences of an Iranian bomb are less what Iran will do with the weapon than the rush toward nuclear proliferation that would result. That is about as inevitable as anything in international politics, certainly in the region. An Iranian bomb will not be acquiesced in by the Turks, the Saudis, the Egyptians, maybe even by the UAE.

To compare it with North Korea is a mistake, because North Korea is unique. It's unique in the countries that surround it. Iran is a very different case. But preventing it by force, you have to look at the consequences. There's already a deep suspicion in the region of the United States as basically anti-Muslim. An attack, even only on the nuclear facilities in Iran, would have tremendous geopolitical consequences in the region. And it would immensely complicate our problems there.

BRZEZINSKI: An attack on Iran would create a situation whereby the United States is involved in a war that spans Iraq, Iran, Afghanistan, and increasingly Pakistan, and would certainly spill over into the Persian Gulf. The implications of that for our position in the world, for our capacity to use power, for the world economy, for popular emotions, for the world of Islam, and probably much of the world's stance toward us in general would be so calamitous that one could only contemplate such an attack under the most extreme circumstances—most extreme.

SCOWCROFT: To me the situation requires sophisticated diplomacy, subtle diplomacy, careful diplomacy, looking at all of the elements of a very complicated situation. I think we have a chance of success at that. But we can't hold back and think that it's up to others to give and we can just sit back and take. We have to prepare to put our interests on the table in pursuit of a solution we desperately need.

BRZEZINSKI: And for which we still have some time.

—March 19, 2008

THREE

TWO UNSOLVED
PROBLEMS

DAVID IGNATIUS: Let's turn to the most intractable perennial problem of the Middle East in our lifetimes, which is the Arab-Israeli dispute focused now on the Palestinian issue. We're now in what may be the late stages of yet another peace process, the Annapolis process. At this moment it's in trouble.

Both of you are very experienced in this subject. Zbig, you helped President Carter achieve the first great breakthrough, the Camp David agreement that provided a peace treaty between Israel and Egypt. Brent, you were a central player in the Madrid peace process, which culminated in a peace treaty between Israel and Jordan. Each of you has experience, then, not simply as practitioners but as successful ones. I'd ask you to step back and look at the story since you left the White House. When you look at Secretary Rice dealing with the Annapolis peace mission, Zbig, what do you think?

ZBIGNIEW BRZEZINSKI: I'm reinforced in my gut feeling that the problem between the Israelis and the Palestinians is too deep, too big, too emotional, too deeply rooted for them to solve it themselves.

I'm very pessimistic about the prospects of peace being achieved by Israeli-Palestinian negotiations that are autonomous and self-sustained. The experience I have from Camp David—but also observing, Brent, what you guys did—leads me to the firm conclusion that only the United States can be an effective intermediary. To me that means two things. One, the United States doesn't become a party to the conflict on one side against the other, and two, the United States doesn't maintain a passive posture but advances its own views regarding what needs to happen, is explicit in advancing them, tries to be as fair-minded as it can, respects the vital interests of each of the parties, but is not shy in making its position clear and in insisting that it be respected.

IGNATIUS: Zbig, when Israelis hear Americans make that argument, they fear we are talking about a peace being imposed on them. When you say it's "too big, too difficult, too dangerous for the parties to solve themselves," that suggests the imposition of an agreement from outside. And maybe that's where we are.

BRZEZINSKI: Well, you know, you can always select the words you want. *Impose* means to force down their throats. The word I use is *help* because I don't think either side is prepared to make the concessions that are needed, and neither side is prepared to take the first step because it's always afraid that the other side will pocket the concession.

So you have to have someone who's prepared to step forward

and make the best possible case for a solution, and be really ready to make that case. In Camp David I, all the negotiations were based on highly prepared, detailed American papers which outlined alternative arrangements. And they were guided by a president who knew his stuff and was very insistent.

If we want progress today, we have to be willing to state publicly at least the general parameters of a settlement, and then say, "The rest is up to you as you negotiate the details."

And these four parameters are, first, no right of return for the Palestinians to Israel—a bitter pill for the Palestinians, a very bitter pill. One has to understand what a big, bitter pill this is, because the whole structure of Palestinian identity is built on the notion that they were unjustly expelled from Israel.

Two, real sharing of Jerusalem, a bitter pill for the Israelis. There will be no viable peace if the mosque with the golden dome, if a part of the old city and east Jerusalem, are not the capital of Palestine. The peace will not be viewed as legitimate. There will be no point of departure for reconciliation.

Third is the 1967 borders, with mutual adjustments to allow the big urban settlements on the other side of those lines to be incorporated into Israel, and with equitable territorial concessions in Galilee and Negev by the Israelis so that the Palestinians don't lose any more land. The Israelis and the Palestinians are almost equal in population. Before too long the Palestinians will have more. The Israelis already have seventy-eight percent of the old Palestine. Palestinians have only twenty-two percent.

Fourth is a demilitarized Palestinian state. I have recently proposed that we even have American troops along the Jordan River to give Israel a sense of strategic depth against any threat.

The rest is up to the parties, but this is what the United States should stand for. I happen to believe that Bush still isn't willing to make the push that's needed. If not, the next president should do it.

IGNATIUS: Brent, you talk often with Secretary Rice about her efforts to get her mind around this problem. Tell us what the lessons are from your peacemaking efforts during Bush I.

BRENT SCOWCROFT: I'm not sure how relevant they are right now, in part because the situation is different. We started the peace process during the First Gulf War. Before the war, Saddam was trying to get the Palestinian issue on the table. He wanted a region-wide discussion and we said, "No. We deal first with your invasion of Kuwait."

And we told the Arab world, "Stick with us. Do this with us, then we'll take up the peace process." I think we gave the Arab world confidence in our evenhandedness by being willing to take on a case of aggression against an Arab state. The process was still difficult, but that paved the way for the Madrid process—the first time both sides sat down officially and said, "We need to work on a process."

IGNATIUS: Brent, you and President Bush were quite tough on Israel, to the point of withholding U.S. loan guarantees for the Israeli government because of your anger over settlements and housing issues. How important do you think that was, that demonstration that in our efforts to be evenhanded we were prepared even to withhold money from our ally?

SCOWCROFT: I think it was important because it doesn't happen often. It has not happened—

BRZEZINSKI: Since.

SCOWCROFT: —too often over the last sixty years. The fact that we refused to guarantee loans for settlements in the West Bank had a big impact on the Arab world. I don't know whether it had an impact on Israel.

BRZEZINSKI: I think it did, because after that Shamir fell. Rabin came to power and it was one of the least active periods of settlement construction in the entire history of the occupation, until he was killed.

SCOWCROFT: You know, Rabin is an interesting case in the way this whole thing has evolved. When I met Rabin, he was ambassador to the United States, and he was as hard as any hard-liner. In the course of being foreign minister, defense minister, leader of the army—all of these things—he matured until the last time he became prime minister he had the vision that, had he lived, would have allowed him to make a deal. It was a great evolution.

Israel is making something of the same evolution, from the days in '48 when they founded the state, to the period after the '67 war when they embraced the vision of a greater Israel, and now back to a two-state solution.

BRZEZINSKI: Let me jump in here. When I first met Menachem Begin as prime minister, he told me flatly, "There's no such thing as a Palestinian. That's a fiction. There's no such thing as a Palestinian. These are all Arabs. And their natural home is across the Jordan." The concept was *Eretz Yisrael.*

Twenty years later, Ariel Sharon accepts a two-state solution. Okay, he's vague about the problem of territories, but he basically accepts a Palestinian state in Palestine. There's a lesson in that. Even extreme parties evolve if you're willing to be patient and talk to them. And I think of Hamas in that connection. Hamas is not prepared to accept Israel, but it is prepared to accept a ten-year truce. If we are intelligent in manipulating Hamas, they could end up like Fatah, growing more moderate with time.

IGNATIUS: Let me ask you both one of the questions that will be most vexing for a new president, and that is whether the United States should encourage contact and discussion with Hamas. This is an organization that refuses to recognize Israel's right to exist, that Israelis feel is bent on the destruction of the state of Israel. And yet there's no question that it is deeply rooted in Gaza. Israel's military attempts to destroy it have failed, and there's every reason to think they'll keep failing. Should we seek some contact with that organization, try to pull them toward a peace process?

SCOWCROFT: When I first became involved in this overall issue in the early '70s, we weren't allowed to talk to Fatah because it was a terrorist organization. We had to go through Morocco or others to communicate with them. This is the process we're going through. I think we need to be prepared to talk with Hamas. Hamas has suggested a cease-fire. I don't know what it means. But we'll never find out if we don't talk to them.

My sense is that if we can make progress on the peace process— I'm pessimistic like Zbig is, but if we can—Hamas will decide it cannot afford to be left out and to end up, at best, with control over Gaza, which can't survive by itself. I think their call for a cease-fire is a tactic and they may not mean it. But I believe shutting Hamas off only makes Hamas stronger and undermines Fatah.

BRZEZINSKI: I agree with Brent completely on the political level. But I don't think we should lose sight of the moral dimension. On the moral level, not talking to Hamas means boycotting them. It means cutting them off. It means punishing a million and a half people where there are really serious humanitarian problems: illness, starvation, general disintegration of the community. I find it troubling. I don't think this is a good way to negotiate unless you're engaged in some mortal conflict.

If we were in a serious war with a country, of course we would have to be prepared to impose hardship on the population. We did that during World War II. But the million and a half people who live in Gaza are not our enemies. We can't forget that.

Somehow we have become indifferent to that, to a degree that I find troubling morally but also politically, because that creates a sense of grievance and hatred for us in the Middle East that we cannot disregard. We have a vital interest in the Middle East. But we are creating increasingly widespread resentment of America. At some point those chickens will come home to roost.

IGNATIUS: Israelis and their supporters would want to interject at this point, "What about us?" Doesn't America have a special relationship with Israel, a special commitment to Israel's survival that means that the kind of evenhanded policy you're both talking about leaves Israel at a disadvantage? If Israel had fifty powerful friends, that would be one thing. It has one powerful friend.

BRZEZINSKI: Excuse me. I don't buy that at all. The notion that we have to prove our friendship to Israel by starving the people in Gaza I just find immoral in content, and not practical politically.

SCOWCROFT: We've talked frequently about a special relationship with Israel. I think we have a relationship that is natural with a small, courageous democracy in a hostile land. I don't think we have any special commitment there. And I think we have an equal commitment to Palestinians, many of whom are spending their third generation in refugee camps. Camps which are, among other things, a breeding ground for terrorism. I think we have a moral responsibility, given who we are, to try to solve this problem.

BRZEZINSKI: Beyond that, there's a practical question. How long will Israel endure if we're driven out of the Middle East? So, you know, I have absolutely no hesitation in saying what I've been saying.

Ultimately I think what I'm saying is in the best interest of Israel. If we can get a fair peace, and we have to do some things to get a fair peace, Israel can become an enduring part of the Middle East and prosper there. If we're driven out of the Middle East, how much would you bet on Israel's survival?

IGNATIUS: The two presidents you worked for, Jimmy Carter and George H. W. Bush, were both criticized by the pro-Israel community as being insufficiently supportive. President Carter was denounced when he published his recent book for using the word *apartheid* in talking about Israeli policy toward the Palestinians.

This is a very emotional issue. It's one of the live wires in international politics. How would you advise a new administration, Brent, to walk that fine line between pursuing an evenhanded policy and maintaining this traditional friendship?

SCOWCROFT: If this goes to the next administration we could face another crisis in the region. We have an unusual moment now. I agree with Zbig: I'm pessimistic about our being able to take advantage of it. But we have an Israeli government that is weak. We have a Palestinian entity that is weak. And, really for the first time, we have Arab countries ready to support a solution.

BRZEZINSKI: And public support.

SCOWCROFT: Public opinion on both sides. What we do not have are two sides that by themselves are able to come to an agreement. They can't now. They're not strong enough. There's too much opposition back home. They need a heavier hand by the United States than we have traditionally practiced.

IGNATIUS: When you say a "heavier hand," what are you thinking of?

SCOWCROFT: We have to put forward, carefully but firmly, an outline based on the Taba accords, as Zbig laid out, and say, "This is a fair and just solution. We present it as a just solution drawn up by the Israelis and Palestinians in 2001. Anything you both can agree upon to modify it, we're happy with. But we need to move now."

If this administration leaves office without an agreement, there will be a big letdown. And the region is incredibly fragile right now. Lebanon is ready to explode. How long can Abbas survive? If we think, well, we'll get a better person if Abbas leaves, we could be fooling ourselves. I think there's a huge danger there and elsewhere in the region. It is very, very fragile.

It will take any new president time to reevaluate, to get settled, so you're looking at a year to eighteen months from where we are now. That time could be costly.

BRZEZINSKI: Let me add to what Brent said. Hopefully President Bush, of whom I'm very critical, will still do it. He keeps saying mysteriously that he expects a peace settlement to be signed this year. He can't keep repeating it without somehow meaning it. And if he means it, he has to do something.

I don't see what else he can do except what Brent and I have been saying. Maybe he'll still do it, and we'll be reading about it as this book goes to press. So be it. But if he doesn't, I agree with Brent but I'll even go a little further. I would say the next president will have to take the bull by the horns right away, because this is an issue which is domestically divisive.

Any president, whether his margin of victory is small or large, comes into office with a certain new legitimacy. He has that first year or eighteen months to do something on this issue. If he doesn't, he won't be able to do it later, so he might as well try. It's a high-risk thing.

But as Brent said, we have several factors in our favor. The Arab states are at last much more rational and are prepared to go for a compromise. The Israeli public is much more flexible on this issue than the right-wing leadership of the large American Jewish organizations, which are strongly committed but which don't reflect the views of the majority of American Jews, who are much more liberal. And public opinion in Palestine and Israel is more flexible. So I think the next president, if he's daring and determined, should be able to pull it off. If he doesn't, he's going to have a mess on his hands.

IGNATIUS: If someone from the Israeli defense ministry were sitting here with us, he or she would say, "Gentlemen, you're forgetting that we pulled out of Gaza unilaterally. And we did so in the expectation that that gesture would be reciprocated. Instead we have missiles falling every day. As the missile range keeps expanding, more and more of our coastal cities are within range of the missiles. We don't have a partner we can deal with for a lot of this problem. There are people who are determined to stop a peace process from working." How do we deal with that?

SCOWCROFT: Opponents of the peace process cannot stop it if the

United States won't let it be stopped. The withdrawal from Gaza was done in a way that made almost inevitable the chaos that followed. Sharon would not talk to the Palestinians, would not make any arrangement for the transfer of territory.

BRZEZINSKI: Or even the facilities.

SCOWCROFT: Or, facilities, anything—

BRZEZINSKI: Because he blew them up.

SCOWCROFT: Security is a genuine problem for the Israelis, and it's one of their abiding fears that unless they themselves are intervening militarily, doing the things they do to keep the Palestinians off balance, they'll be victimized by terrorist attacks. Zbig talked about an American line along the Jordan River, and I think we should consider it.

We also ought to consider something like a NATO peacekeeping force. As the Israelis withdraw from West Bank areas, we put a NATO peacekeeping force in, both to help train the Palestinian security force and to maintain the stability that the Israelis are desperately afraid they'll lose by withdrawing.

IGNATIUS: Let me close this part of our discussion by asking a question that Israelis sometimes talk about late at night when they're really being honest. And that is the question of whether, fifty years from now, there will be a Jewish state in the Middle East called "Israel." I think that really is a nightmare that motivates a lot of the actions that seem to Americans to be extreme. How can that Jewish state be made more secure and more permanent?

BRZEZINSKI: Well, first of all, I understand the feeling. When I first went to the Middle East to push for Arab acquiescence to the Camp David peace treaty between Israel and Egypt, some of the Arabs said to me, "You know, the crusaders were in Jerusalem for ninety years, and they are gone. We're in no rush." So there is a legitimacy to Israeli concern. But they have to ask themselves, "Is that horrible scenario more likely or less likely if there's no peace?" If the peace is somewhat legitimate, that is to say both sides are somewhat prepared to live with it—and I again emphasize Israeli public opinion and Palestinian public opinion have evolved—then that ensures Israel's security.

And you know, the moment Israel and Palestine are reconciled, they have a chance together of becoming the Singapore of the Middle East. If I were an Israeli I would look at Dubai and Qatar and say to myself, "Don't I want a piece of that?" Once there is peace, the intelligence of the Israelis and Palestinians together could make them a dynamo for the region, financially and technologically. Israel is doing very well technologically. But if they condemn themselves to this condition that is neither war nor peace, in an increasingly radicalized Middle East in which we are gradually losing influence, what is their future?

Sure, there will always be Palestinians who will commit acts of terrorism. There will be Israelis who retaliate. Are we supposed to let those people dominate the future? This is where America's responsibility is very high, and where the opportunity for the next president is quite promising if he's willing to stand up and be a leader.

IGNATIUS: Brent, what's your thinking?

SCOWCROFT: It's not without risk, but I think the risk for Israel of concluding an agreement is considerably less than the risk of remaining isolated in a bitterly hostile region and depending on the United States for security. If we can get beyond this deadlock, there's a natural synergism, as Zbig says, between Israel and the surrounding areas, an economic dynamic that can revitalize the whole region.

IGNATIUS: That is such a happy vision. But I'm reminded of a comment of my former colleague, Karen Elliot House from the *Wall Street Journal*, who said that when it comes to the Middle East, pessimism pays.

SCOWCROFT: But let me give you an example. Lebanon is one of the most fragile states in the world. But for a long time, Beirut was the entrepôt and Paris of the region. Lebanon was a fragile, carefully balanced multipolar state. But it was not that Lebanon fell apart; it was that the surrounding situation ripped it apart. I think it's possible for people who don't agree on all the same things to live together and prosper.

▶ ▶ ▶

IGNATIUS: Our subject in these conversations is how the United States can begin to put a badly disordered world back together. As we think about the Middle East, I'd ask each of you to step back and think about the values that you would see us bringing to all of these different problems, from the Arab-Israeli peace process to Iraq to Iran.

One of my memories from my years as a correspondent covering Beirut is the inscription over the main gates of the American University, which was founded by American missionaries in the middle of the nineteenth century. Carved there are the words, "That they may have life and have it abundantly." It's a phrase from the Bible. And it expresses that idealistic American aspiration for the world that led the missionaries into the Near East one hundred fifty years ago and kept them there for so many years.

With that as a starting point, I'd ask each of you to talk about the values you would like to see us bringing to this dialogue with Arabs and Israelis, and how we can change the image our country has today in that part of the world to something more positive. Brent?

SCOWCROFT: The peace process is the place to start. If we can succeed in that we will turn the mood around. We are now seen not as impartial but as supporting one side. The Arabs have largely lost faith in us because of that, and because of Iraq.

If the peace process is driven to a successful conclusion, I think we will change the Arabs' attitude. They will behave more as they did in 1990, when Kuwait was invaded and they joined us in restoring the situation. I think they'll be prepared to play a role in Iraq that they're not prepared to play now.

And it will restore balance with Iran. Iran now thinks it's on a roll. An Arab-Israeli treaty would give confidence to the Sunni Arab world that they can hold their own. It would also be a major step forward in our struggle with terrorism. As I've mentioned, we now have sixty years of refugee camps, with people growing up, living off UN subsidies to survive, with no hope and no jobs. That is a terrible breeding ground for extremism. I believe this is the way to start turning the region around so that we get the moderates, who are, after all, the majority, on our side.

IGNATIUS: Do we need to be less visible in our support for authoritarian regimes? The Bush administration has argued that our support for the Saudi monarchy, for the authoritarian Mubarak regime in Egypt, undercuts any hope we have of connecting with the people in the Middle East. Do you buy that?

SCOWCROFT: No, I don't buy that. Ought we to stand by our principles? Yes. But we can't remake the whole world at once. We need to go step by step.

Giving the Arab world the confidence that we're really supportive, that we're helping them and dealing with the regimes that are there, would get things moving in the right direction. But if we try to do it all at once, we'll end up with a region in which nobody will want to live, which risks being the direction we are headed.

IGNATIUS: Zbig, in your book *Second Chance*, you talk powerfully about the United States turning a page in this part of the world. Walk us through your thoughts about how America comes to stand for different values.

BRZEZINSKI: Well, let me follow on what Brent said, and take as my point of departure that motto you cited. It says a lot about the kind of role we once played in the Middle East, and that we should resume. We were viewed by most people in the Middle East, particularly after World War II, as a liberating force. We were seen as encouraging the disappearance of the British and French without moving in our own forces in their wake. And we were seen by countless members of the intelligentsia as sharing technological know-how, which we had and they didn't, as helping them enter the modern world at their pace and in their cultural setting. That gradually changed, to the point that we've begun to be the new colonialists, particularly through our military intervention in Iraq, our one-sided support for Sharon under George W. Bush, and a kind of generalized indifference to what is happening to the Palestinians. And that was followed by a strange commitment to cultural imperialism through democratization, which we disowned the moment it was tested somewhere.

IGNATIUS: You're referring to our favoring elections by the Palestinians and then, once Hamas won—

BRZEZINSKI: Exactly. If we ask ourselves very seriously what would be the likely result of free elections in Egypt, we know damn well the Muslim Brotherhood could come out extremely well. Will we really want that? I'm not sure the more advanced parts of the Egyptian society would even want it. No one has tested what the masses in Saudi Arabia really want, but I wouldn't want an election in which Osama bin Laden is running against some member of the Saudi royalty.

My point is, we can have a lot of influence, but influence and assistance are not the same thing as cultural imperialism. When we start sending around Karen Hughes to teach the Arabs democracy, we make ourselves the object of ridicule. So I think there's a lot to change.

If we can bring the Israeli-Palestinian conflict to a fair conclusion, I think we can remove one of the major sources of anti-American radicalism in the Middle East. We can again play a stabilizing, constructive role in the Middle East, and as Brent said, undercut some of the social propensity for terrorism.

IGNATIUS: In the category of problems or opportunities in the Middle East, a leading item would be Syria, which keeps advertising its interest in peace negotiations yet isn't at the table. Zbig, you were just there, and talked to President Bashar al-Assad. What did you hear?

BRZEZINSKI: Basically two major messages, which he stated with considerable seriousness. The first one was that he has made a break with Ba'athist Socialism. On this he was very eloquent, although his vice president was much less so. But there's evidence in the country that Syria now sees itself as part of the globalized economy. They understand the need to rely on private industry, to have more trade with foreign countries and more openness. Fewer state institutions running the economy. From what I could gather during a short visit, it looks like this vision is beginning to be implemented on a national level, but with some opposition from the old cadres.

The second point was in response to a question I raised. I said to him, "Looking at your conflict with Israel, would you be prepared to sign a peace treaty with the Israelis in which your territorial aspirations were satisfied but which would not be in any other way conditioned on what happens between the Israelis and the Palestinians?" In other words, something resembling the Sadat-Israeli accommodation. And his answer was an unequivocal, "Yes, absolutely, provided we obtain a full territorial restitution to the lines that existed prior to June 1967."

Now I repeated that when I was subsequently in Israel, and the Israeli answer was a little more complex. They said, "Yes, that's fine. That's good news, but he's got to cut ties with Hezbollah. He's got to cut ties with Hamas. He's got to end all support of terrorism. He's got to divorce himself from the Iranians." So my sense is that's not very much concurrence.

IGNATIUS: Brent, one of the great successes of Bush I was your engagement of Syria to get those peace negotiations rolling, even though they never rolled to fruition. What do you think about the opportunities with Syria?

SCOWCROFT: I think there are opportunities. We have to remember that Syria is not a monolithic state. It's in many ways like

Lebanon in terms of the various divisions. This is a regime that has its own enemies and is very nervous. I think they very much want a settlement. I was approached by the foreign minister, Mouallem, to try to get the U.S. to draw Syria to the Annapolis peace talks by saying the Golan Heights could possibly be raised as an issue for discussion. That, to me, indicates that they want to participate.

For some time after 9/11, the Syrians were fairly cooperative in supplying intelligence and identifying Al-Qaeda operatives. But they're ambivalent. And as I say, they've got their own internal problems. They're partly helping us in Iraq, and partly hurting us, I think for the same reason. They're trying to jockey their own internal situation and protect themselves.

We don't help ourselves by not having a serious discussion with them. For one thing, a solution on the Golan Heights has none of the emotion for the Israelis that the West Bank has. It's more a strategic than an emotional decision.

IGNATIUS: The Syrians will say to you privately that while they don't want to send their army back to Lebanon, they will not tolerate a Lebanon that is not accommodating to Syria's interests. Zbig, is that a reasonable Syrian demand, that there not be a hostile Lebanese government?

BRZEZINSKI: It would depend on the larger context. If there was serious progress between Syria and Israel; if things improved in Iraq so that there wasn't this ambivalence to the role the Syrians are playing, which Brent mentioned. In that context, maintenance of the historic Syrian-Lebanese connection doesn't have to have a hostile effect on us.

So it really depends on the context. This is why so much depends on the degree to which we are prepared, seriously, to move on the Israeli-Palestinian peace issue. That ultimately is a catalyst for the other things we've been talking about. The disarmament or re-moval of Hezbollah would be easier. The fading away or transformation of Hamas would be more likely. The Syrian connection with the Iranians might start fading, especially if there was peace between the Syrians and the Israelis, and therefore a more benign role for them in Lebanon. So the key to it really is how serious are we about really addressing the underlying problems of the Middle East.

SCOWCROFT: Zbig is absolutely right. In 1975, we subtly encouraged the Syrians into Lebanon, to stop a brutal civil war. Lebanon is a creature of the politics of the region. It's another reason for the peace process. If you can put that process together, you can make a deal with the Syrians in which Lebanon resumes its traditional kind of fractious neutrality. But it can only be done in the context of the whole region.

BRZEZINSKI: If I may just add, the view that the Syrian role in Lebanon has been uniformly malignant is just not historically right.

SCOWCROFT: No. Or we never would have encouraged them to go in there in 1975.

IGNATIUS: That may be so. But I've spoken at the memorial service of Gibran Tueni, who was the editor of *AnNahar*, and I've been to the graves of other Lebanese friends who've been murdered, it is believed, by the Syrians.

SCOWCROFT: No question.

IGNATIUS: So a reasonable person might ask, how can we do business with people who assassinate politicians from other nations that they don't like? Don't we have to bring them to justice? What about the Lebanese who grieve so visibly for all the people who've been killed, they think, by Syrian assassins? What should we say to them?

BRZEZINSKI: Well, is the response to change the context, or to take revenge?

IGNATIUS: What should it be?

BRZEZINSKI: I think it should be changing the context. After all, you know, when we promoted Arafat going to Madrid, it was a giant step towards peace. But Arafat did have blood on his hands.

SCOWCROFT: And Lebanese have Lebanese blood on their hands, too. Some of the most brutal killings have been Lebanese on Lebanese.

BRZEZINSKI: The Maronites killing the Palestinians, for example.

SCOWCROFT: What we need to do is what we think will bring all of this to an end.

IGNATIUS: What about our military role? We maintain very large forces in and around the Middle East. We have Centcom with forward bases in Qatar and Bahrain. We continue to sell arms to just about everybody in the region who wants to buy them, except for Iran. Would you recommend that we pull back somewhat from that very visible military presence?

BRZEZINSKI: Well, depends which forces. I would certainly recommend we try to end the war in Iraq.

IGNATIUS: I was thinking more broadly about the deployment of American military forces as a stabilizing factor. And the question every person asks—

BRZEZINSKI: In the Persian Gulf? Yes.

IGNATIUS: —is, "Is it stabilizing or the opposite?"

BRZEZINSKI: If the force is in the Persian Gulf, if it's largely on water, if it's to protect very rich but extremely vulnerable little entities against their neighbors, including Iran, I have no problem with that. It's the larger political packaging that creates the problems, plus this specific war.

SCOWCROFT: I think it's less the troop presence itself than what we're trying to do. It's a turbulent region. Some of our arms sales go back to the cold war. But if we're seen the way Zbig and I both think we ought to be seen in the region—and we can take steps to be seen that way—our presence will not be viewed with hostility. Take the United Arab Emirates for example, a very prosperous country with basically no security—

BRZEZINSKI: Filthy rich, in fact.

SCOWCROFT: The kind of stabilizing presence which gives people the feeling they don't have to worry about security, I think could be productive. But it has to be done with that in mind, and not playing games around the region.

IGNATIUS: The average American in late 2008 looking at the war in Iraq, looking at above four thousand Americans killed, the immense cost, the public opinion polls that show America disliked to the point of being hated by the average person in that part of the world—the average American might say, these people don't like us, and we've been throwing good money after bad. The sensible thing for us to do is pull back. We've overinvested in the Middle East. Enough already. A lot of ordinary folks are feeling we should reduce our presence in that part of the world. So I'd ask you—

BRZEZINSKI: Well, I'd argue with that.

IGNATIUS: It's not just Main Street that thinks that. Richard Haass, the president of the council on foreign relations, has argued that the American era in the Middle East is ending, partly as a consequence of the mistakes we've made in Iraq. So among ordinary folks and even some elite analysts there's an argument that we really are heading into a phase in which American power will be and should be much reduced. From what you both have said, I take it you disagree. So I'd ask you to explain why you think it's important for us to be a strong power in that part of the world.

BRZEZINSKI: Let me qualify the point of departure, because I see it differently. People like Richard Haass are making, to some extent, the case Brent and I are making, that our policy is undercutting our presence. But I don't think the man in the street therefore favors our departure. The man on the street basically feels, first, if we left we'd endanger Israel, and second, we would lose oil. Neither is a good thing.

The real risk is that in this volatile context, the man on the street is going to be responsive to increasingly jingoist rhetoric and demagogy, which will generalize the difficulty into an overall con-demnation of the world of Islam and a kind of fatalistic acceptance of the proposition that we are doomed to World War IV with jihadist Islam—the kind of stuff that Senator Lieberman has been advocating.

That's the real danger. If we don't get a settlement in the Middle East, if the war continues percolating, if something negative happens in our relationship with Iran, the danger could become reality. And that would be simply a fatal maximization of the difficulties that we already confront.

IGNATIUS: Brent?

SCOWCROFT: There's an additional reason for U.S. presence. It's not so much state against state conflict there but factional conflict. Extremism, if you will—a faction of Islam using the sword to intimidate the majority. I think we can bring a sense of stability by our presence there.

BRZEZINSKI: If we redefine ourselves.

SCOWCROFT: If we define ourselves.

BRZEZINSKI: Redefine.

SCOWCROFT: I think what we've learned in Iraq is that you can't pick up a country, create a democracy, turn around and leave. It doesn't work that way. So we need to moderate our presence and the way we operate so that we encourage the right forces in the region, and discourage or provide protection from extremism, which keeps the moderates from speaking out for the kind of Islam that's existed for over one thousand years.

BRZEZINSKI: And extending what Brent was saying, a great deal of that applies also to Afghanistan and Pakistan, where we face similar problems. We have a kind of cultural misunderstanding of the terrain, which leads us to an excessively one-dimensional reliance on force to solve problems that are deeply rooted in history and in cultural differences we don't fully understand, and which require a great deal of time and patience for them to be worked out. Our involvement is a kind of radicalizing foreign intervention which then produces unwelcome consequences.

There was a wonderful article a couple of weeks ago in the *New York Times Magazine* about a platoon fighting in Afghanistan in the wilds near the Pakistani border. These were very brave young guys, totally isolated. There was a village near their camp, and they were occasionally engaging in sniping with the village.

They were at the same time trying to destroy the Taliban base, and so forth. And of course there was an attack on their camp. They finally had a meeting with the elders of this village, where the lieutenant in charge of the platoon put the question very simply: "Do we fight or do we have peace?" And the elders said, "We're going to consider your question. We'll meet tonight and among ourselves, we'll decide." And they did.

The next day they came back and said in effect, "You know, you're foreigners. You're here with guns. Go ahead and fight." Then there was a fight and the platoon suffered heavy losses. The village got pulverized. That, to me, is the kind of fighting that could become more widespread if we're not a little more sensitive.

It has nothing to do with Al-Qaeda. The villagers didn't give a damn about Al-Qaeda. They were interested in their village.

IGNATIUS: In the Muslim world, though, isn't there a sense that all these events that we've been discussing take place under the canopy of a war we didn't start—a war that was declared on us—

BRZEZINSKI: Which war are you talking about?

IGNATIUS: In 1996, Osama bin Laden issued a declaration of war in which he said, in essence, "If you hit the Americans hard, they'll run away." That's what happened in Beirut in 1983 and '84. It's what happened in Somalia. And when you go through that declaration of war the central theme is, "These Americans can be had."

Now, when people in that part of the world read your thoughts about the Middle East, many of them will say, "Aha. You see, the Americans can be beat. They are in retreat. These two wisest of American foreign policy experts are calling for different policies. This very strong attack on America has been successful." I'd ask you to respond to that, because that's what will be on the jihadi Web sites. The sheiks on Al Jazeera will be saying. "Here's one more bit of evidence that the Americans can be beaten."

SCOWCROFT: I think we're saying quite the contrary. We're saying we need to stay there. Bin Laden made clear his attack was not against the United States, per se. He wants to drive us out of the region because he thinks the governments in the region are corrupt and need to be overthrown, and we're protecting them.

So if you're an Arab, do you want us to leave, and leave the region to the mercy of the extremists? We're saying we need the kind of presence that gives heart to the average person in the region who wants to live a normal life, with religion having its place, greater or lesser, but not with a thirteenth-century iron fist telling them what to do.

BRZEZINSKI: There's a famous saying by Sun Tzu: "The best strategy is to let your opponent defeat himself." A great deal of what Osama bin Laden has been saying is similar. He wants to get the Americans involved in such a way that all Saudis will hate us. By concentrating on the presence of American forces in Saudi Arabia, he thinks maybe the Americans will stupidly react and then there'll be a collision. Al-Qaeda says it'd be wonderful if the United States and Iran got into war, because that would spread the conflict.

The ones who attacked us on 9/11 were obviously hoping to so outrage us that we would react in a totally clumsy fashion so that more and more Muslims would be mobilized against us. Unfortunately, in one respect they succeeded, and so we're at war in Iraq.

I think we ought not to get out of the region. But we have to pursue our military policies in such a way that they're politically effective. That means isolating Al-Qaeda, mobilizing Muslim moderates, and creating conditions in which they feel more comfortable in dealing with extremism.

We will not do it if we just apply heavy-handed policies, don't move towards peace between Israel and Palestine, remain stuck for years in Iraq, pursue a policy of expanding military operations in Afghanistan, cut down the poppy fields without giving any compensation to the peasants, attack the Pashtuns, and end up with a wider war on our hands. That's not victory. It's exactly what Osama bin Laden wants us to do in order to defeat us.

IGNATIUS: If I were to summarize this conversation, I would say that you are both arguing for America to stay the course in that part of the world, but sensibly—to stay a course that's sustainable, which is different from our present course. Each of you said emphatically that unless we get more serious about solving the Israeli-Palestinian problem, we are doomed to an ever-worsening situation. Would it be at the top of your list for the next president?

SCOWCROFT: I believe it's number one.

IGNATIUS: Let's turn to another unsolved problem. If there's one part of the world that could blow up in dangerous ways, it's Pakistan, and the Pakistan-Afghanistan frontier. As we remind ourselves so often, Pakistan is a nuclear state. It faces a large and growing Islamic insurgency—its own Taliban. It has a weak, increasingly fragmented political leadership in this post-Musharraf era. So I'd like to ask each of you, how you would suggest moving Pakistan from its present condition—which is pretty dangerous—to something that's less dangerous and more stable.

SCOWCROFT: It's very difficult for me to see a clear path. We have a very dangerous situation. Pakistan, in a sense, got a tough hand in the division of India, in 1947. They inherited the tribal areas, the most fractious areas. They did not inherit the Congress Party, which gave a sense of unity to India that Pakistan didn't enjoy. And they have been unable to deal with democracy. There have been continuing upheavals—the civilian government grows corrupt, or inept, or both, the military kicks them out, runs the country for a while, then turns it back to the civilians. That's been a recurrent theme.

When Pakistan was young, we were one of their closest allies, and they relied on us for security. But after the Second Indo-Pakistan War, we put sanctions on both sides and stopped selling them military equipment. It didn't matter to the Indians, because they had an arms industry. The Paks did not. The sanctions disrupted their sense of security and started the drive for nuclear weapons.

As they started to build nuclear capability, we added more and more sanctions, increasing their insecurity until, eventually, we got the Pakistan we have now, with a military president who has not been willing to give back the country to civilian rule. The political parties are deeply hostile to each other, but these are not like political parties we know. These are dynastic parties with significant tribal bases.

The very fact that Benazir Bhutto could pass leadership in the party to her son and husband is an illustration of the problem. That's what we've inherited. The one key element of Pakistani unity is the army. It's no longer Musharraf, necessarily; it's the army. I think perhaps the best outcome of a very difficult situation is a standoff among the president's party, the Bhutto Party, and the Sharif Party.

Right now, Bhutto and Sharif are together, but that's not likely to last, because the parties are fundamentally hostile to each other. Can Musharraf hang on? I don't know. To me, the greatest danger we face is a crisis over Musharraf in which the army splits. The seniors in the army—the top level—are still the British-trained strong impartial people. But under them—at the colonel level—are the ones who trained the Taliban to go into Afghanistan to fight the Soviets.

I think it's going to take great skill to prevent an explosion. If the army splits, the nuclear weapons are not necessarily secure. And a Pakistan in chaos could be a fatal attraction for India to solve the Kashmir problem. It certainly would have repercussions in Afghanistan.

IGNATIUS: That's a grim forecast. Zbig, do you share that?

BRZEZINSKI: I do, and I am inclined to draw some lessons from what Brent was saying. We have to be extremely careful not to inject ourselves too heavily into internal Pakistani politics. Pakistan is too large, too populous, and too complex for us to be able to deal effectively with its internal politics.

I was not enamored of the U.S. initiative encouraging Mrs. Bhutto to go back. I was involved in some of the discussions with her last year, and I was very suspicious and uneasy. I thought we were trying to mix water and oil, and I was convinced that the result would be either Musharraf would be dead or she would be. By pushing it, we showed that our understanding of Pakistani politics is very shallow. They are terribly convoluted, partially ethnic-provincial and partially, as Brent said, dynastic and competitive, and very much influenced by the army.

There's a saying in Pakistan that the country exists thanks to three *A*'s: Allah, America, and the army. Allah is far away. America's also far away, and also ignorant. The army's on the spot. And therefore the cohesion of the army, for some time to come, will remain the central factor in Pakistani politics. We must be very careful not to inject ourselves in a fashion which risks splitting it.

I think it was too bad that we cut off International Military Education and Training (IMET) for so many years. We didn't have the opportunity to train these younger officers. We have a specific problem, which is the Pashtun area and the frontier area, the sanctuary for Al-Qaeda. We have to deal with it, but we have to be very prudent so as not to galvanize Pakistani politics into irrational anti-Americanism, some of the makings of which are already underway.

To the extent that we have to act, we should act discreetly and avoid publicizing what happens. My guess is if we do that, the Pakistanis in power will see their interest is also in not publicizing it. But if we start boasting, as we are lately, we will make it increasingly impossible for any Pakistani government to accept our actions.

Public emotions will surface. The army may be resentful. And then the consequences are unpredictable. We can probably handle the problem in Afghanistan for quite a while, since we still have some residual sympathy from the help we gave the Afghans against the Soviets. But if the turmoil in Afghanistan spills over into Pakistan, I think we'll be faced with an altogether unmanageable situation. Unmanageable if we get more involved and bogged down, and unmanageable if we abruptly terminate and leave.

So I would say prudence, prudence, prudence over again, and let the Pakistanis sort out their problems. Stop lecturing them on de-mocracy, and be sensitive to their historical geopolitical interests. And emphasize that they have a kind of friend in Afghanistan, which gives them strategic depth vis-à-vis India. But at the same time, we should be careful not to make the Afghans think they're going to be the satellites of Pakistan, which is a difficult game. Be-yond that I simply don't advocate any political activism regarding Pakistan itself.

IGNATIUS: What about in our relations with the Pakistani mili-tary? The new Pakistani chief of staff, General Kayani, has said to our chairman of the joint chiefs, Admiral Mullen, and to the CIA director and others that he is prepared to work with us to train a so-called frontier corps in the tribal areas, to work with people in those very remote villages as a more aggressive counterinsurgency force—

BRZEZINSKI: Yes.

IGNATIUS: —doing economic development. And also using quite aggressive tactics to go out and hit any Al-Qaeda members who are hiding. Obviously that's in our interest, but it also raises the danger of precisely what both of you have talked about: splitting the army. Of being so aggressive that it becomes controversial. What would your advice be about that?

BRZEZINSKI: I would say the Pakistani military leadership really wants it and is prepared to exercise its supervisory role. If we can do it more or less on the QT, without too much visibility, it's probably better than not doing it.

IGNATIUS: Even given the danger that there might be Islamist elements in the army that would look at this and say, "What the heck is our general staff doing working with the United States?"

BRZEZINSKI: That judgment has to be made by the Pakistani generals, not by us.

SCOWCROFT: Right. But I think if we're seen to be helping the Pakistanis rather than insisting that the Pakistani army do A, B, and C—

BRZEZINSKI: Or that we do it without them.

SCOWCROFT: Or that we do it without them. Because remember, this region is one of the most fractious in the world. The British controlled both sides of it for a hundred years and were not able to pacify it. The Pakistanis have to take the lead in dealing with the region and with spillover of the Taliban coming back.

If the Pakistan army wants help, we ought to help. And we ought to encourage the Pakistan army. We ought to start the IMET program again.

IGNATIUS: And get more officers over here for training.

BRZEZINSKI: Younger officers.

SCOWCROFT: Because for a long time, the army is going to be the glue that keeps that country together.

IGNATIUS: Should we decommission the armed Predators that are flying over the mountains of Torah Borah and the tribal areas even as we speak? Are these provocations, these invisible weapons deployed by the United States over the territory of sovereign countries such as Pakistan. Should they be flying?

BRZEZINSKI: It depends on the consequences of their flying. If they engage in strikes which kill a lot of locals in addition to suspected Al-Qaeda, then it may not be productive. You may breed more Al-Qaeda members than you destroy. But it's one of those judgments where it's very hard to generalize.

If we have really hard-nosed evidence that some senior Al-Qaeda officials are in some area, and we really have a chance to knock 'em off, I suppose we should do it. But I would say to any commander who gives the order to do it and in the end kills fifty locals, you're going to pay a price.

IGNATIUS: That sounds like the old admonition, if you shoot at the king, don't miss.

BRZEZINSKI: That's right, and don't kill too many of his relatives.

SCOWCROFT: I think Zbig's right. First of all, we shouldn't brag about it. Better to pretend innocence. "What Predators?" But if we can target them carefully, I think it's a useful thing to do. It shows quietly the awesomeness of U.S. power. And it could breed some respect among the Pakistani army: "These guys are really, really good."

IGNATIUS: So if I hear the two of you, the prescription here is like the Hippocratic oath: First, do no harm. With a situation as delicate as this, in a country we understand as imperfectly as this, be careful. Brent, am I expressing that—

SCOWCROFT: Yes, don't be ham-handed, which I'm afraid we've been frequently in the past.

IGNATIUS: Zbig, people often liken the situation with Musharraf and the dangers of a post-Musharraf Pakistan to something you faced as national security advisor with the Shah of Iran. One of the haunting things when I look at Pakistan is that I think back to the Iranian revolution. I see the nightmare that flowed from that crisis, which we're still living with. I see the nightmare that could flow from a post-Musharraf Pakistan, but even now, I'm not sure what the right course was then, or would be by analogy, looking forward. How about you? You must have thought about this for many hours.

BRZEZINSKI: Well, that gets to be terribly complicated, because it requires rethinking the history of modern Iran, going back even to the days of Mossadegh. But let me make one point. The Shah was running Iran, and the Iranian army was not. In Pakistan, it is the army, and not Musharraf, that runs the country. Musharraf doesn't even dominate the army.

Zia-ul-Haq probably dominated the army more than Musharraf. But the point is, it is the army that runs Pakistan and that is the more viable institution. The moment the Shah crumbled and his will crumbled, the army fragmented. It didn't really stand up on its own. There was no attempt at a coup.

I take the Pakistani army seriously now. I do fear that if we're not careful, we could turn it hostile to us, especially the younger officers, who have had no contact with us and are very nationalistic. That would be terribly counterproductive to us.

IGNATIUS: Having recently visited the headquarters of the Pakistani chief of staff, General Kayani, in Rawalpindi, and talked with some Pakistani military officers, I would say that he's doing all the right things in terms of restoring a sense of professionalism to the army. I'm curious, Zbig, Brent, whether you have the same sense as you look at the evolution of the army since he took over from General Musharraf as chief of staff.

SCOWCROFT: I feel very good about him. I think he's doing it right. He's trying to reprofessionalize the army, where professionalism has been neglected for a time. He has another problem, and that is, in a sense, reorienting the army. The Pakistan army has always faced India, because that's where the problem's been. He has to get them to face their northwest territories, not because the United States wants it but because that's the new threat.

IGNATIUS: I take it, in conclusion, as a good sign that General Kayani hired as his military spokesman the brother of two of the most prominent, courageous journalists in Pakistan. A gentleman who does that can't be all bad.

BRZEZINSKI: Or shortsighted.

SCOWCROFT: But he's one of the most promising things to happen in Pakistan in a long time. At least it looks that way.

—March 27, 2008

FOUR

THE VIRTUE OF
OPENNESS: CHINA AND
THE FAR EAST

DAVID IGNATIUS: It's a truism, for those of us who think about foreign policy, that the great challenge of the twenty-first century is to find a way to bring a rising China into the global community of nations in a way that is stabilizing, that adds to the integrity of the system instead of weakening it. There's no question that China will get bigger militarily and stronger economically and generally become a more dynamic player in the system. Many people feel that that will threaten the United States. Zbig, how do we turn China's growth into something that's in our interest?

ZBIGNIEW BRZEZINSKI: Well, let me confess to being somewhat

optimistic. First of all, the United States' concerns about some aspects of the Chinese rivalry, for example in trade, in business, or potentially in the military area, are quite legitimate. And there is a bipartisan desire to assimilate China into the international system.

That, of course, implies an American willingness to adjust to reality. Assimilating China into the international system is not like absorbing some small country. It requires gradually changing the international system and redefining the meaning of American preeminence. In that regard, I think America's attitude is much more farsighted than the attitude of the major imperial powers in 1914, when Germany was using its elbows and trying to become a major world power with serious imperial and colonial aspirations. We are acting much more intelligently.

Secondly, part of my reason for optimism is my sense that the Chinese leadership is not guided by some Manichaean ideology in which their future depends on the imposition of their value system on the world like, for example, Stalinist Russia or Hitler's Germany. They're guided much more by the thought that they have to be part of the world and are trying, within reason, to figure out how to do it. I think if both sides remain reasonably sensible and nothing very disruptive happens, this process will go on.

IGNATIUS: Brent, on this great big wooly question of how we bring a rising China into the global system in a stable way, what's your starting point?

BRENT SCOWCROFT: I, too, am optimistic. From the U.S. side, the process started back in the early 70s when we reached out to China at the heart of the cold war—and we reached an understanding with China that we would join together to oppose Soviet hegemony. That put a different coloration, in the eyes of the American people, on China and what it was about.

We also established, mostly after World War II, a kind of new world order governed by open systems. We did that in part as a reflection of the mistakes of the world between the wars, though we required Germany and Japan to democratize before we let them back into the world order. So we constructed a kind of open system. For example, we let the communist Chinese assume the China seat in the UN, despite the nature of its system. It was a welcoming environment from our perspective.

On the Chinese side, after 1949 they became a hermit nation. They didn't really seek relations with anybody except the Soviet Union, and even that grew pretty acrimonious. Only gradually have they come out of their isolationist shell. In their economic development, they are now realizing that they need the world. First of all, they're becoming increasingly dependent on imports of raw materials. Secondly, they're very dependent on foreign markets for their manufacturing. That means they need a stable international structure to assure reliable access both to raw materials and to market output.

Unlike Germany before World War I, they don't want to overturn the system. They want to join the system, and it just happens to be a system that's pretty open and congenial, so while there's a lot of nervousness around, and you can read negative statements from either side, I think we have a better chance than the world has seen in a long time to incorporate China into the system.

IGNATIUS: But in a world where a rising China wants access to raw materials to maintain its economic growth, and wants to be assured of a stable environment, why isn't it a natural rival of the United States? Raw materials are in finite supply. There will be competition for them. We see the Chinese pursuing their self-interest rather ruthlessly in their trade dealings with Iran and other countries, contrary to U.S. foreign policy interests. Why aren't we on a collision course?

SCOWCROFT: That's a very good point. Our desired structure is a trading system that is open to everybody. If the Chinese seek exclusive relationships, that's a problem. But so far, they've been prepared to enter an open system.

Now there are some troubling notions. If the United States insists on a formal position of primacy—that we are the number one and everybody else is insignificant—as we sometimes hear nowadays, then that's a real danger signal. But so far, we haven't acted that way. On energy, for example, we've taken the position that there's x amount of supply in the world, y demand in the world, and we're prepared to support an allocation system which is open to all.

BRZEZINSKI: Let me just add two points to what Brent was saying. You, David, referred to China as a rival, and I think you used the word *ruthless*.

IGNATIUS: A potential rival.

BRZEZINSKI: Yeah, potential rival, ruthless in the pursuit of their interest. When you say the Chinese are ruthless in the pursuit of their interest, aren't you also describing the United States? Our business operations internationally are very energetic, to put it euphemistically. And we are not disinclined to promote our interest to the maximum.

But inherently the notion of a rival, business rival, includes the notion of restraint. It's not the same thing as ruthless imperial military competition, which ends up in a collision. And I think that thought, that realization, guides both us and the Chinese. We both realize that we will not benefit by a collision that approximates the great collisions of the twentieth century.

There is a second point. We know more or less how our leadership operates. We know much less about their leadership. But my own experience in dealing with their leadership is that it is remarkably sophisticated, eager to learn, and quite deliberate in its effort to understand realities. That was my first impression when I met Deng Xiaoping. At the time we were able to develop a quasi-secret alliance against the Soviet Union which involved joint intelligence operations and joint assistance to the resistance in Afghanistan.

And while generally I'm impressed by the very deliberate nature of the Chinese leadership's efforts to educate themselves, let me cite you one specific example that has been intriguing me. For about five years now, the Chinese leadership has held, at the highest level, a seminar for the top leaders. Just for the top leaders like our national security council.

It's a full-day session led by some specialists. All the top leaders have to attend, and here are some of the topics they have addressed: One session is called "The Importance of the Constitution and Understanding the Rule of Law"—something very alien to their communist dictatorship. Another session: "Better Understanding of the World Economy and Particularly of Globalization Trends." "Trends in Military Technology," another session. "Overview of World History with an Emphasis on the Rise and Fall of Imperial Powers." I wish our president had spent some time in sessions like that.

Another one, "International Trade, Investment, and the Importance of China Going Global." "Urbanization and Economic Inequality," "Intellectual Property Rights," "Governing through Science," "Democracy and the Rule of Law," "How to Democratize a One-Party System."

This kind of leadership means that the Chinese understand both the potential of their power and also the dangers of exceeding its limits. And, therefore, unless there is some domestic upheaval in China, I rather think that the adjustment is not going to be all that difficult, even if it's occasionally painful to us because China is being more competitive. If there *is* a domestic upheaval, all bets are off.

IGNATIUS: Let's examine that in a little more detail. The Chinese leadership does have this Confucian element—wise men meeting together, seeking to inform themselves in the way you described—as the leadership of this modern mandarin elite. But out in the countryside, there is increasing ferment.

We've just lived through a few weeks of serious unrest in Tibet that spread to some other Chinese cities that have Tibetan minorities. My friends who study China carefully tell me that there's a growing problem with people who come to the cities from the provinces who can't find work or can't find work with which they can support themselves. They're either living in poverty in these cities or going back home angry and unhappy.

Brent, there are people who look at that kind of evidence and say, "China just isn't going to be able to hold together. The autocratic, Confucian elite is not going to be able to impose its will on the country, and this China is just going to break up." And that's the danger. It'd be nice if it would hold together, but it won't.

SCOWCROFT: If you look back at Chinese history, you find recurring periods of going from a highly centralized, very tightly knit country to chaos. My sense is that the Chinese leadership is deeply fearful of instability. I think that fear is one of their driving motives. It's behind their fears, for example, of opening up the system politically: they're afraid of instability. And I understand why instability is a specter they are concerned about.

There's tension between the countryside and the cities, and tension between rapidly growing wealth in the country as a whole and extreme poverty at the lower end. Increasingly, there is the question of how to deal with the rape of the environment that has accompanied their remarkable economic growth. These are huge problems. They almost certainly will concern the leadership more than they have before. I don't want to predict what might happen, but they have tremendous problems.

But I think one of the least likely directions for any instability is outward aggression. Chinese history indicates that the Han Chinese have not been unusually aggressive. When China has been aggressive, it's usually after they've been conquered from the outside and are run by "outsiders."

BRZEZINSKI: Or humiliated.

SCOWCROFT: Yes, or humiliated. One of the things for which they really do bear a grudge against the West is the humiliation of the nineteenth century. That's deeply burned into their historical consciousness.

IGNATIUS: So how do we play that card, if you will, Zbig? Should we be gentle with this Chinese leadership and not exacerbate its problems by encouraging the kinds of things that would lead to unrest and, over the long run, change, such as more democracy? Or do we keep the pressure on, saying to the Chinese, "This system you have, this wooden Communist Party–based autocracy is not going to work in the modern world"? What's the right line for us to take?

BRZEZINSKI: Just a footnote to what Brent said, and then an answer to your question. When I was last in China a couple of months ago, a dinner was given for me by Jiang Zemin, the former president. I asked him, "What is the biggest problem you face in China?" And he said, "Too many Chinese."

In a way, that's a good answer. The floating unemployed population now is about two hundred million, except that it floats from place to place because there's all this going on. New cities growing, huge interstate highway system, fantastic, like ours.

IGNATIUS: But no cars on it yet.

BRZEZINSKI: No cars on it, that's right. But a system already of about forty thousand miles. Ours, built in the 1950s and 60s, is sixty-five thousand miles. The Russians are building their first superhighway from Moscow to St. Petersburg right now, their very first. And you still drive on gravel when you try to drive from Moscow to Vladivostok.

But on this larger issue of how we deal with the Chinese. First of all, with respect. This is not a civilization that's going to accommodate easily to hectoring or lecturing from us. The Chinese are profoundly conscious of their history and culture, and with justification. It is one of the great histories and cultures of the world. If we're going to lecture them on how to conduct themselves, I don't think they're going to be responsive.

Secondly, they are intelligent. The leadership is very intelligent. One of the things the leadership is conducting right now is a public discussion on how to infuse "more democracy," whatever that means, into a nondemocratic system. They know they have to accommodate the popular desire for a more open government. I think at the margins, we can discuss this with them as friends. But if we do it arrogantly, we're just going to get rebuffed and nothing we say is going to be considered.

The last time I was in China, they were terribly worried that Taiwan was going to be the source of disruption for the Olympics. I said, "I don't think that Taiwan will be but Tibet could be." And I said to them, "Look, you know I'm a friend of China. You should talk about this with the Dalai Lama. He accepts Chinese sovereignty over Tibet, and he's against the boycott on the Olympics." And they said, "No, no, he's an enemy of China."

Right now, as we talk, the situation has gotten out of hand, and perhaps it is wiser to talk to others. But if we lecture the Chinese about the Tibetans and tell them what to do, they're likely to say to us, if they respond, "What about your problem with the blacks? What about the injustice in America? What about the disparities in income which are so fantastic and getting wider?"

I don't think we can teach the Chinese how to conduct themselves. But we can find ways of living together, if we have a foreign policy that doesn't intensify economic and social frictions into geopolitical collisions, and if at the same time we try to create a framework of stability that pertains not only to our relationship with China but also to some of China's neighbors: Japan, South Korea, perhaps India, and the countries in the Pacific ranging from Australia to Indonesia. A diversified American policy of creating a web of relationships and of preventing the Chinese from excluding us from the mainland is a policy we can very successfully pursue. This is why, again, I'm a cautious optimist.

IGNATIUS: Brent, do you think that, say, ten years from now, China will be more democratic, that the party will gradually loosen its control? Or should we look forward to pretty much a continuation of what we see now?

SCOWCROFT: I think there's a growing struggle. As they started on their economic development program around 1978, Deng Xiaoping said, "To get rich is glorious" and "I don't care whether a cat's black or white as long as it catches mice." I think they started it because they thought the key to stability was a steady increase in the Chinese people's standard of living. If they could deliver that, then they would have security.

They delivered quite brilliantly on their economic program. Their political structure has not kept pace. My sense is they know it hasn't kept pace, but they're not sure what to do about it. They're toying with rudimentary democracy in some of the villages. Some are saying that democracy should perhaps exist inside the Communist Party. In the election to the central committee last fall, I think they had some 29 more candidates than the 371 seats being contested. So there was a slight—

IGNATIUS: A little bit of competition.

SCOWCROFT: —a slight bit of competition. But as I said before, I think they're leery of opening up the system because it frightens them.

IGNATIUS: And we shouldn't be in the business of pushing.

SCOWCROFT: I don't think so, because as we just said, they're facing enormous problems. If there's a great eruption of unrest, if riots break out, if there's lawlessness, they could easily turn sharply right and crack down very, very hard and say, "Look, this happened because we loosened up."

▶ ▶ ▶

IGNATIUS: Zbig, you could argue that the cold war really turned on the alliance with China that was begun by Henry Kissinger, and on the joint effort that you helped structure as we and the Chinese tried to stop the Russians in Afghanistan. Through that whole period, the flashpoint has remained Taiwan.

In the last few months, there has opened up the possibility of resolution of that source of tension, with the election of a nationalist government in Taiwan and a new president, who says he wants to negotiate with Beijing on normalization of relations. Do you think that's realistic? How can the United States help that process?

BRZEZINSKI: Just one minor technical correction. When you say nationalist, you mean the Kuomintang. You don't mean nationalistic Taiwanese.

IGNATIUS: I don't mean nationalistic Taiwanese. That's who they just got rid of.

BRZEZINSKI: I think the new leadership in Taiwan recognizes the subtle nature of their relationship to China. Taiwan is both part of a broadly defined China and yet separate, and they are prepared to increase the connection between Taiwan and China, to encourage family and social contacts, facilitate investment across the Taiwan Strait, increase air travel—in brief, to promote normalization.

On one of my visits to China, Deng Xiaoping used the occasion to use me almost as a prop for this notion of "one China, two systems." In one China there would be diversity in the sense that Hong Kong would have one system of government and of course the mainland has another. I have repeatedly suggested to the Chinese that the time has come to revise that, and it should be "one China, several systems." Because Taiwan again has a different system. Taiwan is a democracy, for example. I don't expect the mainland to be a democracy like Taiwan in the near future, for the reasons Brent described, and I don't expect Taiwan to regress into an authoritarian system. But it can have increasingly close contacts with China, Cross-Strait's investment, and movement of people and students and businessmen, much of which is already happening. And in effect, create a situation in which a growing China is a patron for several systems.

Tibet is a more difficult problem, because Tibet has a really distinctive ethnic culture. It is the cradle of Chinese Buddhism. The problem is not so much that China controls Tibet, since even the Dalai Lama is prepared to accept Chinese sovereignty. But the

Chinese are beginning to swamp the Tibetans by development and settlement. Maybe the development is well-intentioned and the swamping is not deliberate. Probably it is partially deliberate. But in any case it happens, and that is where the friction arises. The Chinese still have to work out a real accommodation with a significantly different ethnic and religious entity that has to be respected if it is not to be rebellious. That is an important, difficult challenge.

IGNATIUS: Brent, if the Taiwanese government does succeed in normalizing relations, the flashpoint we've all worried about for a couple of generations would be effectively gone. Wouldn't that open the door to a quite different way of thinking about China and the threat it poses?

SCOWCROFT: It might. But Taiwan has already gone from being the most likely flashpoint for a conflict to something less than that. Instead, rising in the background is this growing power rivalry. Taiwan might occasion a conflict, but it wouldn't necessarily be the cause.

I don't think there's going to be a resolution of the Taiwan issue in the near future. But it may diminish substantially as a possible flashpoint. There was a real danger that the outgoing president, Chen Shui-bian, who tried very hard to move toward independence, might do something that would bring us into direct confrontation with Beijing. That is much less likely now.

BRZEZINSKI: Even though there may not be a *de jure* resolution of the issue, there may be a progressive *de facto* accommodation.

SCOWCROFT: And that's an interesting thought. Ten years ago, the Chinese believed that, with respect to Taiwan, time was not on their side. They feared that the Taiwanese would grow more and more independent as the mainlander Chinese died off. So there was a big effort in the 90s to push reunification while Jiang Zemin was still in office. Gradually they have come to realize that time is probably on their side. The economy of Taiwan, the major industries, were moving wholesale over to the mainland, and cultural ties were developing very strongly. The Taiwanese became the ones who began to think time was not on their side. I think we may be heading toward a peculiarly Chinese solution to the problem. There could be something like what Zbig mentioned, a greater China of which the mainland is a part, Taiwan is a part, Hong Kong, Tibet, and so on.

BRZEZINSKI: Even Singapore someday.

SCOWCROFT: A kind of brotherhood of indistinct relationships. But it won't happen overnight.

IGNATIUS: For some, that raises the specter of a new Greater East Asia Co-Prosperity Sphere, to use the term the Japanese coined for their Asian imperialism. And that does frighten people. Even as China solves its problems with its neighbors, it becomes more of a regional superpower. Should we worry about that?

BRZEZINSKI: We should worry about it because it implies, if not exclusion, then a significantly diminished American role on the mainland of the Far East. And we have, in a way, stood up to the Chinese in the debate over what should be the free-trade area in the Far East. Should it be Asia and China, or should it be Asia, China, Japan, and the United States?

But what is important about that kind of discourse is that it's not likely to lead to anything remotely similar to a politically motivated war. It's more an ongoing bargaining and adjustment as China fits itself into the new system while hopefully we respond intelligently, protecting our interests as we engage others subtly in helping us to maintain a more polycentric Far East. This is where our relations with Japan are still very important.

This is also where India can play a role. India is not quite Far Eastern, but it is certainly on the margins. It will be a challenge to our diplomacy and our business to make this complex game work in our interest, without the apocalyptic, almost Manichaean views that are a legacy of the twentieth century.

IGNATIUS: Brent?

SCOWCROFT: We do have to be concerned about it. I don't think we have to be fearful, but we have to watch. There are several things, like the Shanghai Cooperation Organization grouping of Asian states, which the United States has not been invited to join, that we should keep an eye on.

The Chinese reaching out to the ethnic Chinese community in other states could be a danger. But it would also be a danger for the Chinese, because it could increase anti-Chinese sentiment in those states. They might fear the indigenous Chinese as a possibly subversive element in their populations, or as provoking a reaction like the one in Tibet, where the protests seem to have been directed against Han Chinese. This is a complex situation of concern for both China and the United States.

▶ ▶ ▶

IGNATIUS: Each of you has said in different ways that this is, as an economist would say, a positive-sum game, a situation where each side really will benefit substantially from cooperation with the other. If they fail to cooperate, it's bad for both. The question then becomes, how do these two superpowers, the United States already dominant, China rising, find a way to cooperate with each other on issues that matter?

Let's take the most difficult regional challenge at present, which is North Korea, a country that has recklessly moved to become a nuclear state, despite repeated warnings, and has actually tested a nuclear weapon. Through the six-party talks created by the Bush administration, the United States and China have been struggling to find a diplomatic solution to the North Korean nuclear problem. How successful has that effort been? Perhaps more important, what does it tell us about China's ability to be an effective partner to the United States on security issues? It's seemed to me, as an observer, that the Chinese are not willing to risk that much to solve this problem. Zbig, am I wrong?

BRZEZINSKI: I think you're partially wrong, at least in your wording. I'm sure the Chinese haven't done everything we would like them to do. They have not joined us in making explicit threats to the North Koreans in order to obtain their compliance. But the fact of the matter is, without the Chinese we wouldn't have made the progress we have. They have been the critical player in getting the North Koreans at least partially to comply, even though we haven't had full compliance.

IGNATIUS: What have the Chinese done that may not be immediately visible?

BRZEZINSKI: Basically they have told the North Koreans they cannot count on Chinese protection if push comes to shove, and that's terribly important. Besides, the North Koreans have a very serious domestic economic problem. Their trade window to the world is China. So the Chinese have been very helpful. They were the ones, more than anybody else, who made the difference. The Japanese have been with us, but their leverage with the North Koreans is limited. The Russians have been going along, but not decisively. It's the Chinese.

Whether we'll get the full accommodation we seek is still uncertain. We are dealing with an unpredictable regime that shifts its mood dramatically. As we talk, they've just made a scorching threat against South Korea. So the North Koreans are difficult customers. But we and the Chinese are the ones who have moved them to make the concessions they have.

Now, why did the Chinese do that? I think largely because they don't want a flare-up right next to them. And probably because, as Brent said, they feel that time is on their side. If there is ever a unified Korea, it probably will eventually gravitate towards China rather than towards Japan and us. From that standpoint, the Chinese have a long-range interest in the outcome being both constructive and peaceful.

IGNATIUS: Brent, how would you evaluate U.S.-Chinese cooperation in the six-party talks?

SCOWCROFT: There has been an evolution on both sides. I don't think the Chinese want the North Koreans to have a nuclear capability any more than we do. A decade ago, if you asked the Chinese—and I have—about North Korea, they would say that they had gone their separate ways and no longer had much in common. As a result, they had few dealings with the North Koreans anymore.

BRZEZINSKI: And they would laugh.

SCOWCROFT: And say that it was not their problem. Then, gradually, they said that they would agree to the six-party talks, furnish the meeting room, provide the tea. But we would have to do the negotiating. But as we on our side have moderated our position from regime change to discussion of the whole strategic framework, they have become more forthcoming. For them, regime change meant chaos on their border, the last thing they want. Now they've become engaged in the negotiations.

Could they do more? Of course they could, because they are North Korea's lifeline, in general trade and certainly in energy resources. But I think we're working quite well together. The North Koreans are still the North Koreans. And we still haven't uncovered their bottom line.

Do they think they have to have nuclear weapons in order to defend their independence? Or are they prepared to trade those weapons for a security system in which they would feel comfortable? We're close to finding out. Right now, we're demanding that the North confess all their sins, and they're saying, "We won't confess our sins, but we promise not to do it anymore." So there's still some tough negotiating to do. But we and the Chinese are fairly close to a common path on North Korea.

IGNATIUS: I'm reminded of one of Zeno's Paradoxes, where you keep getting halfway to your goal, but never get there. North Korea has tested nuclear weapons, retains nuclear weapons, retains an estimated thirty to forty kilograms of fissile material. Should Americans just accustom themselves to the idea that North Korea's going to have one or several nuclear weapons for the foreseeable future? Is getting them to relinquish those weapons just an unrealistic goal?

SCOWCROFT: No, I don't think so. First of all, the kind of nuclear weapons they have—I'm getting out of my depth now—but the kind they have are from reprocessed fuel. That's plutonium. They're much more difficult weapons to manage, to make explode, than weapons made from enriched uranium. Making a uranium bomb is pretty simple stuff. This is not. And their test was—

IGNATIUS: Was in large part a failure.

BRZEZINSKI: Right, exactly.

SCOWCROFT: So they can't be that confident of being able to make a useful weapon. There has to be some doubt in their minds.

IGNATIUS: Zbig, should the next administration think it can complete this job and get those nuclear weapons under international control?

BRZEZINSKI: I think it should persist in the effort. But it depends a great deal on how well not only the Chinese work with us, but also the South Koreans. There is a new South Korean government that is far less inclined to accommodate the North Koreans than its predecessor.

If intra-Korean relationships deteriorate, it may be more difficult to get the compliance you're talking about. But certainly the next administration, whatever it is, ought to keep this process going, because it's better than the alternative. Unless we are prepared to go to war with North Korea, it's better to have this partial arrangement whereby they have some weapons, but they are so unreliable that it would be crazy to start a war with them. They may be usable as their last defense. But it certainly doesn't give them much to work with if they're planning an attack.

In these circumstances, being patient is going to be more productive than anything else. Before too long, there's going to be some change of leadership in North Korea. It's kind of a curious hereditary regime, but I doubt it can go on to the third generation. Therefore, there's got to be some sea change in North Korea, probably within the next decade.

▶ ▶ ▶

IGNATIUS: Let me pull the camera back a bit further and bring in Japan, the existing economic superpower of Asia, recovering from its long slump. You could argue that the Bush administration's greatest foreign policy success has been managing to improve relations simultaneously with both China and Japan. The Japanese were feeling unloved and excluded. They were worried that we were so dependent on making an accommodation with this rising China that they'd be left out. Now they feel much more reassured.

Brent, you've watched this process closely. The effort began under Secretary of State Colin Powell and Richard Armitage, who made it a key issue during President Bush's first term, and it's continued. How can it be sustained? Can America manage that juggling act so that we have good relations with Japan and with China, without the whole structure breaking down?

SCOWCROFT: I think it can be sustained because we have reassured the Chinese that the Japanese aren't a threat, because our security treaty with Japan means that Japan does not have to develop the military strength to defend itself against outside threats. For the Chinese, that's reassurance. For the Japanese, we've given them the confidence that we're with them, that we have not shifted our partnership across the straits, and that Japan is part of the bulwark of our presence in Asia.

It's a balancing act, and we could fall off one side or another without too much trouble. But if we can maintain it, it not only reassures China against Japan, and Japan that we are still there when they need us, it also gives breathing room to the rest of Asia. Without that U.S. presence and the balance it provides, they might feel as though they have to choose between Japan and China. That's a choice none of them wants to make.

This was all carefully deliberated. Some of it might have been accidental as we stepped along near the end of the cold war. Nonetheless, it's a carefully balanced system, and it's working very well. I don't see any reason it can't continue. The security alliance is a great deal for both China and Japan.

IGNATIUS: Zbig, you've written in at least two books that you worried we weren't paying enough attention to Japan. That we were sort of letting Japan go. Do you still have that worry?

BRZEZINSKI: No, I think that has altered in recent years. Under the present administration there has been a kind of reawakening of the American-Japanese connection in relation to global security, which has compensated for some of the lapses earlier on. I subscribe very much to the view Brent just expressed, that we don't need to choose between China and Japan as our principal anchor point in the Far East.

China is clearly our most important mainland Asia partner. Japan is our most important Pacific Ocean partner. Japan is more involved with us in international security, but it is carefully expanding that scope of activity, not rushing headlong. The Chinese are beginning to do the same. There are now Chinese forces serving in UN peace-keeping missions in Africa and other places. Beyond that, and to me this is interesting from a historical perspective, both China and Japan are avoiding what drove European powers to self-destruction during the twentieth century, which was a political competition reinforced by an arms race, leading to eventual collision.

China has had nuclear capability now for forty-four years. To this day, it practices minimal nuclear deterrence. We have thousands of weapons aimed at China. It has only a handful targeted on us—and implicitly also against Japan.

The Chinese at the same time have tolerated a Japanese military posture that is deliberately undefined. The Japanese have a limited military capability in terms of conventional forces, and they are a cryptonuclear power in the sense that they have the capability to weaponize extremely quickly, and they have delivery systems and guidance systems already.

So both powers are acting intelligently in terms of assuring their security but very deliberately avoiding outright provocation to the other. That provides a context in which we can further an Asia mainland–oriented partnership with China and a more global partnership with Japan. It gives us the opportunity to start revising the arrangements within the international system so that both countries get greater recognition: China in terms of voting rights and leadership in a variety of economic and financial institutions; Japan, hopefully, in the UN Security Council.

This still leaves one very major issue wide open, and that's how the Chinese-Russian relationship will develop. If our relationship with China were to deteriorate, there could be a temptation to revive the old Sino-Soviet alliance. I personally think that's not overly likely. But the other alternative is one we should think about hard, namely, is the Chinese-Russian relationship going to be stable over time? When you look at the border between China and Russia, the demographics and the demands on natural resources are such that there's something almost unnatural about the map of that part of the world. On one side of the border is a huge space, as large as the rest of Asia, inhabited by thirty-five million people. On the other side, the rest of Asia, inhabited by three and a half billion people, one and a half billion of whom are expanding dramatically, getting wealthier, richer, more powerful, more modern. Is that an enduring situation?

IGNATIUS: Well, the Russians can be the Saudi Arabia of Asia. They can sell the energy to fuel the three billion cars.

BRZEZINSKI: But what if that energy runs out in twenty years, as some oil companies are worried it might?

IGNATIUS: That would be a more difficult world.

I'm struck that each of you, in talking about Asia, has described an American policy that, to use Brent's phrase, is open, an open world. And to use Zbig's formulation, we've tried to avoid tight linkages in terms of security. We've tried to avoid either-or choices, such as *either* Japan *or* China. I'm struck by that because it contrasts so sharply with the American policy in the Middle East, where we're always making either-or choices, and where an open system seems intolerable to us.

BRZEZINSKI: That's not accidental.

IGNATIUS: I wonder whether we'll be able to maintain this openness, this approach to Asia that, as you both have said, has been really successful.

BRZEZINSKI: Well, let me jump in here because you touch a sore point. The marvelous thing about the Far East is that we have been able to shape our policy in terms of a broad analysis of our national interest. In the Middle East, our policy is very vulnerable to domestic pressures and divisions. Look at the policy prescriptions that got us into the trouble we're in in the Middle East today.

IGNATIUS: Well, but Taiwan was an external power represented by a very potent lobby, the China lobby, that tried very hard to force its preferences on the government.

BRZEZINSKI: It wasn't strong enough.

IGNATIUS: And it failed.

BRZEZINSKI: Yes, exactly.

IGNATIUS: But not for lack of trying.

BRZEZINSKI: It will be interesting if there develops a huge China lobby in this country, representing not Taiwan but the mainland. For some reason, the Japanese lobby doesn't seem to be in the making. But there is already an incipient China lobby. There is also, incidentally, a growing Russia lobby, which operates not on the basis of traditional voting strengths but entirely on the basis of money.

IGNATIUS: Brent, are you optimistic that we can maintain this open structure?

SCOWCROFT: Yes, I am. We've talked about China and Japan, but there are other players in Asia. ASEAN [Association of Southeast Asian Nations] values its independence, its bargaining position with the others. Farther south you've got Australia, which is a close ally of the United States. To the west you've got India, which is sort of a new player in East Asia. But all of these—China, Japan, India, Australia, and ASEAN—are amenable to open and flexible relationships with each other.

There's a great deal of suspicion among them. But it can be tempered, again, by our presence, because in Asia, unlike in other parts of the world, we're not seen as having narrowly nationalistic objectives. We're a stabilizing presence in the region. And I think that is more the direction the world is going in, rather than the old, narrow alliances for and against particular countries.

BRZEZINSKI: That's a very important point. And it seems to me it might be useful even to sharpen it. In Asia, we have the interplay essentially of three dominant powers, the United States, Japan, and China. Peculiar to all three powers is a stabilizing orientation. If you go back to our discussion in the previous chapter, in the area we called the global Balkans, the United States is playing a destabilizing role. India is preoccupied with its conflict with Pakistan and is certainly not capable of playing a stabilizing role, even if it is not actively destabilizing. You have Iran, which is a disruptive force. It's a totally different configuration.

This is why I think the Far East Pacific area is, on the whole, promising. We can play a constructive role and others can interact with us. Whereas the other part of the world is the fulcrum of potentially disruptive global conflicts. It is the one area in the world where, if we make a major mistake, we could pay a huge historic price for it—as we have already, to some extent, paid in Iraq.

IGNATIUS: We assume the Chinese will change in our direction— become more democratic. But much of the world looks at China and concludes that there's a lot to be said for authoritarianism. The Russian embrace of democracy produced chaos and near economic ruin in the 1990s under Yeltsin, and the world doesn't want any part of that. When I travel to Iran I find Iranians saying, "We'd like to be like China. We want that stability. We want our economy to grow." And there's a suspicion of democracy. What's the danger that the world will look at China and say, "We think a healthy dose of authoritarianism makes sense"?

SCOWCROFT: I don't worry about that. First of all, I don't think any democracy is going to turn itself into a dictatorship for the economic benefits. There's no doubt, if you look at the development of

China, that they have had a strong authoritarian government and have done a great job modernizing their economy.

Conversely, the Russians first modernized their political system, made it more democratic, and as a result they had insufficient central power to force transformation of the economy. India is another interesting case. India is becoming an economic powerhouse, but they're doing it almost in spite of themselves. In its early years, many of the Indian governing elite were educated in England in Marxist economics. They had a socialist orientation. As a result, the government still continues some residual suspicion of entrepreneurship. And yet they're doing reasonably well. And the China model hasn't finished working itself out, as we have discussed. One of the advantages of an authoritarian system is that you can move at a breakneck pace. But it might be into some directions that turn out to be very harmful.

BRZEZINSKI: That's a key point. I have no particular sense of anxiety about countries deciding to emulate the Chinese model. If one looks at the collective experience of countries in which intelligent economic development originated from the top in a highly authoritarian setting, it is striking to note that once the economy becomes successful it creates pressures for democratization. Look at the South Korean experience. It was hardly a democracy until about twenty years ago. And yet its economic success paved the way for an established democracy.

In a different way, that is even the Japanese experience. The Meiji Restoration was a highly mobilized system of economic and technological innovation organized from the top down. It created the preconditions for what we did in Japan after the war, and then produced a democracy that's now constitutionally entrenched.

Taiwan also started as an authoritarian system—not very different, actually, from the Chinese in terms of economic development. The government promoted a fair amount of free enterprise in rural areas, low-scale business, then liberalization. Economic development took off and democracy followed.

And look at China itself. The big debates in the communist leadership today are less about fundamental economic choices and increasingly about how you democratize the system without an explosion. You don't compress it too much, but you also don't release too much pressure too quickly. I don't know whether China will avoid an explosion, but there's no doubt that economic development, which has been very successful for most Chinese, nonetheless creates increasing pressures for democratization. And in an interactive world I think that pressure is also reinforced by outside forces.

IGNATIUS: Do you think we'll be comfortable as Americans living in a world where other countries, notably China but also many of the countries that look admiringly at China's success, choose a different balance between freedom and order? The Chinese have tilted that balance significantly more toward order than we would.

And the Chinese people seem to go along with it. When I travel in China and ask them about the knockoff version of Google they have, which filters out things that are politically unacceptable, the Chinese attitude is, "What's the big deal?" They're willing to accept a restricted universe of Google searches if it comes with a nice apartment and maybe a new car. That's a fundamentally different way of ordering the world than what we as Americans tend to think is the natural and appropriate way. Can we live with it?

SCOWCROFT: What direction does this represent for the average Chinese? I would argue that it's in the right direction. Twenty years ago there'd have been no Googling even if Google existed. I think this is a question that is academically fascinating, but there's very little that we're going to be able to do about it. You can think of a model of any kind. Singapore is a very unusual model. Zimbabwe is a very different model. Nations and cultures are going to find their own way and take advantage of their particular talents. But as they look around the world for examples, I don't think many of them would say, right now, "I'd rather live in China than the United States."

IGNATIUS: So we shouldn't regard the Chinese model tilted more toward authority and order as threatening to us? Or as an example that may divert the world's aspirations away from what we'd like to see?

BRZEZINSKI: Well, if China stimulates the appearance of mini-Chinas in other countries, it doesn't follow that these countries emulating the Chinese will necessarily be more antagonistic towards us than those following the American model. I don't think that follows.

Second, in a lot of countries, the choice is not authoritarianism versus democracy. It is stable development with control from the top down versus chaotic freedom that's economically totally disruptive. And I'm not sure it's such a good choice.

Look at Egypt and its population, and the Muslim Brotherhood. If Egypt were to plunge headlong right now into American-style democracy, would it be politically stable? Would it be stable economically?

IGNATIUS: I think anyone who knows Egypt would say no, it would be chaotic. There's a wonderful essay I read years ago called "The Hydropolitics of the Nile," which said that a society based on the annual flooding of rivers has to be extremely well-organized; it demands central authority, and what are we doing pushing a model of a society built on endless wilderness and fertile land everywhere you look. So I'm sure Egypt isn't going to look like America.

SCOWCROFT: One of the ways we could make this a bigger problem than I think it's going to be naturally is to try to develop this notion of a community of democracies and divide the world into democracies and nondemocracies. I think that would be a very dangerous direction to take.

IGNATIUS: But, Brent, isn't that precisely the course President Bush has been following? Some of his rhetoric about democracy makes Woodrow Wilson sound like a cynic. And it sort of universalizes our particular form of democracy. I take it that you both would feel quite strongly that that kind of rhetoric—as Brent put it, dividing the world into democracies and nondemocracies—is a mistake.

SCOWCROFT: I think we should make clear to the world that we believe democracy is the way to go, and we're prepared to help anybody who wants to go in that direction. But we should not seek to impose it. We should encourage it and help others who seek to emulate the best parts of our democracy.

When we have tried to export it, sometimes it's been successful. In the Philippines it's been successful. In Iraq, so far, it certainly hasn't been. And that was one of the announced reasons for going in. I think we should stand for democracy. We should not try to impose democracy.

IGNATIUS: The Chinese do share the dream for more openness. And many are frustrated and angry that they aren't getting a piece of this fabulous pie that everybody else is eating. What do we do in that inevitable moment when they come into the streets, as they did in Tiananmen Square in 1989, by the tens of thousands, or maybe by the millions? And the Chinese government panics as it did in Tiananmen Square and sends out the troops, and the kids in the streets are determined to provoke a confrontation, and the troops open fire? There will be a lot of dead kids. The question will surely be, what is America going to do about this? What's the answer?

SCOWCROFT: It would be a terrible crisis, and a terrible human problem. It's very difficult to know how to steer a course through a crisis like that. I was around during Tiananmen Square. We did put sanctions on the Chinese, especially the military. But we reached out quickly to the Chinese and said, "Look, we don't like what you did. We don't agree with what you did. But our relationship is so important for both of us that we must see our way through this." It took some time, but we salvaged the relationship at some measure of cost to our human rights image.

IGNATIUS: Did you ever think, Brent, that if you'd made a different choice, you might have cracked the communist system to the point that it couldn't repair itself? And that we might see a transformation like what we saw in the Soviet Union and Eastern Europe?

SCOWCROFT: No, I didn't think that would have happened. What happened in the Soviet Union and Eastern Europe was not a revolution, but more an evolution which we supported at a pace that didn't bring about a crackdown this time from the Soviet Union.

IGNATIUS: Zbig, what would you do when those kids come out in the streets, as they will in the Chinese crackdown?

BRZEZINSKI: My judgment would be very much affected by what I discerned about the people on the street. I think the key to success for a prodemocracy movement is, to some extent, a single word that was once very well-known globally.

The word is *solidarity*. What was unique about the Polish anticommunist movement Solidarity is that it was not just university kids in the streets. University kids have been on the streets many times. In Mexico City in 68, they got mowed down. They were on the streets in Tiananmen Square and they got mowed down. But where was the rest of society? Some were empathetic. Some were indifferent. Some were hostile.

The key to the success of democracy in Poland was solidarity of intellectuals and the working class. All of them imbued with democratic ideals, which they had internalized. They were determined to create a democracy. And they wanted a peaceful transition, which, in different ways, was repeated in the Orange Revolution in Ukraine or the Revolution of the Roses in Georgia.

There is an important lesson here. Democracy is a nurturing process which cannot be institutionalized simply on the basis of a relatively isolated social force. It has to reflect a social maturity. Clearly, the people in the Polish Solidarity movement were not all on the same intellectual level. Lech Walesa was a very simple but intuitive leader. But you also had people like Professor Bronislaw Geremek who were sophisticated and understood democracies. There were former communists who realized Marxism was deceitful and had rethought their world view. And you had, literally, workers and intellectuals, peasants, working together.

That's how democracy comes peacefully. If the students go out in the streets in Beijing, I will do whatever I can to convey to the Chinese my sense that they should be restrained in response. And that there should be an effort to avoid bloodshed.

But I will also look very carefully and see whether the workers and peasants have joined the protests. Do they have some unified doctrine that can guide them in establishing democracy?

IGNATIUS: One gauge of whether a democracy movement is going to be successful is whether the army in these situations is prepared, in fact, to open fire.

BRZEZINSKI: The army always senses who it is aiming at.

IGNATIUS: The army senses who it's aiming at. If it feels it's a relatively small segment of society, they will start shooting.

BRZEZINSKI: Especially if it's a privileged segment.

IGNATIUS: But what's striking about the countries where these solidarity revolutions succeeded is that, in many cases, the army was told to open fire, and wouldn't.

BRZEZINSKI: Exactly. And I think that makes your point. They were opening fire on a whole society, and they won't do that. Armies are drawn from the people as a whole and won't attack people as a whole.

SCOWCROFT: It depends on a societal condition of maturity.

▶ ▶ ▶

IGNATIUS: We haven't talked much about India, and that's typical of foreign policy discussions. This enormous, increasingly prosperous democracy in the heart of South Asia just doesn't hit the American radar screen. We worry about the Middle East. We worry about China and Japan. We often forget about India.

The Bush administration has worked very hard to cement a new strategic relationship with India, to make real accommodations to

India as a nuclear power, in effect to grandfather their breakout nuclear weapons program into the nonproliferation treaty. Do you both think that was wise? And do you think it was successful?

The Indians, to my surprise, at this writing seem unwilling to close the deal. It's a very favorable deal for them. But something in their nationalist character keeps them from signing on the dotted line. Zbig, why is that? What's going on with India?

BRZEZINSKI: Well, the Indians are very difficult customers. They have been that way for fifty years. They certainly were not helpful during the cold war. They weren't helpful during the Afghan War. I'm not sure how helpful they are right now, because they're obviously interested in limiting Pakistani influence in Afghanistan. And that's driving the Pakistanis into some of their more rash actions. So that is worrisome.

Secondly, I feel very uncomfortable about the nuclear deal we signed with India. I think we are legalizing what might be called preferential and selective proliferation. The exclusion of their fourteen reactors from international control damages our credibility on the nonproliferation issue.

These fourteen reactors are producing weapons. Excluding them from international control has potentially significant implications, even in terms of the military balance in the Far East. If the Indians were to significantly increase their nuclear arsenal, would the Chinese stick to their minimum nuclear deterrence posture? I don't think we have thought through the strategic implications of this.

IGNATIUS: Brent, the administration saw this as a real breakthrough agreement.

BRZEZINSKI: But for what?

SCOWCROFT: They did.

IGNATIUS: For the opportunity it presented to make a strategic alliance with a rising economic superpower in Asia that was also a democracy.

BRZEZINSKI: Against whom?

IGNATIUS: It wasn't against anybody. It was, again, a positive-sum game. It was premised on these two great democracies, the United States and India, making common cause and putting aside their differences. How well do you think that's worked out? Zbig's skeptical of it.

SCOWCROFT: I don't think it has worked out. It was, at best, premature. I don't know what deliberations went into this emotional surge toward India. Maybe because Russia was no longer a pillar for India, they were available. There may have been some calculation about needing a counter to growing Chinese strength. I don't know. But obviously, we embraced India very strongly. As it turned out, that had negative implications for Pakistan. We're paying for that right now.

BRZEZINSKI: There may have been anti-Muslim feeling, too, among some of the people who were for it.

SCOWCROFT: I don't know. It's possible. I'm puzzled by it. But from the Indian perspective, they obviously felt they needed partners other than Russia. But part of the reason they have not fully embraced a close relationship may be that the Indians don't want to be a small boat floating in the wake of the great United States, because one of their other alternatives is to lead the developing world. And as we've seen in the Doha [Development] Round discussions, they have played that role quite seriously.

So we've got a whole situation in flux right now. My own sense is that it's good that the nuclear deal is now on the shelf. I think it was premature at least. But what's going on with India is a much deeper issue.

IGNATIUS: Do you both regard India as essentially a benign force? We focus on the Chinese economic miracle, but some people argue we're looking in the wrong place. The country that will really be increasingly dominant in technology and will really compete with us is India, not China. Do you think there's a malign underside to this story of India's growth?

BRZEZINSKI: Maybe there's a vulnerability rather than a malign reality. India is a remarkable success as a democracy, but it's also a deceptive success. India's social disparities are far more acute than China's. The poverty, for the lower portion of the population, is far graver. That is something that still has to be overcome. The Indians are way behind the Chinese in developing a respectable modern urban sector and even in their transportation system.

The second problem is illiteracy, in which India is again way worse than China amongst women—somewhere near fifty percent. Among men it's somewhat lower, but still staggeringly high for a country that aspires to be a technological pioneer.

And then there is a third aspect, which is again very different from China, and again to India's disadvantage. China is ninety percent Han. India is really diverse ethnically—180 million Muslims. I think there are more Muslims in India than in Pakistan.

Think what will happen when the masses get literate and politically activated. That hasn't happened yet. The system works on the basis of dynastic political parties inherited from British colonial rule, with a democratic tradition but with the masses relatively easily molded in one direction or another. Once the masses begin to be motivated by their personal or group preferences, ethnic dislikes, religious phobias, and social resentments, India could be a very troubled place.

▶ ▶ ▶

IGNATIUS: Let me turn the bright and generally optimistic light we've been shining on East Asia to a somewhat darker color. I base my argument on simple economics. Rising China and an already risen and very strong Japan have increasingly financed American consumption. We have been spending significantly more than we produce. The Chinese and Japanese have been writing IOUs to cover the ever-widening trade deficit that we run, and have now accumulated enormous amounts of U.S. debt that they hold. This makes us very vulnerable should the Chinese decide they have a fundamental conflict with us over some issue.

With a trillion dollars or more of our debt, they're in a position to exert some leverage. And as the American economy enters what's looking like several very difficult years, I do wonder if the American people won't rudely discover the extent to which we've become indebted to these East Asian economic powers, and if there aren't going to be greater frictions in this world as we make adjustments from our present unsustainable economic situation to some sort of rebalancing.

It wasn't all that long ago that people were taking sledgehammers to Japanese automobiles in Michigan towns where big automaking facilities were suffering from foreign competition. Are we heading toward a period when America's anger at our indebtedness and dependence upon this Chinese economic superpower is going to be a big, painful issue?

SCOWCROFT: I doubt that will happen, for a couple of reasons. First, while the Chinese have over a trillion dollars in U.S. Treasury notes, they can't use them as a weapon against the United States without destroying their own wealth. In a sense, that makes us partners. We depend on each other.

Second, international business is moving from a vertical model, which it was when we were bashing Japanese cars, to a horizontal model in which so-called Japanese cars are built in South Carolina and there is coming to be no such thing as an American car or Japanese car.

We're looking with some fear at sovereign wealth funds as well, but in a way, they're a vehicle for rebalancing the world economy without the catastrophe of deep depression. They're keeping the world economy liquid. I'm not sure we understand how to deal with all these new forces, but to me, they're stabilizing forces that can even out the ups and downs in national economies. But I'm not an economist.

IGNATIUS: Zbig, do you see any danger of an American reaction to our growing indebtedness and dependence on East Asia? Could it trigger a backlash in this country?

BRZEZINSKI: I suppose it could. On the symbolic level, the situation's even worse because we are financing the war in Iraq by borrowing from the Asians. This is the first war we have financed by borrowing from foreign peoples rather than paying for it ourselves.

SCOWCROFT: This is the second.

BRZEZINSKI: The second? Which was the first?

SCOWCROFT: First Gulf War.

IGNATIUS: Well, we didn't borrow. They wrote us checks.

SCOWCROFT: They donated.

BRZEZINSKI: You guys were smart because you—

IGNATIUS: You made our allies pay cash up front.

BRZEZINSKI: You created the coalition in which they were participants. Whereas now in Iraq, we're alone. But a lot depends on how the next president plays this. I think one of the important roles of the next president will be to educate the American public about the new global realities.

My sense is that the public is living in some sort of nirvana. They don't really understand what's happening in the world. They don't know how financial, economic, and political relationships have been shifting, and how much we now depend on a good, stable, intelligent relationship with the Far East, most notably China and Japan. I can understand the rage among workers who lose their jobs to foreign competitors. But that rage really is not anti-Asian. At one stage it also manifested itself against Mexicans.

But it is an understandable rage in part because we haven't done enough, one, to prepare the country for these shifts, and two, to try to deal with the consequences of these shifts for specific sectors of our society through programs that would seriously attempt to upgrade the qualifications of our labor force for new enterprises. In other words, taking seriously the social consequences of technological innovation and the imperatives of making technology the trademark of the American global economic role.

That's where the next president will have to really exercise the office's influence. Today the logical allies of the United States are Europe, which is simultaneously a competitor, and several Far Eastern countries, notably Japan, China, South Korea, which is becoming a powerhouse economically, and some of the smaller ones. The new Korean president has started talking openly about South Korea's global economic role. This is a country of fifty million people or so, and it's really becoming significant. We now have a signed free trade arrangement with the Koreans. It's important that these relationships have public support. We are a democracy, but domestic moods are driven by where the shoe pinches, and they can be exaggerated by fears and ignorance. That's where leadership is needed.

SCOWCROFT: I must say there has not been much leadership in an instructive way, and the domestic reaction, for example, to hardship in the United States has been a demand for tariffs against Chinese and other goods. That compounds the problem.

IGNATIUS: If you insist, as a country, on spending more than you make, and then get angry at the consequences of other people bailing you out—that's an unsustainable position.

SCOWCROFT: That's what I mean. Zbig talked about educating the American people, and that is a real necessity. There has not been much effort toward educating people in this country to the current situation. Quite the contrary.

IGNATIUS: Let's return to the theme with which we began, the consequences of this rising Asia, symbolized by a rising China. Is it fair to say that the adjustment to that fundamental change will necessarily change the United States? That we will end up being a different country in some ways? The shorthand people sometimes use is that the future speaks Chinese. That overstates it, but it's a future in which our role will have to be a little different, won't it, Zbig?

BRZEZINSKI: Yes, but in the past we have been capable of responding. We transformed ourselves from an industrial pioneer, industrial innovator, industrially dominant state into a service-providing state very successfully. I think the next question is whether we can become a technologically pioneering state. Can we build our economy around creating and innovating? If we can do that, we'll be viable. If we don't, we'll become what Great Britain gradually became before its recent burst of innovation, precipitated by Thatcher. The alternative is to become a nation of decaying industrial wastelands.

SCOWCROFT: I think Zbig has put his finger on it. We have to realize that this is a much more interdependent world, and it's going to get more so. We have to integrate our economy with others more closely. We'll depend more on others for certain things. Our particular national skill is the ability to turn science and technology into engineering. As Zbig says, innovation. Right now our tendency is to try to hold on to things ourselves and impose export controls. We think we're the center of everything, when what we need to do is stay ahead. If we release our energies, I think it's our natural talent to take ideas and turn them into practical products. That's where we're good.

BRZEZINSKI: And we have to bear in mind that in the interactive age, xenophobia is a psychological phenomenon of retardation.

IGNATIUS: What do you mean by that?

BRZEZINSKI: People who were condemned by lack of innovation to make defective cars, and who therefore couldn't compete with a country that was making very good cars, took refuge in dislike of the other country for doing better. If you don't do as well as someone in a field, you leapfrog them. We haven't put enough emphasis on this, if we want to be number one.

IGNATIUS: Again, I'm struck by the consistent theme that emerges from our discussion of Asia, which is the need for openness, now the need for flexibility, for suppleness in the way we respond. Brent, are you confident that political leadership can keep America supple, flexible, open in what's likely to be a pretty messy next few years, in which a lot of chickens will come home to roost and the country will feel under pressure? There's going to be a natural impulse to ask who's to blame. How can our leaders help us maintain that essential flexibility?

SCOWCROFT: I don't think by any means that the United States has burned itself out or that we're a declining power. We're still full of energy and optimism, but leadership is key. The current debate focuses on the capillaries, not on the arteries. We need a more thorough and thoughtful discussion of the kinds of things we've been talking about. What is really going on in the world? And how do we react to it, stay ahead of it, cooperate with it, rather than resist or pretend it isn't happening? That debate has not really taken place.

I believe the American people can respond. And I think our future should be bright. But we have to step forward to do what is necessary to take care of those whom technology and economic development have left behind. We have the resources to do that and we can preserve a leadership position. But if instead of embracing the change which is taking place we try to prevent it through tariffs and other restrictive measures, we will simply be left behind.

BRZEZINSKI: For us in the twentieth century, Europe presented the challenge of war or peace, and that's what we had to concentrate on. For us in the twenty-first century, Asia presents the challenge of competition or decline. It's a different challenge, and I think Brent and I agree that we will not get into some sort of twentieth century military collision with China. The problems nonetheless are massively complex, but they're qualitatively different. If we're intelligent in responding to the challenge of Asia, we'll do all right. But if we go into a kind of xenophobic shelter, a gated community of fear, we lose.

IGNATIUS: You, Zbig, have written in your most recent book, *Second Chance*, your fear that the United States remains, in some ways, intellectually backward in a world that's undergoing what you call a global awakening. It's happening most noticeably in Asia, where there's been just a stunning improvement in standards of living, in people's opportunities and aspirations. You've expressed concern that in our education system and in the way our leaders talk to our people, that we are being left behind. I wonder if you'd speak directly to that—that in some ways the American people have to really lift their game. They have to embrace a changing, challenging world in a way they haven't.

BRZEZINSKI: There's a paradox here. We are the most globally involved country in the world, and yet we have one of the more parochial publics in the world. In part it's because we're large, in part because we're confident, in part because we have been self-sustaining for such a long time, in part because we hadn't been invaded by others until 9/11.

As a consequence, I think the American people have a better sense of what's on TV than what's happening of importance in the world. That's not sustainable any longer. How can we undertake the necessary reforms domestically in response to the external challenge if we don't have a clue to what that challenge is?

IGNATIUS: Brent, what's your feeling about the American people now? Apart from our leaders, are we really rising to the challenge?

SCOWCROFT: I think it's too early to say, but it doesn't look good right now. We've had it easy for so long, and the average American hasn't had to worry about these things except in time of great crisis. Right now there's no great crisis, and he's more worried about what's going on in his particular city, county, state, than he is about what's going on in Washington, let alone the outside world.

Many Americans spend their whole lives without having any real contact with a foreigner, somebody who thinks very differently from the way Americans think. We assume everybody thinks just like we do. That makes it very difficult to react in an enlightened way to this novel world where we're being swamped with multiple waves that are generated elsewhere.

IGNATIUS: When I travel around the world, I'm struck by the American ability to live with and really harness diversity. Even the countries we've named as such great successes—China, Japan, other countries in Asia—have enormous difficulty bringing outsiders in and making them feel welcome and making them productive. In a way, that is the American genius.

And although we've mentioned some reasons for pessimism, I believe that as long as we remain open to our own diversity and retain that gift of making other people who come here looking for opportunity feel welcome, I can't help but think that we will respond and change. Do you share that, Zbig?

BRZEZINSKI: Hopefully, yes. But—hopefully. There are a lot of people in this country who favor deporting eleven million people because they arrived here illegally. Even though many of them have been here for years and have their children here. Moreover, all the restrictions on access for foreigners, scientists, students, and so forth, how will that affect our intellectual life and our ability to innovate? The great burst in American innovation came significantly as a consequence of the massive immigration to America of intellectual talent from Europe in the 20s and 30s.

IGNATIUS: You've traveled in Silicon Valley. Take a spin through Palo Alto or San Jose, and see how many Indian-Americans—

BRZEZINSKI: Precisely.

IGNATIUS: —and Chinese-Americans and Vietnamese-Americans have gotten rich.

BRZEZINSKI: This is—

IGNATIUS: And I mean super-rich.

BRZEZINSKI: Let's hope it continues. And, if it continues, yes, it will be one of the keys to America's capability to keep up with growing economic competition from East Asia. But we have to be willing to make these people feel that they're part of America. And that operates not only on the level of Silicon Valley but also on the level of the poor Hispanics in this country who are increasingly under attack.

SCOWCROFT: Our history is one of diversity. We've had influxes of people of different cultures, different ethnic groups, and we've always assimilated them. So we tend less to look askance at somebody whose skin's a different color or who speaks with an accent than they do in Europe, for example.

It's very hard, if you're in France, Germany, Netherlands, to assimilate someone who's different. Because everybody you know has been just like you in an ethnic and cultural sense. We're much easier in that regard. But now we've developed this—it's almost a fear of the outside. That is very alien to us, traditionally.

You can see it in our visa system. You can see it in the attitude toward immigration. We're here now; let's not let anybody else in. I hope it's temporary. Basically, we're not as reflexively ethnocentric as most cultures have been.

BRZEZINSKI: There are hardly any countries in the world where someone with a name as difficult as mine can sit at the same table as Brent Scowcroft. So I'm very aware of how good America has been to people like me. It's important that we stay on course.

—*March 31, 2008*

FIVE

THE STATE
WITH UNNATURAL
BOUNDARIES

DAVID IGNATIUS: When we think about Russia, we sometimes forget that we're dealing with a new country, a country that's reborn—but is proud, prickly, struggling to figure out how its government will work and what its relations with its neighbors and the rest of the world will be. I'd like to start our discussion of this new Russia by asking each of you to talk a little bit about how it was born. Like every country, it's shaped by the circumstances of how it came to be. Both of you were key figures in the long, cold war struggle that led to this amazing transition.

Brent, let me start with you because you were in the White House at the moment the Soviet Union disappeared and Russia was reborn. Tell us about your perspective on how this country came to be.

BRENT SCOWCROFT: When Bush Sr. came into office, there was a lot of ferment in Eastern Europe, and we reviewed what our policy there ought to be. In the past, each time Eastern Europe had erupted in one place or another after the iron curtain came down, the Soviet Union came in and crushed the movement, killed the dissidents and reimposed iron rule. Then, after a time, unrest would bubble up again. It happened in Germany in '53, in Hungary in '56, in Czechoslovakia in '68. And it was beginning to percolate again.

We decided to change traditional American policy toward Eastern Europe. The U.S. had been encouraging the satellites that were making the most trouble for the Soviet Union, so Romania and Nicolae Ceauşescu had been at the top of the U.S. "good" list. We decided that was the wrong approach; that what we should do was encourage the movement from within to broaden the system to make it more open. So Ceauşescu went from the top of our list to the bottom, and Poland went to the top. We saw real possibilities in the way Solidarity was behaving.

We tried to act in a way that did not provoke in Eastern Europe another cycle of uprising and repression. We wanted to move liberalization forward, but at a pace that would be under the Soviets' reaction point. Of course, we didn't know exactly what that pace was. But we tried to avoid causing either a crackdown by the Soviet Union or an internal disruption within the Soviet Union in which the hardliners would kick Gorbachev out because he wasn't tough enough.

That was our policy. While that doesn't really answer your question about how the new Russia was born, our attitude toward its evolution was that we wanted to nurture liberalism in Eastern Europe and encourage Gorbachev in his Glasnost and Perestroika. We saw Gorbachev trying to build little Gorbachevs in Eastern Europe, and we wanted to encourage that process.

IGNATIUS: There's a view that in the Gorbachev years, the KGB, understanding how weak the system was, tried to encourage little coups around the country, to shake up a bureaucracy that it thought was failing. That they felt that unless there was some kind of revolution from within, they were in terrible trouble.

SCOWCROFT: I think Gorbachev saw glasnost not as leading toward democracy but as a way to increase the efficiency and effectiveness of the Soviet Union. Starting with Brezhnev, the country had had a series of sick or senile leaders, and it had stagnated for years. Gorbachev, I think, saw himself as rejuvenating the system, not replacing it. One of the ways to rejuvenate it was to lift the burden of terror and repression. The problem was, he couldn't get the party to do what he wanted, so he threatened to hold party elections and throw out the bad guys. That's really what started the slide. Gorbachev sowed the seeds of his own destruction and that of the Soviet Union in the way he went about his responses.

IGNATIUS: Did you ever imagine, as you began Bush Sr.'s term in office, that you would see an end of the Soviet Union as a confederation of republics?

SCOWCROFT: No, I can't say that I did. When I came into office, one of the things which imbued me was the danger of excessive expectations. Because the first time I was in the White House was during the period of détente. I think we lulled ourselves into thinking that détente, which was a good tactical maneuver, had fundamentally changed the environment. By the time Zbig came in, the Soviet Union was talking about the correlation of forces in the world changing—in their favor.

And I thought, we shouldn't allow ourselves to be swayed by our own rhetoric this time. So I was very hard-nosed about Gorbachev.

His rhetoric was terrific, but there were no accompanying concrete measures on the ground, when Bush Sr. came into office, to indicate the cold war was over. To me, the cold war was fundamentally about Eastern Europe, and the Soviet army was still there. The sinews of control were still in place.

So I was a skeptic. Did I think the system was going to collapse? Eventually, yes. But during that time? No.

IGNATIUS: Zbig, perhaps because of your Polish background, I had a sense over the decades that when people scoffed at those who talked about a rollback of Soviet power, you believed it was possible. I can remember talking with you in the late 1970s about the feelings of nationalism in the republics, the feeling that they were not Soviet but real countries. And I have the sense that you never lost hope that this Soviet empire was a temporary phenomenon. When did you first begin to think that a breakup was really possible, and that the United States might encourage it?

ZBIGNIEW BRZEZINSKI: When I was a graduate student I wrote my MA dissertation on the issue of Russian nationalism and Soviet imperialism. My thesis was that Russia under the name of the Soviet Union was not really a national state but an empire ruled from Moscow, and that its history comprised four hundred years of territorial expansion which reached its apogee in 1945, when the empire ranged from the river Elbe to Kamchatka.

But in an age of nationalism, I felt that empire would not endure and that, paradoxically, by transforming a dynastic empire ruled from Moscow into a fictitious federation of national states—national in form but socialist in content was the slogan—the Soviet Union was actually stimulating nationalism among the non-Russians. That was much more true of the larger Soviet bloc, when nations that had an independent history were also subjugated. I was of the view that at some point in the age of nationalism, the Soviet Union would have a crisis. I then reached the conclusion, after the Soviet Union occupied Czechoslovakia in 1968, that the communist ideal was spent and national sentiments would become stronger and stronger, and that our policy should be guided by that reality.

I disagree somewhat with Brent when he says that under the first Bush administration America's traditional priorities were changed, and that prior to his tenure in office, Ceauşescu was the favored object of American policy. That may have been true of Reagan, but it certainly wasn't true of us. Early in the Carter administration we made the very deliberate decision to support those East European states which while loyal to Moscow were liberalizing domestically, like Poland or Hungary, as well as those that were opposing its domination, like Tito's Yugoslavia or Ceauşescu's Romania.

We weren't favoring just the extreme nationalists. Our goal was to promote diversity in the Soviet bloc in the context of détente without treating détente as a static arrangement but rather as a dynamic process that would promote a dismantling of the Soviet Union.

And this is why we supported the rise of Solidarity so much. Solidarity arose not in the late 80s but in the late 70s. It really challenged the integrity of the Soviet bloc because its dismantling of communism in Poland then led to repetitions in Czechoslovakia and Hungary, to the isolation of East Germany, and to the collapse of the Berlin Wall.

To make a long story short, to me the whole process represented the termination of something that had defined Russia for four hundred years: an imperial expansion from a clear center to create a multinational state. And then suddenly and abruptly, when Brent was in power, we had the emergence of a national state whose boundaries and national identity were both very vague and had to be formulated. And that brings us to the dilemmas Putin confronted, and to the present.

▶ ▶ ▶

IGNATIUS: Let's move toward the present. I'd ask you, Brent, to look at the birth of this new Russia through Russian eyes. We Americans see it as a great triumph for our foreign policy, our values: the end of an "evil empire," as Reagan put it. But in Russian eyes it was a very different event. It's a nation born in humiliation and dismantlement. Speak a bit, please, about what that birth process means in terms of how Russians think about their country and how Russia's leaders conduct their foreign policy.

SCOWCROFT: If, instead of Gorbachev, the Politburo had put in, for example, another Brezhnev in his prime, these events would not have happened in the same time frame. The Soviet Union would have continued. Eventually it could not have sustained itself, politically, ethnically, or economically. But Gorbachev and the way Gorbachev went about it had a lot to do with the timing of the breakup.

BRZEZINSKI: He was an accelerator.

SCOWCROFT: Yes, absolutely. And when Gorbachev ran for president after the end of the Soviet Union, he got about one percent of the vote. He is one of the most detested people in Russia. That says something about this transformation we're talking about.

IGNATIUS: Why do they detest him? What do Russians feel—

SCOWCROFT: Because he destroyed the glory of Russia.

BRZEZINSKI: It was a glory built on an imperial ethic, imperial tradition, imperial pride.

SCOWCROFT: And then comes Yeltsin. I don't know whether Yeltsin was a small *d* democrat or not. He was a populist who had his fingers on the pulse of this movement, and he rode it. He was not a manager, not a governor. Politically he told the provincial governments to take all the power they thought they could handle.

He dismantled the state economy and sprinkled out economic control so that the oligarchs were able to gather it up at bargain-basement rates. Putin, I think, was appalled by all this. Whatever his motivation, he is a centralizer, and he tried to gather back the sinews of the Russian state, and preserve what he could of the remnants of the Soviet state. Maybe his motivation—I don't know—is to recreate the Soviet Union. I doubt it. But he certainly wants to recentralize power in Russia.

I think that's partly because, for the Russians and I think for Putin, this whole experience was a huge humiliation. Former President Bush went out of his way to avoid the concept, "We won the cold war. The Soviet Union lost it," because—

IGNATIUS: This is your boss, Bush Sr.

SCOWCROFT: Bush Sr. He didn't want a World War I syndrome again. So what he said was that everybody had won by the dismantling of the cold war. He was criticized when the wall came down for not wanting to go to Berlin and dance on the ruins.

IGNATIUS: And for the famous "Chicken Kiev" speech, in which he was seen as insufficiently tough.

SCOWCROFT: That particular issue was your colleagues in the press.

That speech was not about Ukraine staying with the Soviet Union. It was about Ukraine not breaking up into its constituent parts, as Yugoslavia was already starting to do. It was a warning against the perils of disintegration—which is why it was made in Kiev and not in Moscow.

IGNATIUS: Zbig, when I talk to Russians, they often express a feeling that the United States took advantage of Russia's weakness during the 1990s, in this period of disarray under a weak president who, as Brent says, was prepared to let power diffuse from Moscow to the provinces and to the oligarchs. They feel we pushed for all the advantages we could while Russia was weak. And Russians still seem angry about it. Do you think there's justice in that? Did we take advantage of their weakness?

BRZEZINSKI: I don't think we did that deliberately, although the events, as they unfolded, could be interpreted by the Russians in that fashion. But I would, first of all, take a more generous view of Yeltsin's role. Don't forget that the disintegration of the Soviet Union, the fragmentation of power, was a very dynamic and unpredictable process with a possibility of significant reversals.

There was, after all, the coup attempt against Gorbachev, which was led largely by the secret police with the support of the army and the party bureaucracy. Who prevented it from succeeding? It wasn't Gorbachev. His role was a little ambiguous. He refused to resign, but he really didn't take them on. It was Yeltsin who did. And Yeltsin, in a sense, saved the process of transformation from a dramatic reversal that probably would have resulted in a lot of brutality. Secondly—

IGNATIUS: Do you think that the dismantling of the old communist regime could have been reversed so that the old guard returned to power?

BRZEZINSKI: Since the coup attempt failed, it's easy to argue that it inevitably had to fail. But the fact is that for several days people in Moscow and a lot of other places in what was still the Soviet Union thought it had already succeeded. And it was Yeltsin in Moscow who mobilized the opposition, forced a confrontation, caused the fragmentation of the coalition, and reversed the coup attempt, but also precipitated the removal of Gorbachev.

Remember, shortly after Gorbachev returned to Moscow "in triumph," there was a joint appearance by Yeltsin and Gorbachev on Soviet television. Yeltsin was already the president of the Russian republic in the Soviet Union, which was a new post. He very dramatically pulled out his pen and announced that he was issuing a decree for the dismantling of the Communist Party.

Gorbachev objected on television, and Yeltsin said to sign it. The same day, militias surrounded central committee offices and all the communist bureaucrats left the building pell-mell. Some of the conspirators committed suicide. That was a very decisive moment. There was a later showdown when Yeltsin was president, but this was the critical one.

The result was chaotic, but what else could it have been? This was a centralized political and economic system in which, all of a sudden, political centralization was ended. The economy started fragmenting, and then swarms of Western consultants appeared on the scene giving advice but also enriching themselves like crazy, while the Russians joined in. You remember how suddenly all these fortunes were made. People who were nothing all of a sudden became multimillionaires—billionaires. And that of course created resentment in Russia, in the public, particularly since the relatively secure, but not very wealthy, Soviet middle class was devastated. Those are the people who suffered the most.

So there was a tremendous amount of resentment. When Yeltsin increasingly became drunk and incompetent and there was pressure to push him out, Putin became president. We know what happened under Putin, but we don't quite know for sure what motivated him. But we have some indirect clues.

First of all, what is his world view? He has given us some indications of that. He's said the end of the Soviet Union was the greatest geopolitical calamity of the twentieth century. Now that's a century in which there were two world wars in which hundreds of millions of people were killed; a century in which there was Hitlerism and the Holocaust; a century in which there was Stalinism and the gulag. But to him, the relatively peaceful dismantling of the Soviet Union was the greatest geopolitical calamity of the century.

Secondly, there's an interview early in his presidency in which he talked about his family antecedents. The person he admired the most in his own family was his grandfather. Who was his grandfather? That hasn't been picked up very much by the Western press. His grandfather was a security guard for Lenin and then for Stalin, in fact his food taster. This is the man Putin admires the most.

Then, about a year after he became president, he went to an annual celebration where all the senior generals of the KGB were assembled, retired and new ones. He walked in, stood in front of them, saluted, and said, "Comrades, mission number one accomplished." Maybe it was a joke. But remember, he came from the KGB elite, the KGB agents who were stationed abroad. These were the pampered children of the Soviet Union. They had access to Western books, they could travel abroad, they were trusted. They were on special missions. I can well imagine their mood as they watched the Soviet Union disintegrate. And I can well imagine that a group of them—vigorous, younger, ambitious—said, "This has to be brought under control." So my sense of Putin is that he is reacting to what happened. I don't think he has assimilated the fact that the old imperial system cannot be recreated. He's motivated a great deal by nostalgia.

He's also rational, and he's not going to try to create a new Soviet Union. But he is going to do two things. First, he's going to try to isolate central Asia in order to keep the West out as much as possible. He's doing that very effectively by making all of the oil and gas of central Asia funnel through Russia. Secondly, he'll try to subordinate states such as Ukraine and Georgia because they are geopolitically critical. Ukraine, because if Ukraine goes there's no longer any chance of a Slavic Union and Russia becomes only a national state. Georgia, because it's critical in the Caucasus, and the Baku-Ceyhan pipeline gives us access to the Caspian, which the Russians would like to cut.

SCOWCROFT: Let me give you a few vignettes about what Zbig just said, starting with the coup against Gorbachev. That was a surprise to us. We were trying to figure out what had actually happened, what the real situation was. For example, we tried to find out who had possession of the codes for missile launch in the Soviet Union. We couldn't find that out.

There was a lot of confusion for the first day or so. We tried several times to get through to Gorbachev, and couldn't. I don't know whether it was the president, or me, or somebody else, who said, "Let's put in a call to Yeltsin." Strangely enough, the call went right through. And Yeltsin was right then in the middle of Moscow standing on that famous tank. Yeltsin was very courageous, and he did consolidate the opposition. But what was really remarkable about the coup is that the people we had feared—the head of the KGB, head of the military, and others—were so inept they couldn't even mount a coup.

BRZEZINSKI: And they started committing suicide.

SCOWCROFT: Yes. They couldn't have mounted a two-car motorcade. They were totally inept. But when Gorbachev came back from his internment in the Crimea, as Zbig said, they had this joint meeting. Yeltsin humiliated Gorbachev, just humiliated him. The hatred that had developed between those two is one of the keys to what happened. They had been colleagues for some time and then, in 1987, Yeltsin broke away. He gradually became determined to get rid of Gorbachev. I have a hunch that the Soviet Union disappeared when it did because that was the way Yeltsin could get rid of Gorbachev.

IGNATIUS: When did President Bush decide that Yeltsin was the horse to ride here?

SCOWCROFT: One of the things Gorbachev never understood relates to a point Zbig made about the role of nationalism. He grossly underestimated nationalist sentiments in the various parts of the Soviet Union. He had this notion of restructuring the Soviet Union into a kind of confederation. He actually developed a framework, and the various republics voted on it. When Ukraine voted against it, that was the sign that Gorbachev was finished. It was a paper project. It didn't deal with the realities of what was developing in the Soviet Union.

IGNATIUS: And Russians themselves were feeling nationalistic and I think were sick of having to think of Uzbeks and Tajiks as their fellow countrymen. You don't think that's right, Zbig?

BRZEZINSKI: Not at all. Not at all.

IGNATIUS: I certainly heard it from Russians. You'd see these comical shows on Soviet television, this parade of nationalities. Russians would just sit there laughing at it.

BRZEZINSKI: Yeah, but they got enormous satisfaction from having this territorially impressive empire. It's one of the major sources of their identity. "We're the largest country in the world." But if you begin to peel off these countries, they're no longer so large. This territorial sense is one of the mystiques that has to be redigested and rethought today. And this is why the process is so painful: The boundaries of Russia that exist today are not viewed as natural. In fact, the Russians have deliberately resisted demarcation of the boundaries in order to prevent their consolidation. It's the new former Soviet states that keep demanding that the borders be demarcated.

You have no idea what a trauma it was when it collapsed. I was there shortly afterwards, visiting the presidents of the different republics. At the end of one of these visits I was taken to the airport. The president was bidding me goodbye, and there were a number of planes parked there. And they were painting new names on the planes. They were no longer Aeroflot, but let's say, "Air Uzbek" or "Air Kyrgyzstan." I asked the president, "How did you divide the Aeroflot fleet?" And he said, "It was very simple. The day the Soviet Union dissolved, any plane on our ground became part of our fleet." It was a chaotic, confusing, painful process.

For non-Russians it was an unexpected emancipation because it moved more rapidly than they were historically prepared, whereas in Eastern Europe it moved more slowly than the people expected. And that's a fundamental difference.

IGNATIUS: Brent, let's come back to Putin. Zbig said Putin described the breakup of this old Soviet empire as a calamity. What does he want? What does his generation want?

SCOWCROFT: I don't disagree with Zbig's description, but I don't think Putin is a one-dimensional figure. He was a favored member of the KGB who probably had that mentality built into him. He was also the deputy mayor of Leningrad under Sobchak, who was the first demonstrably democratic mayor trying to put in a democratic order. Now what rubbed off? I don't know.

BRZEZINSKI: But sad to say, Sobchak was also quite corrupt.

SCOWCROFT: Well, democracy and corruption are not mutually exclusive.

BRZEZINSKI: No, no. But the point is that it was not only democracy that was rubbing off. It was this wheeling and dealing too.

SCOWCROFT: I don't disagree with that. Among the interesting moments in Putin's sort-of autobiography is that he says that one of the most moving moments of his life was when his mother spirited him off in secret to the cathedral to be baptized. Now what does that mean? I don't know. But here's a guy with a lot of things swirling around in his mind. One of the things he's done best is to appeal to Russian nationalism. He is popular. The Russian people like him. And as for that image of the calamity of the Soviet collapse, most Russians feel exactly that way.

BRZEZINSKI: But I think one also has to face the fact that his definition of Russia as this very proud national state, which, as he claims, emerged in the wake of the greatest calamity of the twentieth century, has made it more difficult for Russia to come to terms with the negative legacy of Leninism and Stalinism. The Germans have gone through that process, and they have in a sense expurgated the Nazi experience as something very evil. Putin has created a situation in which there's very ambiguous, hesitant, and partial condemnation of Stalinism.

And there is a sense of semijustification, or sweeping it under the rug, that delays any genuine, constructive, positive redefinition and gives the nationalism a xenophobic, nostalgically imperial aspect. And that has not only delayed the transformation of Russia, it has infected Russian nationalism with a bacillus that could be quite ominous—you know, the black-shirted youth, the anti-Western, anti-Asian, kind of racist quality. I'm actually optimistic about Russia's long-term evolution. But we are in the middle of a very contradictory and ambiguous phase in which Putin on the one hand consolidated Russia and brought back order but on the other hand delayed some of the self-redefinition that I think will eventually open the doors of Russia to Europe and Europe to Russia.

SCOWCROFT: That self-definition could take a generation. I think there will be more Yeltsins, more Putins, maybe more Gorbachevs as the Russians settle in to who they are and what should their structure be. All I'm saying is I don't know how much of Putin's behavior comes from a desire to recreate the old Soviet Union rather than an appeal, as he sees it, to Russian nationalism.

A year ago I heard him give a speech in Munich. There were three parts to the speech. The first two parts were widely publicized, and the third was almost not mentioned by the media. He said something roughly like the following: "When we were weak, when we were flat on our back, you in the West"—this was to a NATO audience—"you walked all over us," and he detailed that. Then he said, "Now, we've regained our strength and we're not going to be run over anymore. We're going to stand up for ourselves."

And third, he said, "But now's the time to cooperate. We ought to cooperate on nuclear weapons, we ought to cooperate on non-proliferation, and we ought to cooperate on nuclear power so that no nation feels the need to enrich uranium nationally." We ignored that.

Putin has indeed gotten popular by kicking us in the shins. It is an appeal to Russian nationalism. I'm not sure how much we can reach out now, and how much he is prepared to respond. The Russians love strength, power, and assertiveness. Whether we can work through that to a cooperative atmosphere, if we treat them as if they matter, I don't know.

IGNATIUS: Let's turn to that question of how the United States should deal with this new Russia and its prickly nationalism, its sense of grievance about the dismantling of the old empire. There has been, from one U.S. administration to the next, a desire to push NATO outward to include the former republics of the Soviet Union. And one of the things Putin has been angriest about is this process of NATO expansion to the very doors of the Russian heartland. The proposal to expand NATO to Georgia and Ukraine in particular seems to have really upset the Russians.

In a sense that shouldn't surprise us. If the United States was facing a potential adversary that was expanding its alliance to include Canada and Mexico, we'd be pretty concerned.

SCOWCROFT: We would invoke the Monroe Doctrine.

IGNATIUS: Well, yes, we have a celebrated national policy going back more than one hundred fifty years, saying that this shall not pass. So let me ask you, Zbig, what is a wise policy for the United States going forward?

BRZEZINSKI: Let me try to formulate it as I would if I were responsible for policy. If I were advising a president, I would say, first of all, we have to identify areas of common interest and try to see if we can promote them. For example, arms control is an area of common interest. It's in both their interest and ours for the arms race not to get out of hand as it did during the cold war. So I would start with that.

I think that would logically lead to nonproliferation. And again, I think there's a shared interest here. How one pursues nonproliferation could become an area of disagreement, especially, for example, in the case of Iran where we were seriously tempted to use force. I'm not sure the Russians would formally go along with that, although I suspect they would see some benefits for themselves if we got entangled in a conflict with Iran. They would assess the benefits and risks to us, and I think conclude that either we would end up paying a very high price or else they wouldn't be that negatively affected. Nonetheless, there is a common interest here as well.

I think by and large the Russians don't want the area we talked about earlier, the global Balkans, to become massively unstable, because that could spill over into Russia. While we talk of Russia as a national state, the fact is that twenty to twenty-five percent of the Russian citizens are not Russians, including about thirty million Muslims. So there is a potential spillover that gives the Russians an interest in the stability of the global Balkans.

The Russians are also concerned about China and America becoming allies, because that would give China greater leverage against Russia. That gives us some diplomatic opportunities which can be constructively employed.

But we must not deceive ourselves into thinking that propitiation of Russian leaders on a personal level is a substitute for strategy. Praising individual leaders, honoring them in a fashion that creates misconceptions as to what Russia really is, for example labeling it a democracy when it isn't—I don't think is helpful. What is really important is to create a geopolitical context that reduces the likelihood that a nostalgic desire to be a great imperial power again becomes realistic, and which, over time, gives Russia the overriding option of becoming more closely associated with the West rather than creating its own competing imperial system.

On a practical level, that means several things. First, we have to make deliberate efforts to establish more, and more direct, economic links with the central Asian nations as energy exporters, and not agree to their being sealed off. So the Baku-Ceyhan pipeline was an important strategic accomplishment. We are considering the Nabucco pipeline as a reinforcement of that access. We should persist in that. At some point, probably not that far off, pipelines from central Asia through Afghanistan and Pakistan to the Indian Ocean will become feasible. Those are good things to do.

That brings me to your question about NATO expansion. Just think what the situation would be today if the Baltic republics were not in NATO. It would probably be as ominous as it is between Russia and Georgia. Look at how the Russians reacted when the Estonians decided not to have a monument honoring the Soviet occupation of Estonia in the middle of their city, but moved it to a cemetery. The fact is that the expansion of NATO eastward first of all included countries that didn't want to be part of the Soviet bloc, wanted to be part of NATO, and by and large have a much better relationship today with Russia than ever before, Poland particularly. So I don't think the expansion of NATO has been disruptive, quite the reverse.

That brings me to the difficult issue of Ukraine and Georgia. I think these countries should not be foreordained to be in the shadow of Moscow. On the contrary, if Ukraine moves to the West, first to the EU, eventually maybe to NATO, the probability that Russia will move towards Europe is far greater than if Ukraine is told in advance that it can never be part of the EU and NATO because Moscow doesn't want it to be. That keeps alive the notion in Moscow that Ukraine, Belarus, maybe the Central Asian countries can again be part of some Russian-dominated entity.

I would say of all these things, seek areas of cooperation and avoid special provocations, such as an explicit American-Chinese anti-Russian alliance. But also create geopolitical contexts in which the Russians will eventually say, "Our future will be safest, our control over the Far East territories will be most assured, if we are related to the West, if there is a kind of Atlantic community that stretches from Lisbon to Vladivostok." I think more and more younger Russians, beyond the Putin generation as Brent said, will be attracted by that, if we are capable of sustaining such a complex strategy.

IGNATIUS: If I hear you, between the lines you're saying don't push too hard, especially at a time when we're hearing loud Russian protests on the speed of NATO expansion into Ukraine.

BRZEZINSKI: Yes, but don't take decisions which preclude that expansion. For example, the issue right now is not NATO membership for either Georgia or Ukraine. The issue is whether they should have that option at some point in the future. Ukraine has a program, adopted not by President Yushchenko but by his pro-Russian rival, Yanukovych, who has set the following target dates; 2006, two years ago, for obtaining a membership action plan (which is the big issue today), 2008 for accession into NATO. That's Yanukovych, not Yushchenko.

IGNATIUS: Brent, how hard should we be pushing NATO outward, and how hard, by implication, should we be pushing Russia?

SCOWCROFT: One of the things we've left out of this discussion is the EU. It seems to me that we are mixing up NATO and the EU. We do want these areas to be incorporated into the greater region of Europe. To me, the EU is quintessentially designed for that job. The

EU is supposed to remake nations' internal structures and get them ready to join its community, and it has done a wonderful job at this.

When we substitute NATO for the EU, we're using a very different instrument designed for very different purposes. I think we have come to completely confuse the two organizations. Now, I agree with much of what Zbig has said. But I want to comment on two points. First, there are probably more areas in the world where we and the Russians have generally common interests than where we have fundamental conflicts. The "near abroad" is an area of tension for Russia, and so is the issue of democracy, as we define it. The Russians are not going to turn democratic because we hector them about it. That probably slows the process. They're going to come to their own conclusions. We ought to make clear where we stand, but to punish and hector them only adds to their sense of martyrdom.

The issue of the Ukraine and Georgia is interesting. I was not a great fan of NATO expansion in Eastern Europe because I feared it would dilute NATO's unity of purpose. But I think it has worked well. The Baltics, which were the most sensitive issue in the breakup of the Soviet Union, were a special case. They were the most sensitive issue, both for the Soviets and for us, because we had never recognized their incorporation in the Soviet Union. For the Russians, unlike the rest of Eastern Europe, they were a part of their Soviet Union. We've resolved that issue.

But now come Ukraine and Georgia, which clearly were part of the Soviet Union. They were not satellites. And with respect to Ukraine and Russia, there is a deep historic tie. Kiev was the heartland of Russia until the Mongol invasion in the thirteenth century, when the Russians fled north into the forests where the Mongols wouldn't follow them.

So there is a sense here in which this is different. And I think, contrary to Zbig, that bringing Ukraine into NATO would be seen by the Russians as a further attempt to humiliate them. We should proceed cautiously and encourage the EU to reach out. If we start to rethink what NATO is and where it's going, then a parallel approach to Ukraine and Russia by NATO may be reasonable. Pushing membership now will cause a problem, especially since the eastern part of Ukraine is, I think, majority Russian.

BRZEZINSKI: It's Russian speaking, but it's not Russia.

SCOWCROFT: The western part has a very different history. And Ukraine itself, as I understand it, is divided about the issue.

IGNATIUS: Some polls show a majority of Ukrainians opposing NATO membership, and there certainly is a sharp division.

BRZEZINSKI: That's absolutely correct. And the Ukrainian government, which has sought this so-called membership action plan—which is not a decision to join NATO but only to prepare for an eventual membership—took the initiative in going to Brussels and asking for this arrangement, in part because a previous government, the one supported by eastern Ukraine, initiated those steps several years ago. But the Ukrainian government has also stated that it will not ask for membership unless a majority of the people approve it in a referendum. So the issue at this stage is not membership. The issue is whether the possibility of eventual membership should be excluded or not. If there's no membership plan, then in effect it is excluded. It's a contingent approach.

IGNATIUS: Well that doesn't much reassure the Russians—

SCOWCROFT: It's not a contingent approach.

BRZEZINSKI: Ultimately the Ukrainians are the ones who should decide their future, not the Russians. Otherwise you're placing a country of forty-five million people in a subordinate position to its neighbor, who determines whether it should—

SCOWCROFT: Oh, no.

BRZEZINSKI: —or should not take a certain decision.

SCOWCROFT: No. You're the one who's saying NATO is not taking action because Russia won't let us. I don't think we have to take that position. If we don't take any action on Ukraine it doesn't mean they're barred from membership. It doesn't mean anything.

BRZEZINSKI: But the point is—

SCOWCROFT: But the membership program is like getting on an escalator. It doesn't necessarily mean you want to go to the second floor, but it surely is a good indication.

IGNATIUS: That's the marked destination.

BRZEZINSKI: But that is something the Ukrainians have asked for. We didn't go to them and say, "Ask for it, and then we'll support you." The sequence is the opposite. The Ukrainian president, prime minister, and speaker of the parliament wrote a joint letter saying, "We now feel we are ready to have this membership action plan. We would like to have it. But we're not going to join NATO unless a referendum in the country approves it."

IGNATIUS: But, Zbig, how many times can you poke a stick in Russia's eye without their fighting back? We've gotten in the habit, through the years of Russian weakness under Yeltsin, of poking them a lot and getting away with it. Isn't that period ending? Don't we have to take them seriously when they say, "This is fundamentally contrary to our interests and we are going to resist it"?

BRZEZINSKI: I believe that if Ukraine is not placed in a position of subordination to Moscow, but oscillates towards the EU and NATO, it actually increases the probability of Russia doing so as well. If we create conditions in which there is this fear of Russian sovereignty, which we have to respect at the cost of the sovereign rights of other countries, we are in effect reinforcing their imperial nostalgia.

SCOWCROFT: I don't think that's the choice at all. I'm all for the EU pushing hard on Ukraine. The Europeans are not enthusiastic.

BRZEZINSKI: The Europeans are divided.

SCOWCROFT: They're divided. But I'm certainly in favor of EU membership for Ukraine, which would do all the things you're saying without antagonizing Russia. NATO is a different instrument. For Russia, it has the symbolism of the organization that during the cold war was a mortal enemy. We don't think of it that way anymore. But why be provocative? Let's push EU in those areas and just let the situation develop gradually.

BRZEZINSKI: I have no problem with the EU part. The problem arises when an important country like Ukraine wishes to be part of NATO, or at least wishes to have that option. One has to ask, "Why do they feel that way? Why do they want that option?" We have not instigated the Ukrainian interest in being part of NATO. The Ukrainians have shown that interest.

IGNATIUS: *Some* Ukrainians.

BRZEZINSKI: Including the leader of the party which represents the east and who had a timetable officially approved. Why do the Ukrainians feel that way? I think they think their security would be enhanced if they were generally part of the Western community.

They would thereby consolidate their independence, which in the back of their heads they know the leaders in Moscow have not resigned themselves to. As recently as three years ago, the official organ of the Russian foreign ministry published a series of articles by historians designed to show that the Ukraines are really not an authentic nation but essentially an offshoot of the Russian people.

It is this kind of insecurity that motivates those Ukrainians who are saying, "We'd at least like to have that option in the future, once our country as a whole approves it." I am in no rush to fulfill that desire. But I certainly feel uncomfortable denying it simply because the Russians declare that this is somehow an invasion of their rights.

IGNATIUS: The common theme between the two of you, as I hear it, is that it should be an American goal to draw Russia toward Europe, to let Russia have a European identity and future, and that a European Ukraine is a necessary precursor for that. As Ukraine moves into the EU, Russia will likely move with them. So we want to draw Ukraine into Europe, but in a way that doesn't create a crisis and confrontation. Am I summarizing that correctly?

SCOWCROFT: No. Not for me.

BRZEZINSKI: Yes, and no. I think you have created a kind of umbrella of consensus under which there are some disagreements.

SCOWCROFT: That's not my feeling at all. I think Russia and Ukraine ought to be considered quite separately. And I do not believe that if we draw Ukraine into Europe, Russia will necessarily follow. Quite the contrary. Russian pride of place and their feeling, if you will, that Ukraine is a little brother plays in quite the opposite direction. I would keep them on separate tracks.

IGNATIUS: So you think a European Russia, or Russia as a future member of the EU, is an unrealistic prospect?

SCOWCROFT: No, I don't. Look, I would not rule out eventual Russian membership in NATO, if and as NATO evolves into something else. I wouldn't rule out Russian membership in the EU either, but it is so complicated that I think there is not much point in talking about it right now.

BRZEZINSKI: Well, I wouldn't rule it out either. But I think it's unlikely for quite a long time, and it's altogether unlikely if we exclude Ukraine, because that will significantly revitalize the Russian notions of some supernational entity emerging first as a Slavic union. And it would help the Russians seal off central Asia, which they are very energetically doing.

They have yet to accommodate themselves to this new reality of the post-Soviet space, and they would like, to the extent possible, to create some new arrangement whereby the central Asians are cut off from the world, and the Georgians and Ukrainians are subordinated in some degree. But I don't think they have the means for doing it over the long run.

If we're intelligent about it, if we don't force confrontations but instead create options, Russia will have to face the fact that it cannot indefinitely control that huge space, potentially so mineral rich, without being part of something larger. And that something larger essentially is the Euro-Atlantic community. I don't see Russia becoming a junior partner of China. If it does, it will lose the Far East someday, perhaps cataclysmically.

That is a difficult process of accommodation that, in the short run, makes the Russians terribly worried. Worried about China, fearful that we'll try to exploit them, uncertain as to whether they can really be part of Europe. That is the background of the dilemmas the Russians are quietly discussing among themselves. But the more intelligent, articulate ones that have spent some time in the West, I think, are increasingly leaning to the proposition that Russia has to oscillate towards the West. But they haven't yet crossed the Rubicon.

SCOWCROFT: The Russian-Chinese relationship is a very interesting one that's gone through several stages. The Russians are still selling China almost any kind of military equipment they want. But in my view, if Russia has a geopolitical enemy, it's China. Siberia is one of the most likely places for a national conflict among great powers.

I cannot imagine over the long run that those two can be partners. And yet they're acting that way now, both in the Shanghai Cooperation Organization—this council among Russia, China, and some central Asian states, ostensibly to resolve border disputes—and in their arms relationships. I think this is very short-term thinking on the Russian side. They want to keep their arms industry going, so they're prepared to sell anything to anybody who will buy.

BRZEZINSKI: The Shanghai Cooperation Organization is really a double-edged sword for the Russians. Initially they were in favor of it, and in fact they sponsored its creation as a way of putting a check on the Chinese. But the way it's worked out, it has actually legitimated the Chinese presence in central Asia.

SCOWCROFT: It has.

BRZEZINSKI: For the first time since the Mongol invasion, Chinese troops have been in western Kazakhstan and on Russian soil over there, participating in joint exercises. Which is a very symbolic, new reality. This was recently brought home to me somewhat comically. When I first visited Kyrgyzstan, many decades ago in the Soviet era, the main street in Frunze, the capital, was called Lenin Prospect. When I visited independent Kyrgyzstan, whose capital is now called Bishkek, the street had been renamed Mao-Deng Xiaoping Prospect.

IGNATIUS: Get out.

SCOWCROFT: That's incredible.

BRZEZINSKI: If you go to these bazaars in central Asia, they're just filled with Chinese goods and Chinese traders. And if you go to the Amur River on the Russian-Chinese border, you see these wonderful old Russian-Ukrainian villages on the Russian side, with unpaved streets and sidewalks made of wood. Meanwhile, just across the river, the Chinese have constructed several towns, with twenty- and thirty-story aluminum and glass buildings, illuminated at night, and streets with cars driving around on them. You just look at that frontier and say, "What the hell's going on here?" I think to some extent it's deliberate. And there are more and more Chinese illegally in Russia on the other side of the river, leasing farms from Russian peasants who are either too lazy or too drunk to make them work, or leasing forests, or doing small retail trade.

If you go to Harbin, in Manchuria, which used to be a Russian city—particularly after the Bolshevik Revolution, when a lot of White Russians fled there—there's a district for trading with the Russians. All the street signs are in Russian and Chinese. And what do you see? You see the Chinese selling cars, television sets, iPods.

And the Russians are selling matryoshkas, nested wooden dolls. That just tells you a great deal. And then you go to a restaurant in the evening and you have all these Chinese filling themselves with food, and you look around the room and notice there are rows of chairs along the walls, with these rather beautiful Russian girls sitting, waiting for customers.

▶ ▶ ▶

IGNATIUS: Let's talk a little bit about central Asia. Traveling to the *stans*—the central Asian republics—you get a sense of enormous restlessness on the part of their leadership, that they're eager for greater contact with the United States and anxious about Moscow's attempts to subjugate them and to draw them into joint energy policies, security policies. You find that in every capital in central Asia now. What should we do about it? Is this an opportunity for America? Should we be trying to develop closer relationships with Uzbekistan, Kyrgyzstan, and the other former Soviet republics in that part of the world?

BRZEZINSKI: It depends what we do. I don't think we ought to try to establish some sort of a political-military relationship with them, except maybe on a tactical basis to help us in Afghanistan. What we really ought to be doing is what we have been trying to do, but ineptly and without real effort at a high level in the government, and that is to gain greater direct access for trade, particularly for energy exports. And that means pipelines—gas and oil.

SCOWCROFT: That is what we really need to focus on. Not the political so much as the economic. To give them access to the rest of the world.

BRZEZINSKI: For example we should already be planning pipelines throughout Afghanistan, down through India or Pakistan to the Indian Ocean.

IGNATIUS: When I was in that part of the world, I kept thinking that what we really need is a new Tennessee Valley Authority for the water resources of that part of the world.

BRZEZINSKI: In Kyrgyzstan.

IGNATIUS: You have the greatest hydroelectric power opportunities on the planet with all the snow in these amazing mountain ranges, you have a desperate need for electrical power, and we ought to create a TVA that ties together the Stans and Afghanistan. Your point that the Great Game, circa 2008, is about pipelines I am sure is right.

BRZEZINSKI: Yeah, because energy is their main asset. The rest of the world wants it. And if they can deal directly with the rest of world, they will consolidate their independence. This is one of the reasons why Russia put so much pressure on Georgia to prevent the Caspian pipeline we were talking about. It's not Saakashvili, it's not the Revolution of the Roses, it's the Baku-Ceyhan line. Look where it runs. It runs from Azerbaijan and the Caspian Sea, through Georgia, to Turkey, and to the West.

IGNATIUS: Is it conceivable that people will fight wars in the future over pipeline politics?

BRZEZINSKI: I think it's quite conceivable that access to energy will be a major source of political leverage. There's no doubt there's a growing interdependence between the EU and Russia in terms of energy purchases and sales. And the Russians need Western investment. But there is a time lag in the event that the energy is cut off. The consequences in the West would be immediate. The financial consequences in Russia would be felt three, four, five years later, which gives the Russians a short-term advantage in applying pressure.

IGNATIUS: But they could shoot themselves in the foot rather easily.

BRZEZINSKI: In the long run, assuming the West didn't cave in in the meantime. So that is a little unbalanced. This is why the West has to insist on upstream access—buying the fields, being co-equal investors—which it's not getting in Russia—even gaining access to distribution of energy, the way Lukoil's getting it. Right around the corner from this office there's a Lukoil station. We don't have Texaco stations in Russia.

SCOWCROFT: Energy is an area where we need to inject more geopolitical sense. We ought to sit down and calibrate world supply and demand, and try to develop a world energy edifice that will reduce the chances of all these irritants overwhelming us.

IGNATIUS: Well, there's something for the in-box of the next president: a dialogue with Russia, and really a global dialogue involving many countries, about energy and energy security.

SCOWCROFT: Absolutely. Take the Chinese and Iran, for example. The Chinese say they don't want Iran to have nuclear capability, but they have to preserve their access to Iran's oil. What we ought to say is, let's create a system so that if you're cut off somewhere, we will share the shortage, so that nobody has to suffer disproportionately. So that no one has to be hostage to their dependence on oil.

▶ ▶ ▶

IGNATIUS: Let's talk about Russia's political future. They have a new president, Dmitry Medvedev. When I talk to Kremlin officials they tell me that it's a mistake to see Medvedev simply as a puppet of Putin, that he is really the first Russian leader who represents the new generation, that Putin was a transitional figure shaped by his KGB experience. In that sense he is very much a child of the cold war. Medvedev is not; he is Russia's first post–cold war leader, and my Kremlin contacts tell me we should see him that way and take the opportunity to work with somebody who represents the new generation. Brent, what's your sense? Have you had a chance to meet him or any of his people?

SCOWCROFT: I have not had a chance to meet him. All I know about him is what I've read. I think he's an interesting figure. He didn't get where he is by being soft. He's obviously a tough character. He seems to have a more international approach, if you will, than Putin.

My guess is that we're in for some interesting times in Russia. It seems from the way Putin went about this and the fact that he selected Medvedev and not, for example, Sergei Ivanov, that he thought Medvedev was more manageable. But once Medvedev becomes president, he may wake up one day and say, "I'm the president." This relationship of Medvedev being a puppet of Putin is not cast in stone.

BRZEZINSKI: In any case, since we can't be too sure of what is behind the curtains, we should treat Medvedev as if he is the president.

SCOWCROFT: Yes.

BRZEZINSKI: And we should try in dealing with him, in effect, to boost him. It is true that his biography is quite different from Putin's. His training is in a different profession, and that's all to the good. I am, however, not too optimistic that treating Medvedev as if he is really the president will yield fruits very quickly, because he is Putin's choice. He was Putin's sidekick for a number of years in Leningrad. In fact he sat in the outer office where Putin was sitting next to Sobchak, and he was essentially Putin's office assistant.

I think Brent was quite right in saying that Putin chose him over Sergei Ivanov because he knew that Ivanov, if he became president, would reinforce presidential powers with the realities of power, that is to say, with the kind of cliques that control the instruments of power: the FSB [the Federal Security Service], the military, and the oligarchs who have been subordinated into the Kremlin. It's unlikely that Medvedev can quickly create his own instrumentalities of power. I think Putin is going to be running the show for some time. It's not an accident he agreed to be prime minister. And he has already talked about executive power being vested in the prime minister.

Beyond that, there is still the remote possibility that at some point, for example, Medvedev could get sick and could resign from office. Under the Russian constitution, Putin could then run for the presidency.

IGNATIUS: How should we react to that?

BRZEZINSKI: We couldn't do anything about it, and we would have to live with it. But the point is that until Medvedev can translate a nominal supremacy into real power, Putin's going to be in a position to make choices. Medvedev's power is not going to rest on the constitutionality of the office, as our president's does, but on the realities of power.

IGNATIUS: Yes, although it's striking that Putin has wanted so much to be seen as working within the Russian constitution.

SCOWCROFT: Yes.

BRZEZINSKI: That's right, and that's good.

SCOWCROFT: He does not want to be illicit, and we can probably count on that. So might he happen to mind becoming president again—

BRZEZINSKI: And that's not illicit under the Russian constitution.

SCOWCROFT: It's not illicit.

BRZEZINSKI: And that option, therefore, is there. Medvedev could get sick.

IGNATIUS: Yes, he could get hit by a bus one day or take an accidental overdose of polonium.

BRZEZINSKI: Exactly. You can't dismiss that. The point is he was handpicked by Putin, and the question that arises is, why did Putin pick him rather than the guys who were with him in the Kremlin, much closer to him in terms of power?

IGNATIUS: What Kremlin handlers and fixers tell me is that Putin recognizes that power should pass to a new generation. He's a transitional figure. I'm not saying I've drunk that Kool-Aid, but that's the official line.

SCOWCROFT: But none of us know. Putin was handpicked by

Yeltsin, and my guess is that didn't turn out the way Yeltsin thought it would.

▶ ▶ ▶

IGNATIUS: Let me ask each of you to turn to the broadest question the United States faces in thinking about Russia. What should our goals be in dealing with this country? Zbig, what are America's national interests and goals as we think about Russia?

BRZEZINSKI: I think in different ways, both Brent and I have already at least implied what we think it ought to be. We would like to see Russia, one way or another, closer to the West. I think the Russian political culture is more European than Asian. In some respects one may qualify it as Eurasian. But the predominant lifestyle to which Russians aspire, and the key cultural heritage with which they associate themselves, is essentially a European, Western, Christian heritage. And therefore it is a reasonable goal, even if distant, to think of Russia evolving increasingly towards democracy. I think the next generation of Russian leaders, beyond Medvedev, is going to be more democratic, more worldly, more European than the present, and certainly more than the previous, generation.

I expect someday that the Russian president—maybe the one after Medvedev, if Medvedev lasts that long and Putin doesn't come back—may even be a graduate of the Harvard Business School or the London School of Economics. That's not a fanciful speculation; increasingly, the Russian elite tries to send its children to British and American universities, not to Tokyo or Beijing. And at some point, from the Russian point of view, a "Europe" that stretches from Lisbon to Vladivostok will be a welcome vision, because it enables them to keep control over what they treasure, which is the Far East territories.

The alternative vision of Europe to the Urals, once formulated by General de Gaulle as an enticement to bring the Russians closer to Europe, could ironically come to pass if Russia were to isolate itself. It would then find it increasingly difficult to control that huge space to the east with a demographic crisis, drunkenness, one of the highest mortality rates in the world, immigration, and the pressure from China. Then you could get truly a Europe to the Urals, but it would be a disaster for Russia. Obviously that's a wild speculation, but it's a prospect that I think troubles the Russians. This is why I believe creating a geopolitical context that sucks Russia towards the West, even through some painful stages, is not an unreasonable, though very long-range, goal.

IGNATIUS: Brent, how would you define America's goals in this relationship?

SCOWCROFT: America's goal should be a Russia comfortably at home with its European neighbors. Ever since Peter the Great, Russians have been arguing over where their soul is—whether they are Europeans, or Asians, or Asians with a European veneer. I agree with Zbig. We ought to encourage them to find their niche, and make it easy for them to be comfortable in that niche. Not irredentist, not hostile, not resentful. That may mean going a little bit out of our way to make them feel equal. I think it's likely to be a fairly long process.

At the same time I would resist giving away too much. Zbig talked about pipelines, for example. I think we ought to push very hard for an oil pipeline from Kazakhstan under the Caspian Sea to Azerbaijan. That would not hurt Russia; it merely destroys the chance of a monopoly against Europe.

IGNATIUS: If those are our goals, do you think it's wise for us to push ahead with our plan for missile defense installations in the Czech Republic and Poland—a proposal of the Bush administration that has really upset Putin and the Russian leadership? Will that process advance America's goals as you define them, or will it hurt them?

SCOWCROFT: I'm puzzled by the project. The president has announced that we cannot allow Iran to have nuclear weapons. And yet we ostensibly are building a defense against those weapons, apparently assuming they will be built anyway. So I am confused about the purpose of the deployment. Also it's not clear to me whether its goal is to defend Europe or the United States. And unless the technology is different, I'm not sure you can do both at once.

I am very heartened by our latest direction on this, which is to try to get the Russians on board with something dealing with missile defense. I don't know enough about it, but it seems to me to have a big question mark over it.

IGNATIUS: Zbig, what do you think?

BRZEZINSKI: Well, I am sort of squeezed, because on the one hand the policymaking establishment here in Washington wants me to propagate the idea of missile defense with the Poles and Czechs, while on the other hand the Poles and the Czechs come to me for advice on how to deal with it. So first of all, what I say to the Poles and Czechs is essentially this: It's in your interest to be a close ally of the United States. If the United States really feels strongly about this, you should try to accommodate it. But you have to be practical in how you do it, and that depends a great deal on the political context. If NATO is for this system and Russia accedes to it, then there's no real problem. You can have an arrangement with America and get some compensation, maybe modernization of the armed forces.

The difficulty arises if NATO's lukewarm, Western European countries are against it, and the Russians are strongly against it— and in fact are making threats. You should still go along with it if America really wants it. But then you really have to get compensatory commitments from the United States, that if the Russian threats are real, or if there are political or economic sanctions from the Russians, you will be compensated. That gets to be very complicated since, understandably, the United States is not eager to give such bilateral assurances.

So that's my formal negotiating position. Now, putting on my hat as an American policy strategist, I am, like Brent, a little bit baffled. We say the system now proposed, the latest version, is meant to defend the Europeans. But the Europeans are not asking for that protection. Secondly, the system we want to deploy is nonexistent, and the threat against which it is to be deployed is also nonexistent. So I don't quite see the rush. My guess is that if the Democrats win the elections, they'll certainly slow down the process, reduce the funding. In brief, the issue depends on the actual context over there, how far the United States is prepared to assume responsibility for the consequences of deployment, and finally on our electoral process.

IGNATIUS: Do either of you see a danger that if the U.S. continues to push this despite strong Russian objections, and with some European uncertainty if not outright opposition, that we could create precisely the Russian reaction we want to avoid? Namely a kind of pulling inward, a sense that the United States, whatever it says, still wants to place a threatening missile system on their border? Brent, what's the chance that if we continue pushing this, we could end up producing the worst possible outcome from the standpoint of the goals you talked about?

SCOWCROFT: I think we could, but I'm not sure that would happen. The threat is more psychological than real. In fact the Russians have nothing to fear from this system.

IGNATIUS: Is that true? Couldn't it easily be turned into a missile defense system aimed at preventing them from using nuclear weapons?

SCOWCROFT: It would be ineffective against a Russian missile attack. It's designed to intercept a few rudimentary missiles. It is not designed to work against the Russian arsenal. It would take a revolution to turn it into an actual threat to Russia, and the change would be quite discernable. But obviously, Putin has decided it is deeply offensive to him, and I think he has chosen—and maybe really feels—that this is akin to abandoning the ABM treaty and pushing NATO's frontiers up against them. I don't know how deeply he holds these views. I don't think it's as critical an issue as Ukraine and NATO.

IGNATIUS: Zbig, how hard should we push against Russian objections?

BRZEZINSKI: First of all, I'm skeptical about the urgency of deploying such a system. At the same time, we can't entirely ignore the Russian reaction. Not that we should therefore propitiate them. We ought to say quite clearly to the Russians that if their negotiating style is going to involve threats, that will be counterproductive.

While I have some real skepticism regarding this plan, I do think the administration has tried to talk to the Russians seriously and is trying to reassure them that this is not a system designed against them. I think it's doing that in good faith. And I don't think a proper Russian response is to start saying, "We're going to deploy rockets, target these countries, and target these facilities." That is not conducive to serious discussions. If anything, it's likely to produce intransigence. You just don't resolve issues by threats.

This is, incidentally, one of the elements that makes me concerned about the discussion over Ukraine. It's one thing if the Russians object to the possibility of Ukraine being in NATO on the grounds they are a neighbor. It's another thing to publicly state, as Putin did in a press conference with Yushchenko, "If you move towards NATO, we're going to target you with nuclear weapons." That's pretty rough stuff among so-called fraternal nations. I think that style of negotiating is counterproductive if Russia wants to be a partner.

▶ ▶ ▶

IGNATIUS: Let me close with a subject that's hard to resist when talking about Russia, and that's the Russian soul.

BRZEZINSKI: The one that some presidents are good at recognizing?

IGNATIUS: Well, we all grew up reading great big Russian novels, and each of us traveled to the old Moscow in Soviet times. One of the paradoxes of that Soviet Moscow was that it was the most intellectual city on the planet. Going there was like visiting Greenwich Village. You'd go into the apartments of dissident intellectuals who were so cultured, so deeply read, producing works often in secret, and you'd stay up all night talking with them about big ideas and the dreams they had. You visit Moscow today and it's a boom town. It's got more neon than Las Vegas. And it has a soulless feeling. You see beautiful women in the most expensive gowns, big-spending guys walking into bars and restaurants, but if you try to look for a literature in the new Russia that has merit, forget it.

So I want to ask, in this broad cultural sense, where you see Russia going. Not simply as a nation state but as a culture. Zbig, you in a sense grew up in the shadow of that Russian culture.

BRZEZINSKI: There's no doubt that there is a depth—an intensity—to human relationships in Russian society that is very heartwarming. And there is a sense of communion that is easy to fit oneself into when you're dealing with Russians who are not part of the KGB or the organizers of the gulag, but Russians who are themselves victims of an oppressive system and whose sense of resentment and deprivation nourishes their souls and makes them more genuine human beings.

So I have great feeling for what you just said. It's why I like Russians. I like to be among Russians. You may be surprised to hear that I fit in very well, and most of them are very warm towards me, because I often dislike the same things they dislike in their own country.

It's sometimes said that the Russians are among the most saintly and the most evil of peoples at the same time. There's no doubt that some of the human rights activists in Russia are prepared to put everything on the line, to sacrifice everything. They do it with a commitment that is beyond one's capacity to even remotely equal. And then there's this tradition of insensitivity to suffering, a willingness to brutalize people. Look at what's happening in the Russian army. It is just a monumental scandal, how they treat their own young people. Fortunately there's a rising wave against it. I often think that that brutality is the product of the semi-animalistic level of peasant life, which breeds the feeling that you can mistreat animals and that human beings are no different. You almost get satisfaction from mistreating people because you're so mistreated and deprived yourself.

So that Russian soul has been there. Is it now being spoiled? I fear you're right. The boomtown aspect that you describe matches some of the worst features of America. And I do think that our personal lives don't have the same capacity for warmth, and intimacy, and shared philosophizing that you see gradually declining in Russia. That may be a feature of a technological, profit-oriented society in which the acquisition of material wealth is the primary definition of success. It's what makes me worry sometimes about our own society.

IGNATIUS: Brent, do you think the Russians are losing their Russian soul?

SCOWCROFT: I think it's way too soon to prognosticate on such fundamental things. I agree with both of you on the Russian soul. There's a sensitivity, a warmth of humanity that is very touching. You can see it in their literature and music. But Russia has also had a brutal history. It's a country without many natural frontiers, which has been overrun many times. It has been dominated by ruthless leaders in the interest of security. So this sense of insecurity and of a brutal struggle for survival is inbred. They have sought their survival in expansion—pushed their borders out as far as they can so as to have breathing room against invaders.

The Russian soul is an amalgam of these experiences. Along with their very many assets, they can be overly aggressive when they're strong, and they brutalize other people. And sometimes fawning when they're weak.

It is not a soul whose good parts cannot eventually dominate the bad parts. But I think—and what we're talking about is the evolution of the Russian state—I think the Russian personality will also evolve. If Russia develops a society in which people feel comfortable, secure, not threatened either internally or externally, then there will be a flowering of the better parts of the Russian soul.

—April 1, 2008

SIX

THE INDISPENSABLE
PARTNERSHIP

DAVID IGNATIUS: When we think about America and the
world, we tend to assume that Europe is a static and un-
changing area about which we know everything there is
to know. We forget that over the past twenty years, Europe has
changed as much as any region in the world.

The European Union has been created and has expanded beyond western Europe to bring in diverse new members. Europe has
created its own currency, confounding the expectations of many
who thought it was impossible. It's in many ways a very different
place. What is this new Europe? What makes it different? And
what new security issues does it present for the United States?
Zbig?

ZBIGNIEW BRZEZINSKI: What is new about Europe is clearly the highly institutionalized effort to transcend traditional national sovereignty. That is a remarkable achievement. The United States was "a more perfect union." But at its founding it was a more perfect union of mostly Anglo-Saxons plus slaves and some residual Indians. The creation of the European Union out of so many distinct nations and languages is historically unique.

Looking at it from the American point of view, I would say that it is in our interest that this Europe, one, be larger; two, that it be politically more defined; three, that it have an increased military capability of its own; and four, that it be allied with the United States. Let me just add a word briefly to each.

Europe should be larger in the sense that the creation of a historically and culturally defined Europe is still unfinished business. From the American point of view, it is desirable that Turkey be in such a Europe because an excluded Turkey is likely to become more like a Middle Eastern country and so bring the Middle East to Europe.

Europe should be politically more defined in the sense that if Europe is our partner, we want it to be able to take decisions that are viable in a variety of fields, ranging from the socioeconomic through the political and military.

Third, I would like Europe to be militarily more capable because a great many of our shared problems have to do with security. Sadly, the transatlantic dialogue so far has involved demands from the United States that the Europeans share our burdens—which they're not capable of doing. In turn, the Europeans demand that they share in the decisions but profess to be incapable of assuming the burdens. A militarily more capable Europe would be better able to really act as an ally. Nicolas Sarkozy recently proposed a standing corps of some sixty thousand men to which the six leading countries of Europe—France, Great Britain, Germany, Spain, Italy, Poland—would each contribute ten thousand.

And last but most obvious, I think that while America is still the paramount country in the world despite the costs of Iraq, we really need Europe as an ally because that will maximize our shared influence. But also, in many issues that we're concerned with, the European perspective is a little more historically sophisticated, perhaps in some ways a little wiser. I think we would benefit from a genuine partnership with Europe in which we share decisions as well as burdens.

IGNATIUS: Brent, how would you define the new Europe? And how new do you think it is?

BRENT SCOWCROFT: I agree with Zbig that the new issue is the transcending of national sovereignty. It is new and in many respects unique. The EU is fundamentally dissimilar organizationally to the United States. Although the U.S. is frequently looked at as a model, the EU is breaking new ground. It's very much a work in progress. There's a lot of ambivalence both in Europe and in the United States about where it's going and even about whether it's desirable.

The United States has been ambivalent about the EU for a long time. On the one hand, we argue as Henry Kissinger did: If you want to call Europe, what's the telephone number? On the other hand, we're very leery of a unified Europe. In many respects we would rather deal with Britain, France, Germany, and so on separately.

In Europe, the ambivalence is over whether they want to develop the [European] Coal and Steel Community established in 1948 into a union, like the United States of America, or something looser, more of a confederation? This question has gotten into the debate over deepening or broadening the EU. Do you focus on adding more countries or strengthening the ties among current members? The French, for a time, wanted to do both. Well, it's extremely hard to do both because the more you broaden, the more you diversify the interests and attitudes and perspectives that you have to bring together into a union that can really coalesce.

IGNATIUS: Do you think, Brent, that this broader Europe will retain the coherence that the tighter EU used to have? I sometimes hear Europeans asking, what do we really have in common with Slovaks, with Cypriotes, with all these diverse people we've brought into the new Europe? Have we fundamentally weakened the character of our union?

SCOWCROFT: That's the dilemma. As Zbig says, there's a lot of desirability in extending Europe. Turkey is a classic example because Turkey geographically straddles Europe and Asia. But the broader you get, the more likely it is that you will have a less cohesive structure. That not withstanding, I think it is critically important to have Turkey in the EU.

Let me say one other thing, on the military side. Zbig talked about a European military. But one of the real conflicts with the U.S. that has come out of the development of the EU is over its military role and that of NATO. That conflict is being somewhat sublimated now, partly because the European states are not prepared to put money into their defense establishments. But for a long time, the French especially were trying to persuade the EU to create a military organization separate from, and in some respects in competition with, NATO. Operations jointly with NATO would be on a completely voluntary basis.

These particular currents are not so prominent right now. There's kind of a lull, because Europe is somewhat exhausted with taking on so much and trying to absorb it. And the military issue is relatively quiescent. But these are the issues we face. They're unique because we've never before faced the creation of a great power by deliberate action.

BRZEZINSKI: The paradox in all this is that the European Community, as it expanded, renamed itself the European Union. But what's really happened is that the European Union has become the European Community as a consequence of enlargement.

The European Community of ten or less was much more cohesive. In fact, if a real European Union had been created back in the late 50s, we probably could have had a single European state involving France, Germany, and several others. Now we have a much larger Europe which calls itself a union. And it is economically and socially very successful. But it has yet to define itself politically, and from the American point of view, it would be good if it did. I think probably it will, because it is moving slowly in that direction.

The question arises most acutely in the defense area. Europeans don't want to spend too much on defense. They're willing to support and be part of NATO, which gives them a sense of security. But it is growing increasingly clear that the Atlantic Alliance, facing the kind of global problems we have been talking about in these sessions, is not going to be able to act if only one party makes the decisions and assumes the major burdens. Europe has to recognize that. I think we have learned that our power, while decisive, is not conclusive. A closer relationship between America and a more defined and militarily self-sustaining Europe is beginning to be perceived by both sides as a mutual interest.

That will raise, of course, the question, where does this Europe end? I happen to think Ukraine should be part of it. And almost all the members of the EU are members of NATO. Therefore, if Ukraine ever becomes a member of the EU, it will seek to be a member of NATO.

That, at some point, will raise some complicated questions about the nature of the European relationship with Russia, which we discussed rather fully in the last chapter. But I see this historic progression as something that far-sighted leaders on both sides of the

Atlantic now recognize as desirable. And I think it is almost inevitable, unless the West commits suicide.

IGNATIUS: But is it really in America's interest that Europe have its own strong, independent defense force? We keep calling on the Europeans to do more of this. But if they really did have their own independent defense capability outside NATO, wouldn't that raise problems for us?

BRZEZINSKI: One has to ask, "Independent for what?" I don't think it's likely that Europe is going to have an independent capability for a really large new war. I don't think Europe is going to have an independent capability to deploy hundreds of thousands of troops abroad. But the Europeans can certainly have much more capability than the expeditionary forces, essentially the size of a battalion, that they selectively dispatch to some parts of Africa—often requiring help from us even with transportation. Europe can do much more without straining itself, but also without becoming so independent that the security linkage between America and Europe would grow diluted or even be ripped apart.

SCOWCROFT: My sense is that the Europeans are strategically exhausted. In the twentieth century they fought two grueling, lengthy wars that have taken a toll on their populations, their politics, their whole outlook. And they can't bring themselves to see the need for strong military force, especially since we have so much. So while I agree it would be useful if they did more militarily, it seems to me that for some time, while they recover their élan, we should accept a division of labor in which we do more of the military part and the Europeans do the things that they do well, which includes rebuilding and reorganizing states in the way that they do to bring them into the European Union. We should work very closely with them but recognize that hectoring them about the need for more forces is not going to be helpful.

BRZEZINSKI: Right, but I have a bit of a reservation here. The reservation is not in the merits of the case you're making, Brent, but more in the political consequences if we have that kind of division of labor. Take Afghanistan, for instance. The Europeans will be in Afghanistan doing good things, building roads, schools, whatever—which maybe they can do better than us. And we'll be there fighting and bleeding.

I don't think the American public will view that as an alliance in the long run. We will resent it. I think we have the right to expect the Europeans, in spite, as you say correctly, of their strategic fatigue—we have the right to expect them to be more responsible for the state of the world. They are lagging behind us. But incidentally, I also see the British being willing to take that responsibility, the French increasingly willing, as well as some of the smaller allies like the Poles and the Dutch. The real problems are Germany and probably Italy. I think that can be overcome.

SCOWCROFT: I'm not talking about a division of labor. I'm saying that all of the members have to participate in all aspects, though perhaps not equally.

BRZEZINSKI: Okay, I agree with that.

SCOWCROFT: But I'm saying that they can do and are willing to do much more on one side. And we ought to recognize and not demand an equal effort because if we do, the eventual consequence will be separation.

BRZEZINSKI: Fair enough.

IGNATIUS: Brent, what would that mean in practical terms in Afghanistan?

SCOWCROFT: Well, for example, a Paddy Ashdown kind of figure might have gone in and been able to play the role Ashdown played in bringing Bosnia together politically and economically. He might have been able to attract more economic resources than the United States, as a way of balancing our military presence, and, in addition, really unify our collective effort in Afghanistan.

BRZEZINSKI: Let me be clear, then, about what you're saying. Even if America assumes the larger share of the burden of fighting and leading, would you expect the Europeans to increase their role? Or would you give them an exemption?

SCOWCROFT: I would not give them an exemption, no. I agree with Bob Gates when he says we cannot have a two-tiered NATO. But we should not just continuously beat up on them for not carrying their share of the military burden because it's much more complicated than that. We need to be understanding and realistic so that the alliance as a whole can maximize its impact.

BRZEZINSKI: So the military burden doesn't have to be shared equally.

SCOWCROFT: That's right.

BRZEZINSKI: But there has to be some significant sharing.

SCOWCROFT: Absolutely.

▶ ▶ ▶

IGNATIUS: Turning to some of the things that worry Europeans, I think at the top of the list is what we sometimes refer to as Eurosclerosis—the sense that this old continent, even as it remakes itself and the European Union expands, just has demographic problems. It's not reproducing its population in many key European countries. The Scandinavian countries, Germany, Italy, have such low birth rates that the need to import labor will grow and grow if their economies are going to work. That makes some Europeans very pessimistic. Zbig, as someone who was born on that continent and came to America as a young man, do you share that fundamental demographic pessimism about Europe?

BRZEZINSKI: I don't have, from the top of my head, the remedy for the demographic problem. And I have to confess that I don't know too much about it. But it does seem to me that there is some evidence to suggest that demographic projections should not be viewed as one-directional. If one projects a declining population, one should not assume that will always continue, nor the opposite, that a population increase will continue. Most of the projections of the size of the world population have been drastically revised over the years. I think that some European countries are already beginning to see some changes in the number of children per marriage.

But, yes, there is a problem. I imagine Europeans will try to deal with it somewhat like others are trying to deal with it, through social policies that encourage larger families and by accepting larger numbers of immigrants. Countries that are not accustomed to assimilating outsiders will probably exercise caution about accepting a large numbers of immigrants with religious and cultural differences. I think this is why, for example, workers from places like Lithuania, Romania, Slovakia, and Poland are more welcomed in the west. Romanian peasants are now, quite literally, filling empty villages in

Spain where the native inhabitants have either died off or moved to the cities. In Ireland there's a huge Polish community, and not only masses in Catholic churches but radio broadcasts of soccer matches and so forth are also in Polish.

IGNATIUS: But they're not being welcomed by European labor unions.

BRZEZINSKI: That's a different issue. European unions, of course, don't like it. But the countries are welcoming them. I accept the proposition that Europe has been badly hurt by the traumatic experiences of two world wars and is now deeply aware that war should be the last instrument of policy, and that this has led to a reluctance to think of security problems that are distant from Europe. Yet today, most of the problems Brent and I have been discussing are problems that not only challenge America, they also challenge Europe. If America doesn't deal well with them, Europe and its way of life are going to suffer. And that could mean the end of the West. Among those who think about the future, there is an awareness that neither the traditional geopolitical problems nor the new global problems will be addressed effectively unless America and Europe really work together.

SCOWCROFT: That's a very important point, because it's critical that the countries that have common views about man and his relationship to society and the state—and that means the Atlantic community—work together. These ideas are not commonplace to much of this new globalized world. Working together, we advance what we think is the fundamental truth of how to organize society. If we're not together, we have much less chance of success.

IGNATIUS: When you say *common views*, I take it you mean ideas about individual freedoms, in contrast to the more collectivist view of how life and society work that we see more in Asia. Am I right?

SCOWCROFT: Yes, though I don't know if I would put it that way, because it's not just individual versus collective. It is protection of minorities as well. It's many things.

IGNATIUS: Rule of law?

SCOWCROFT: Rule of law. Much of the world has not, historically, developed that way. It's not that one's right or one's wrong, necessarily. But we believe deeply that the world is made up of individuals, and that government should seek the maximum good for the maximum number. I think that by joining together, with our different skills, Europe and America can promote those ideas better than if we're squabbling the way we have in recent years.

BRZEZINSKI: The bottom line is, if America and Europe do not consult and act together in some systematic fashion, there will soon be no West, because neither America alone nor Europe alone can sustain a new world, turbulent and changing as it is. So it is critically important that America and Europe fashion a truly workable decision-making process.

That requires two things. It requires, first, that Europe itself develop a decision-making process that really is coherent, sustained, and operational. That's not going to be easy, but the recent constitutional changes are beginning to significantly move Europe in that direction. We will have, before long, a European president. In fact, who ought to be that president is already becoming the subject of an interesting political discussion.

We'll have a European foreign minister. And if some of the plans for a large European military capability move forward, there will be something that begins to approximate a European army—which nonetheless will not be capable of significant independent action without American participation.

Secondly, we have to have a transatlantic decision-making process that actually gains legitimacy and respect, and proves that it is operational. For example, I think the G8, or the G7 as it used to be, has become discredited for a variety of reasons, including its misuse of the term *democracy* to define membership. But we should strive for some transatlantic organization like that, involving America, probably Canada, and the EU. I don't think it can come into being instantly. But if we were willing to take the initiative, I think we'd find more and more Europeans responsive. It might even push Europeans towards a more deliberate decision-making process. I think our next president would find this a very fertile area for really historic innovation.

The Atlantic Charter, incidentally, provided for this. The Atlantic Charter was a little bit lost in the 1945 division of the world into spheres of influence. So this is not a new idea. But it may be a timely one.

SCOWCROFT: That's an interesting idea. Europe, in past years, has strongly resisted that kind of thinking—especially the French, who for a time wanted to drive the United States out of Europe because they felt that was the only way Europe could unify. As long as we were around, we were the big guys and Europe would never develop the way the French thought it should.

That's one of the reasons I say the unification of Europe is very much a work in progress. There are any number of currents and countercurrents. I think we have to be cautious. But we should at least improve our collective decision-making. NATO used to play a much more central role than it does now. During the cold war, the NATO Council was a serious decision-making body.

BRZEZINSKI: Because we dictated the decisions.

IGNATIUS: And we had a common enemy.

SCOWCROFT: And common objectives. We don't have anything like that now. I still bear scars from discussions with Europeans who were proposing particular points of view. If we countered those points of view, they would claim we were objecting because we didn't want them to consolidate into a community.

We also can't forget what's going on inside Europe. I spoke to a Polish group about two years ago, and they told me they didn't regain their independence as a sovereign state only to turn it over to Brussels. Europe is ending one phase and maybe beginning another. The phase which is ending is the French notion that they will dominate Europe through a Franco-German entente. What we're seeing now instead is the French under Sarkozy talking to the British and worried about the Germans as the big power in Europe. And the current trends in Germany are not exactly conducive to a vigorous, stimulative Europe.

Over the short run, there are going to be these starts and stops. The best course for the United States is to welcome progress toward consolidation but to be very patient and prepared to make the most of the transatlantic community, whatever its current state and mood may be.

▶ ▶ ▶

IGNATIUS: What about how the two powers relate to the rest of the world? Does the European system of democracy travel better than America's? We're often a bit messianic in our promotion of democracy. We have specific ideas about how it should occur. Are the

Europeans more effective in promoting democracy because they're less evangelical? Do they provide a better model for transition to democratic government?

SCOWCROFT: There have been three general trends in America on this issue. The first I would call the Washington-John Quincy Adams trend, in which we saw ourselves as the shining city on the hill. We believed democracy was the way to go. We were an example of man's ability to live in peace and harmony with his fellow man. If others wanted to adopt our system, fine. But, as John Quincy Adams put it, we go not in search of monsters to destroy. We're the well-wishers of all who seek freedom and liberty. We're the guarantors only of our own.

The second trend began with Woodrow Wilson, who found the Washington-Adams foundation too constraining and believed we needed to be evangelizers of democracy. There's been a debate ever since about whether we accept countries as they are and work with them, or try to turn them into democracies.

The third takes place after 9/11 with the Iraq War. It constitutes an emendation of the Wilsonian ideal. It's now our goal or our mission to spread democracy, if necessary even by force. The Europeans, on the other hand, possibly from their experiences with colonialism, are much more modest in what they do.

IGNATIUS: Zbig, when you look at the European success in absorbing the former communist states of Eastern Europe so rapidly in this expanded European Union, you do have to see it as, among other things, an astonishing success in inculcating the values of democracy and very quickly providing and encouraging democratic forces and structures. We brag about being the city on the hill, and we're talking about democracy every other minute in our foreign policy promotion. What can we learn from the Europeans, who've actually been building democracy in formerly communist Eastern Europe?

BRZEZINSKI: Well, I would qualify the message inherent in your question. For one thing, the United States was far more supportive of the democratic movements in the former Soviet bloc than the Europeans. The Europeans tended to try to ignore it. Chancellor Schmidt even said he fully understood why martial law had to be imposed in Poland. And so the Solidarity movement was then crushed. We supported these movements, whereas Europeans tended to be more accepting of what they thought was an unavoidable reality.

Secondly, some of the central European countries have traditions of democracy that are as deep as western Europe's. Poland had the Magna Carta just after Britain. It had the second constitution in the history of political systems, after the American and before the French. Czechoslovakia was a viable democracy before it was overrun by the Nazis. There are traditions in central Europe that were revitalized when the Iron Curtain disappeared. Western Europe certainly encouraged and helped consolidate this revitalization.

Generally the Europeans have not been evangelical in their promotion of democracy. They tend to view it as inherent to themselves and to be somewhat skeptical about trying to proselytize it. We have been proselytizers. But also, like the Europeans, we have been oppressors. We tend to forget that aspect of our history. We overran Hawaii, threw out the local queen, and destroyed the local culture for the sake of agricultural interests.

SCOWCROFT: But we called it Manifest Destiny.

BRZEZINSKI: It's Manifest Destiny, exactly. Look at what we did in the Philippines after the Spanish-American War. Allegedly we were liberating the Filipinos. But we actually waged a war against their guerilla-type resistance, a very energetic and bloody one. And we only gave them freedom some forty years later, after the Japanese overran them and drove us out. When we came back the second time, we weren't so oblivious to Filipino aspirations for democracy. So while our record of evangelizing democracy is on the whole not that bad, it has had its downsides, both in terms of using democratization as an excuse for other objectives, as in Iraq, and in terms of some significant departures from a universal commitment to democracy when it was convenient to us to do so.

Still, there is a difference. Americans are a more outreaching people. Americans tend to a kind of universal activism. Europeans are more preoccupied with what they are and would like to nurture and preserve it. Maybe by combining the two, we can achieve a closer transatlantic communion that would be healthy for both of us.

IGNATIUS: Do you, Brent, see any areas where we can learn from the Europeans? Rather than this American hyperpower, as the French like to say, assuming it's got the answers to everything, are there areas where Europe has answers that you like better?

SCOWCROFT: I think Europe has a much more methodical, organized—sometimes to the point of tedium—way of doing things. We tend to start and stop, either go full-speed ahead or do nothing. And that's why I say we ought to take advantage of those European talents for encouraging people, showing them how to change, showing them how to modernize, showing how to run an economy and a political system. They do that better than we do. The leadership issue, I don't know. It's changing so rapidly on both sides of the Atlantic that it's hard to generalize.

IGNATIUS: The Europeans are good at orderly rule sets. It's easy to make fun of Brussels and all of these people endlessly writing little rules and regulations. But the reality is that they establish a very reliable platform for doing business in these recently communist states.

BRZEZINSKI: Absolutely. There's no doubt that Brussels and its emphasis on regulation and orderly procedures is a wonderful contribution to the transformation of eastern and central Europe.

I would say we can learn from the Europeans more in terms of internal affairs than in the kind of issues we have been discussing. In the more developed parts of Europe there is a real absence of the kind of social iniquities and disparities that exist in the United States. These disparities are not healthy. I don't think they are in keeping with our values. But we have been rather indifferent to them for specific historical reasons. I think we have a lot to learn there from Europeans, who in that respect have moved towards a more just and genuinely democratic society than ours.

The Europeans have also done better than we have in dealing with some fundamental infrastructural problems. A lot of what we once associated with American dynamism during the industrial age has now become antiquated. The absence of railroads, for example, is scandalous. I take the Acela to New York quite often. It's like sitting on a third world train, shaking, moving slowly, always late. European railroad transportation is a whole different world. They have trains that we're not even dreaming of building yet.

I think some aspects of the health service in several countries, such as France and Switzerland, are pretty good. We could learn from them. But these are all domestic issues.

SCOWCROFT: One of the fundamental differences between Europe and the United States is that Europe has developed in such a way that they've had to get along with each other. As a result of geographical limitations, they've increasingly lived in larger urban units and therefore have had to have rules for behavior, rules for managing people's interaction with each other. People who couldn't stand that kind of confining regulation tended to come over to the United States.

As communities on the U.S. east coast started to develop the same need to manage people's interactions, those who chafed under regulation moved to our open and empty west. As a result, the U.S. has developed a much stronger tendency to resent government. Hence the motto that government is best that governs least.

IGNATIUS: And that's what we've got.

SCOWCROFT: Yes, we have, though the subject of too much government is still a live political issue here. We tend to be intolerant, impatient with each other, and our politics tends to be more volatile than the politics of Europe.

IGNATIUS: Well, Europe remains more orderly, certainly. When you travel there, you see the way they protect their environment, protect their old treasures. Zbig, what do you see and feel when you look at the new Poland? This is the land of your birth. It's been transformed by war and the aftermath of war as much as any country on earth. What do you see there now?

BRZEZINSKI: I think Poland is quite rapidly becoming a genuinely European state. Certainly its current political leadership, which has widespread social support, is very European. And some of its top personalities are, so to speak, of the European class. That is to say, one does not feel that they are culturally or politically inferior to the better elements of the west European political elite. So in that respect, there's a lot of movement. The young people, particularly, are becoming very comfortable with the new European reality.

Physically, the country is changing dramatically. I think the fact that Poland and Ukraine were awarded the Euro soccer championships for 2012 is going to give a lot of impetus to this evolution, because it's also producing infrastructure: new airports are needed, new stadiums and also new highways, again creating the enormous possibility for rapid movement of people.

All of that is to the good. But there are legacies of the past. There was a period in Poland when the political leadership was very extremist, both politically and in its religious values. The country has some very backward, traditional farming regions with almost a peasant culture—which are, however, dramatically benefiting from membership in the EU. When Poland voted for membership in the EU, the farmers tended to vote against. They are now the strongest beneficiaries and the biggest enthusiasts for Europe, a little like the French farmers, who benefit exactly the same way.

IGNATIUS: It's good to be a farmer in Europe.

BRZEZINSKI: Yes. All in all, I'm rather optimistic about Poland. And because of that, I'm also optimistic about Ukraine, which is increasingly similar to Poland in terms of its potential and less and less adhered to Russia.

IGNATIUS: Brent, it happens that a European diplomat came to see me today, doing a study for his government about bilateral relations with the United States. He said to me, "We worry that the transatlantic relationship is breaking down." He was thinking of all the issues we've talked about that pull America's attention away from Europe and towards the Middle East, China, this new looming

Asia. And he said, with a tone of resignation, "We just worry that the next administration's attention inevitably will shift from Europe and our traditional relationships and be focused elsewhere." It's a widely held fear. What's the right answer to give to that diplomat?

SCOWCROFT: That that's more an aberration than a new pattern. I think it is true; our attention really is focused elsewhere. It's partly a consequence of the end of the cold war and thus the end of the glue that forced us to shelve our differences because of the greater common threat.

Once the Soviet threat disappeared, those differences came to the fore. Then there was France's notion, as I mentioned earlier, of itself as the leader of Europe. Finally there was our Iraqi incursion, which split the Europeans.

And even before the Iraqi incursion there was Afghanistan, where NATO invoked Article Five of its charter for the first time in its history. In effect, the Europeans were saying, "We're with you." Our response was "Thanks. If we need you we'll call you. Don't call us."

Our incursion into Iraq was widely unpopular in Europe. The French saw its unpopularity as a way to put themselves at the head of European public opinion and drive the United States out of Europe. Of course, the British did not see it that way.

So we've gone through a period of abjuration. Zbig and I are saying the same thing. A strong Atlantic community is vital for the United States and for Europe. Eventually that idea will come to prevail over the disturbances of the past ten years.

IGNATIUS: Zbig, wouldn't our attention inevitably be pulled toward the Pacific and Asia? Isn't it just a matter of the shape of the global economy?

BRZEZINSKI: It certainly is a fact that the global center of gravity is shifting to the Far East. And the six-hundred-year-long dominance of the Atlantic countries in the world is subsiding. But still, if you look at the combined intellectual, economic, and military resources of North America and Europe, it is quite clear that if they can be mobilized intelligently and focused on a constructive policy, that Atlantic community still has an important, and in many respects preeminent, role to play. But it depends a great deal, overwhelmingly, on what Brent and I have been saying. Can we generate a shared strategic direction? Can we find an equitable balance between the sharing of decisions and the sharing of burdens? Can we define goals that are not just self-serving but which address the larger dimensions of the global economy?

If we can do that, then the West will remain the preeminent region in the world for some decades. Even if we are more attentive to the Far East, Japan needs us at least as much as we need them, and probably much more. China, for all its potential for global leadership, will still be, for the next several decades, a country with massive infrastructural problems and poverty. India has yet to prove that it can sustain its national unity. They're a population of a billion people who are still mostly politically inactive and not yet mobilized. We don't know what will happen when that population, so differentiated in ethnicity, language, and religion, becomes genuinely politically awakened.

So the West has a role to play. But it really requires a kind of leadership that is capable of setting a direction and of collaborating across the Atlantic. Hopefully we will have that.

Will the Europeans have a similar leadership? That's much more difficult. But I do attach a lot of significance to something which in this country has not been given enough attention, the Lisbon Treaty and the fact is it's moving forward. And even the Poles you talk about, Brent—who are leery about giving up too much of their sovereignty so soon after they've regained it—just voted the other day, overwhelmingly, for the Lisbon Treaty even though the nationalist party opposed it. If everybody else in Europe ratifies it too, that will be another step toward real European unity. If they elect even a symbolic president, but one with some stature and historical vision, it's going to be the beginning of a new game.

SCOWCROFT: David, your question may be a product of "old-think." If you look at the trends in the world today, it may not be right to say power is moving to Asia because the global forces at work are diminishing national power, changing its nature, and diffusing it. As a result, a few years from now, where the focus of what we usually think of as power lies may not seem so important. Globalization is redefining the nature of national power.

It may be far more important to be able to present a vision that will attract people toward producing a better world. The world is creating wealth at a faster rate than the population is growing. With the right organization, we ought to be able to take care of more people and give a better life to everyone. So to ask, "Are you worried the West is fading?" may be to pose the wrong question. I think that in terms of culture and ideas that is not the case. And comparisons in terms of national power may be less significant than in an earlier age.

BRZEZINSKI: That's a very good insight, and let me give you an example. Look at the dilemma the Chinese leadership has with the Tibetans. It's the poor Tibetans who have this vast country, with its enormous resources and power, in a tizzy. Why? Because traditional power can't solve the problem. The Chinese could massacre every single Tibetan if they chose. Why aren't they doing it? They're very angry. They're furious, in fact. But they're worried about a lot of other things.

IGNATIUS: They're about to host the Olympics—

BRZEZINSKI: Precisely. But why are the Olympics so important? Because there's a new concept of influence and power in the world. Chinese national dreams and their pride are connected with the Olympics, and they don't want to sacrifice them. This speaks exactly to Brent's point, that we now have a sort of globalized interdependence in which other values and objectives complicate the traditional notion of power.

IGNATIUS: There's no question that the transforming phenomenon in the world these days is openness.

BRZEZINSKI: And interaction.

▶ ▶ ▶

IGNATIUS: As borders open, as electronic pathways for knowledge open, not even the strongest, most authoritarian government is able to control that. We saw that in the Soviet Union and Eastern Europe. We're seeing it now in China.

It's this theme that each of you, in different ways, has addressed in all of our conversations: maintaining openness as a principle, maintaining respect for the rights of individuals in this western European, American sense that Brent's been talking about. It's a crucial value.

Let me raise a final dollars and cents, or dollars and euros issue. As we're having this conversation, international financial markets measure the relative worth of Europe and America, as reflected by our currencies, in rather worrying ways for Americans. The euro is trading many days at about one dollar and fifty cents. Our cities are swamped with European tourists who are picking up clothes and electronic appliances at what for them are ridiculous bargains. But these currency values are telling us something important about Europe and America.

Some people say that the euro will emerge as a rival to the dollar as the world's reserve currency, and that the financial capital of the world is going to be London and not New York because London, for all kinds of reasons, is a better place to do business with this diverse world than New York. What do we learn from this very striking change in valuation of the euro and the dollar and from the growing importance of London relative to New York as a financial capital?

SCOWCROFT: I think we've learned that the world is much more deeply interconnected than we thought. We have tended to think that, especially economically and financially, we are a unit unto ourselves, and we're finding out that's not so.

I think we've made some serious mistakes. But having Europeans buying cheaper American goods means that they will buy more American and fewer European goods. The net will be an improvement in our balance of trade.

There are now new forces that tend towards rebalancing. There's an imbalance growing between the oil producers and the consumers and between cheap producers like China and consumers. They result in new elements, like the sovereign wealth funds, that help restore the balance. But we act as if we're immune from all of these developments. One of the reasons London is becoming the world's finance capital is that we have created restrictions that make it unattractive to do business in the United States.

We have to realize we're an intimate part of a very different world. When we cut interest rates to stimulate the domestic economy, we also increase the price of oil. I think we need to broaden our views and consult more with others rather than acting as if we're completely independent.

IGNATIUS: Zbig, what do you think about the economics of this?

BRZEZINSKI: I'll just add that this is an area where American-European cooperation will be just as important as it is in geopolitics and security. Clearly, the present travails of the United States demonstrate that both positively and negatively. Look at what's happened to some major Swiss banks because of the temptations of the American housing market.

Beyond that, we as a country over the last decade or two have become self-indulgent in how we operate financially. The indebtedness of the United States has reached dramatic proportions. It's raising questions about the long-range viability of Social Security, Medicare, and other government programs. We have waged a war for which we have refused to pay even one cent through social sacrifice, whether imposed on the rich or shared with the poor. We have chosen to borrow instead. It shouldn't be surprising that there is some loss of confidence in the United States, some question marks about the dollar. Fortunately, no one has been rash enough to try to penalize us for this by dramatically shifting large amounts out of U.S. treasuries and into euros. But if we don't begin to respond to this situation, there will be pressures to move in that direction.

We have to ask ourselves whether the lifestyle we have adopted, and the almost exclusive emphasis on the acquisition of material goods as our definition of the good life, is really a healthy response to the reality of an interdependent world.

To take one specific example, for every hundred Americans, we have about eighty-eight cars. For every one hundred of India's one billion people, they have one and a half cars. Just think of the energy shortages, pollution, and climate change that will follow if the

Indians and Chinese and others decide that the way to have a good life is to be like us. So our practical problem, which is part economic and part philosophical, is ultimately a global problem. And that's something we, also, have to start thinking about.

SCOWCROFT: Your example may be a dangerous one, because as I understand it the rate of increase in the purchase of cars in India and China is astonishing. Apparently they *have* adopted our model of the good life.

One of the things we need to remember is that world wealth is being created at a rapid rate, a rate that is historically perhaps unique. What we don't know is how to distribute it, how to use it, how to take advantage of it to make the world a better place.

IGNATIUS: The theme that I hear from both of you is that even as Europe changes and expands, the cultural values that Europe and America share remain strong and essential. They're what defines the West. The question is how we can work with the Europeans to advance those ideas, to work effectively together for goals that we share.

Europeans worry that more transatlantic cooperation means more European deference to American desires. They think, especially during the Bush years, that they're moving in a different direction, toward a society that takes care of its citizens better, toward a culture that's less raucous and violent than American culture. Often they look at us and throw up their hands. They don't want to live the way Americans live. They want to live as Europeans. So this tension between America and Europe, and also the great bond that holds the Atlantic Alliance together, is as much about soft power, about those indefinable cultural values that we share, as it is about hard power and decisions about NATO deployments or an independent European security pillar. Am I right, Zbig, that at the end of the day, when we think about Europe, we're thinking about shared cultural values?

BRZEZINSKI: It's both. There's a quip that I sometimes make, that to make the American-European relationship really viable we need regime change in America and we need a regime in Europe. We need regime change in America because we need to reassess what is happening in the world and to redefine the American role away from the self-serving assertions that became so fashionable with the Neocons. And Europe needs a regime, literally. There is really not yet a genuine political regime in Europe.

The military and political structures we've been talking about are needed to provide a framework in which our shared cultural values can be channeled in positive directions, and a framework which is also capable of defending these values. For all of these things, America and Europe are indispensable to each other.

SCOWCROFT: And to the world.

—April 2, 2008

SEVEN

THE POLITICS OF
CULTURAL DIGNITY

DAVID IGNATIUS: You are both master practitioners of foreign policy, and you agreed to take part in this project in
part because you believe the world is changing and that
the rules under which you operated when you were national security
advisors in the White House are also changing, forcing us to think
in different ways. Today I want to ask you to talk about what's new
in the world. What challenges are different from the template you
both grew up with? Brent, let me ask you to start off.

BRENT SCOWCROFT: I believe we've had a more abrupt change in
the international environment than at any time in recent history, a
fundamental change that goes under the broad heading of globalization. It's a change in the way people communicate and interact. That
is what's revolutionizing the world. The world's people are more

politically active. There have always been immigration flows, for instance, but they're huge now because radio and television allow people to compare their current status with that of others around the world and see where the opportunities are. This is happening around the globe. Some of the consequences are good and some are bad. The important point is that it is really changing the status of the nation-state, how it cares for its people, and how it can manage its overall responsibilities for its citizens. The fact is that the role of the nation-state, while still predominant, is steadily diminishing.

I think that is at the heart of what we're facing. The major challenge is that the whole world is changing at once, and this so-called information age is literally transforming the world we all know and the institutions with which we are familiar. It is most dramatic in the more highly developed countries, and those with access to the most modern technology. It is less acute in Latin America and least acute in Africa. And when it hits Africa, divided as it is into states that have no rational borders and that cut across tribes and ethnic groups, it's going to be even more challenging.

IGNATIUS: In this new world, Brent, it sometimes looks as if the Internet, our new instant communications network, acts as an opinion accelerator. For instance, anger over Danish cartoons can suddenly spread to every capital in the Muslim world and there'll be crowds in the streets. We see that phenomenon throughout politics. What does that acceleration of anger mean for the conduct of foreign policy?

SCOWCROFT: It makes people who have never been very aware of anything beyond their immediate village politically active. And much of the flow of information is without the moderating influence of editors of newspapers or of radio or television. For example, on a blog you can say, this is the way the world is, and nobody edits it, corrects it, or says it is not true. So there's a flood of information coming to people who are not used to questioning or sorting through accuracy and inaccuracy by themselves. It's having a profound impact on radicalism and terrorism.

IGNATIUS: Among other things, it's their command and control system.

SCOWCROFT: That's another aspect of it, absolutely.

IGNATIUS: Zbig, what's new in the world?

ZBIGNIEW BRZEZINSKI: First of all, we have to recognize that the traditional problems of power and geopolitics are still with us. But superimposed upon these traditional problems and also transforming their character are two novel, fundamental realities. One is the transformation in the subjective condition of humanity, what I call the global political awakening. For the first time in history all of the world is politically activated. This is something that started with the French Revolution and spread through Europe and to Asia in the late nineteenth century and throughout the twentieth century, and now it's global.

The second reality is the surfacing of the first truly global problems of survival. The biggest problems of survival, heretofore, were national problems, whether they were man-made like the Armenian genocide or the Holocaust, or natural phenomena such as a drought. Now we have problems of survival of a global character. Let me just amplify both propositions.

On the subjective level, this global political awakening is creating massive intolerance, impatience with inequality, with differentials in standards of living. It's creating jealousies, resentments, more rapid immigration, the things that Brent referred to. Connected with that is a craving for respect for differentiated cultures and for individual dignity. Much of humanity feels that respect is lacking from the well-to-do. On the objective level, the new global problems include such things as the crisis of the environment, the threat to the human condition associated with climate change, and the incredible potential for massive lethality deliberately inflicted by human beings on other human beings. We are now capable of killing a lot of people instantly and very easily.

I once wrote something to the effect that until recently it was easier to govern a million people than to kill a million people. Today, it's much easier to kill a million people than to govern a million restless, stirred-up, impatient people. That danger confronts all of us. It is what makes the issue of nonproliferation so important.

These two novel conditions complicate the more traditional issues we have to cope with. Superimposed on them is this obligation to understand and respond to the unique challenges of the twenty-first century, which involve a comprehensive transformation in both the subjective and the objective conditions of mankind.

IGNATIUS: And yet we confront these global conditions with a system of nation-states that contains very traditional systems for solving problems.

My old professor at Harvard, Daniel Bell, observed more than thirty years ago that the nation-state is too big for the small problems of life and too small for the big problems of life. I wonder if we need to think about new structures, new ways to deal with these problems that transcend the nation-state. What do you think, Brent? That's a dream that goes back to 1945.

SCOWCROFT: We do. I think we've described the imperative for that, that this new world is superimposed on the international structures created by and for the old world, which is very different.

But the attitude in the United States is probably more negative toward international organization now than it's been in decades. It's always been ambivalent, but it's more negative now. I would suggest that if we didn't already have a United Nations, the world as it is right now could not sit down and agree on a useful UN charter.

IGNATIUS: That's scary.

SCOWCROFT: And that's the difficulty. These worlds are clashing with each other and there's not the necessary urgency to take action among politically responsible people.

BRZEZINSKI: Let me add to that. Earlier in our discussions Brent expressed skepticism regarding the notion that some people are propagating regarding some sort of collective or union of democracies. I forget the exact phrase they use, but anyway Brent was doubtful about the utility of such a formation. And I share his skepticism. For one thing, how do we define democracy? Who's in, who's out? A lot of our friends are going to be out, we may have some people in who are not really our friends, and it's not going to work. But as a practical matter, we do have to ask ourselves: Who can we best work with in dealing with the kind of issues we have just been talking about?

My inclination would be to emphasize two propositions: One, we know that certain states share, basically, some of our values and interests, and therefore we have to work with them more closely. I would put in that category, first of all, Europe. This is why I attach such importance to a really serious effort to create a genuinely collaborative partnership with Europe. That requires a lot of work. It's more than a slogan.

Secondly, I would say there are some countries outside Europe that fall in the same category, and therefore we ought to think of how to draw them in. That includes Australia; it very much includes Japan, and that's a more complicated challenge; and increasingly, South Korea, which is now incorporating global responsibility into its policies. There may be some others.

In brief, on the issues we have been talking about, we ought to be interested in shaping coalitions of states that share a responsible interest in solving these problems and not determine participation entirely on the basis of whether or not the states concerned are democracies. We would start with democracies that share our values, but then selectively engage those countries that really are prepared to work responsibly on some of these issues. That's going to be tough, but we won't be able to solve these problems alone in any case, and we'll need coalitions that in some fashion represent a dominant majority of wealth, power, and serious commitment. On some issues, we may want Russia in the coalition, on other issues, China, India, Brazil, et cetera.

IGNATIUS: One question is how that group of like-minded, developed countries can extend the writ of law, order, and security to the world as a whole. Thomas Barnett, a political theorist, has written a book called *The Pentagon's New Map,* in which he distinguishes between these core connected countries with, as he says, orderly rule sets—the countries of globalization, as Brent has described it—and the disconnected periphery of states that are outside this world of orderly rule sets and that increasingly are lawless, ungoverned, often tyrannical. The challenge he presents is how we'll extend connectedness and orderly rule sets to the world as a whole, so we don't have these pockets of lawlessness. Brent, how can we do that?

SCOWCROFT: I think we can do that the way the United States has typically behaved in the past. I agree with Zbig, but I wouldn't start with democracies, necessarily.

BRZEZINSKI: I wouldn't either.

SCOWCROFT: I would start with leadership on issues. Not domination and ultimatums but leadership. The United States has a tradition of leadership. The League of Nations, for example, the UN—these were U.S. ideas. They're attractive ideas, and the United States, with its reputation for having the interest of mankind at heart, if it takes a leadership position, can gather people together and persuade them to move in the right direction. That's been lacking in recent years, partly because the end of the cold war induced all of us to breathe a sigh of relief and conclude that there were no more serious problems and we could just go back to preoccupation with our domestic issues. The outside world was fine—not really threatening.

We're finding out that it is not fine, but I think if we, for example, were to mobilize United States leadership on behalf of climate change and say, "This is a world problem, we really need to move," the world would respond. We have that kind of power or moral authority, to a degree that no one else does. Europe eventually may have it, but it doesn't right now, and certainly no other power centers have it. That's what we can do, that we have not done very much since the end of the cold war.

BRZEZINSKI: Let me also add that to do it, the president not only has to take global leadership, he has to make a really serious effort at domestic leadership because, ultimately, we are a democracy. Ultimately, the United States is not going to be serious about anything unless there is a national commitment by the president, by Congress, and by the public. The issues we're talking about do require a significant rethinking by Americans of what the key challenges are in the world today and what America's principal responsibilities are.

It's very easy, given recent circumstances, to slide into a paranoid mood in which *war on terror* defines everything and struggle against

Muslim jihad is the defining strategy. If we move down that path, we will not be able to touch any of the issues we've been discussing. But it's not enough just to abandon these demagogic slogans; there really is a task of significant public education. More than ever before, the next president will have to be a national teacher on these issues and make a very concerned, intellectually sustained effort to get the American people to think hard about what is new about the twenty-first century, what is unique about the challenges we face, and why America can only respond to them if it manages to shape a whole series of differentiated coalitions that are dedicated to a collective response.

IGNATIUS: Zbig, let's dig a little deeper on that. You've written about this global awakening. We've talked about it in our conversations, and you've described a global yearning for dignity. Not simply a better life or a higher standard of living but for something intangible, which is respect. How does the United States put itself on the side of that aspiration for dignity in a more powerful way?

BRZEZINSKI: First of all, avoiding stigmatizing others. I fear that a great deal of our talk about Islamic terrorism has unfortunately created more hostility towards us among the largest religious formation in the world. We have to be very careful. If we were to use the same terminology, let's say, about the Irish Republican Army and keep talking about how they're trying to establish a papacy in western Europe, that this is a Catholic conspiracy, that this is a Catholic crusade against us, we would certainly alienate most Catholics, including the sixty-five or seventy million Catholics in this country. So we have to be sensitive about the language we use.

Secondly, we have to face the fact that the quest for dignity is related to the awareness of social disparities. People who feel deprived, and who can now see on television how deprived they are compared to others, are going to resent the rich if they feel the rich are perpetuating the status quo.

So we have to identify ourselves with certain specific causes, such as elimination of starvation in the world. Millions of people are still starving in the world, and some deliberate effort is needed to begin to create conditions for self-sustaining development in poorer countries.

We have to do much more in terms of health and medicine and better schooling for people in the poorest parts of the world. It's these kinds of causes where an evident American involvement, a pioneering role, would help a great deal. And that requires, last but not least, asking ourselves whether the unlimited acquisition of wealth is the ultimate objective of life. That applies not only to the people who simply want to have more material goods; it applies particularly to our political elite. I find it disgusting—I'm using the word advisedly—disgusting that chief executives, in businesses that often have adopted destructive, short-term policies focusing on immediate profit, are obtaining payoffs on a scale of hundreds of millions of dollars when they leave their bankrupt financial institutions. There's something fundamentally unjust in a world where that's taking place. And so there's a whole gamut of issues, ranging far beyond the political into the cultural and philosophical, that we have to think about seriously.

▶ ▶ ▶

IGNATIUS: We're talking about living our values better. Brent, part of the mystery of leadership is how a president can embody our values in a way that speaks to the world rather than alienating the world. George Bush certainly thinks of himself as a principled man, but the world's reaction has been to be turned off.

SCOWCROFT: One of the problems is the use of terms. We're throwing around terms like freedom, but freedom means different things to different people. Freedom from what? Freedom to do what? What are the restrictions on freedom? It becomes very confusing. We should be talking, instead, about dignity—dignity of the individual. Dignity is easier to understand. And if you take that idea to heart, it changes the way you look at things. Our current immigration problem, for example, has resulted in pressure on the government to round up and deport illegal immigrants. But these are not animals crawling across our border, they are human beings. They've come to the United States, most of them, hoping for a better life, for a more dignified existence.

If we would focus on human dignity, it would help us deal with the issues Zbig talked about. I don't see anything wrong with getting wealthy, but we need to think about people's dignity and how we can improve their well-being, which is what we as a nation are about.

IGNATIUS: How would a president signal respect for human dignity? What are some practical things that a president could do?

BRZEZINSKI: Well, at the risk of a personal confession, the reason I liked Obama from the very beginning—he may or may not be the president this book will be read by—is that apart from his intrinsic intelligence, I felt that his election would, by itself, signal respect for the dignity of others. I don't mean this to be a political tract for him, but given his biography and his identity, he creates a collective respect for diversity. And for dignity, because dignity entails respect for diversity.

Dignity is not the same for everybody. Yet we have to universalize the notion and not have a sense that the world is divided into superior countries with superior cultures and downtrodden coun-tries with inferior cultures. That will not endure in the twenty-first century. It has the makings of chaos and violence and resentment. Obama represents one way a president could respond, simply through who and what he is.

Another way is simply to address the issue. McCain is an engag-ing personality. You have a sense of heroic decency in the guy. And if he makes it his intellectual challenge, I think he could help a lot. I hope very much that he doesn't make the crusade against jihadism a major definition of his foreign policy, because I think that would be self-defeating for America as well as for him. I think he has the ca-pability, in his personality and intellect and heroic past, to project another message.

SCOWCROFT: It's harder to do than to say. We have said since the country was founded that all men are created equal. Yet those words were written at a time when one-third of the United States popula-tion was enslaved. Only five years before I was born did women get the vote throughout the United States.

Simply to talk about dignity, to assert that one human being ought to be considered as valuable as another, is important, but it also has to be reflected in the way one behaves. I think Barack Obama represents those values, so does Hillary Clinton—and so does John McCain in his crusading about immigration, about Guantanamo, and against mistreatment of detainees. These issues are at heart about dignity, about how you treat other human beings.

IGNATIUS: Certainly in the sense of dignity of the human body and soul, John McCain—who experienced the most hideous insult to personal dignity, being tortured month after month, year after year in North Vietnam—made a decision that what was done to him should never be done to any human being. He defied President Bush to press that issue.

BRZEZINSKI: And that's to his great credit.

IGNATIUS: It is to his great credit. So we have three potential presidents who all speak to the issue of human dignity.

SCOWCROFT: Uniquely. And all three represent it in different ways.

IGNATIUS: The word in Arabic for dignity is *karameh* and it's a very powerful word for Arabs. In my thirty years of tromping around that part of the world, I've realized it's the one thing people won't give up. You can batter them, imprison them, but they won't give that up. In our conversations we've approached a subject that worries all of us, and now I'd like to address it directly: whether, after the mistakes and difficulties of the last seven years, we are becoming locked in a clash of civilizations.

We don't want to be, we don't think it's necessary, but there are hundreds of millions of Muslims who are furious at the United States, for whom the images of those prisoners at Abu Ghraib will never go away. What do we do about that? How do we avoid the crackup that many people fear is ahead of us, despite our nice words about dignity?

BRZEZINSKI: It's not only a question of the new president, his or her personality, his or her words. It's not only a question of how Americans are encouraged to rethink what we ought to be doing in the world. It's very specifically a question of what we do, soon after the inaugural, to deal with the problems in the Middle East which precipitate a long-lasting hatred of America. It will take a lot of effort, but it's a series of issues that cannot be put off. In my view, there should be a sense of urgency in dealing with the issue of Iraq, even though Brent and I might disagree on how rapidly something can be done.

There's certainly a sense that we have been slack and ineffective in promoting an Israeli-Palestinian peace, which both peoples need, but which, more importantly, we need—and we have to be identified with it.

There is the more general question of how we deal with Iran. Last but not least, there's the question of how we deal with Muslim traditionalism and fundamentalism, which should not be reduced simply to Al-Qaeda. If we're not careful in places like Afghanistan and Pakistan, we can get embroiled in something that perpetuates hostility towards us.

SCOWCROFT: It hasn't helped that we have surrounded ourselves with an environment of fear. That has been deadly. We have depicted Muslims in the war on terror the way we depicted Germans in World War I. We dehumanized them, turned them into objects of hatred and fear, the enemy. But Al-Qaeda is a very different kind of enemy. It is a small clique with a certain goal, and we need to remember that. Just because a man going through Customs is named Mohammad, you don't pull him aside and strip search him. But we do because the climate of fear has become pervasive in this country. That's one thing we have to attack.

IGNATIUS: Zbig, what has fear done to us as a people?

BRZEZINSKI: It's made us more susceptible to demagogy. And demagogy makes you more inclined to take rash decisions. It distorts your sense of reality. It also channels your resources into areas which perhaps are not of first importance. I'm struck by the extent to which this country, more than any other, lives in an environment in which everywhere on television, on radio, in the newspapers, you see advertisements emphasizing security and defense and weapons. We have a defense budget that is literally bigger than that of the entire rest of the world combined.

SCOWCROFT: And is less controversial than I think it's ever been in our lifetimes.

BRZEZINSKI: That's right. It's quietly accepted because we're scared. We're meeting in this building in Washington, and we go through this idiotic security procedure to enter it. The implicit message of these precautions is that Bin Laden is sitting in some cave in Pakistan planning to blow up the building in which a few investment banks and law firms are located. We have succumbed to a fearful paranoia that the outside world is conspiring through its massive terrorist forces to destroy us. Is that a real picture of the world, or is it a classic paranoia that's become rampant and has been officially abetted? If I fault our high officials for anything, it is for the deliberate propagation of fear.

When Brent was in office, when I was in office, we lived in a situation in which in six hours, half the population of the United States could be dead. We did everything we could to conduct our foreign policies rationally, to make deterrence credible, to keep the American people secure and confident. We haven't done that in the last seven years.

SCOWCROFT: In World War II, in the cold war, was Washington barricaded the way it is now? No. True, the threat today is different. But we're in danger of losing what has been the ideal of America: the hope that we can make ourselves better, and make the world better.

BRZEZINSKI: We've lost our self-confidence.

SCOWCROFT: And the optimism to go out and do good. That's been the symbol of America, why we've accomplished so much. That's why the world traditionally likes us. Even when we made serious foreign policy mistakes most said, "Well, they mean well." Now there's great doubt around the world about whether we mean well. That's a tremendous change, and we need to recover our image. The next president needs to start on this recovery and make us again the hope of mankind that we've always seen ourselves as being and that much of the world has traditionally seen us as being.

▶ ▶ ▶

IGNATIUS: I'm struck that the two of you, who are often described as foreign policy realists, who put America's national interests first and try to form policy around the advancement and protection of those interests, have been talking in this conversation, and in all of our other discussions as well, about values. How should future American leadership combine those two strands, a realism about our interests and an anchor in our values as a people and a country? Zbig, that's not an easy trick. Jimmy Carter, the president you served, sometimes got that right, sometimes wrong.

BRZEZINSKI: We'll always get it sometimes right and sometimes wrong, because you're right, it's not easy. I entitled my memoirs from the White House *Power and Principle*. And I don't know whether I'm a realist or an idealist—I don't classify myself.

It seems to me that if you're engaged in statecraft, you have to address the realities of power. Power is a threat but also a tool. If you're intelligent and you have the kind of power that is needed, you use it in a way that promotes your national security and interests, but that is not enough. Power has to be driven by principle, and this is where the element of idealism comes in. You have to ask yourself, ultimately, what is the purpose of life? What is the purpose of national existence? What is the challenge that humanity faces? What is it that we all have in common as human beings?

And you try to strike a balance between the use of power to promote national security and interests, and trying to improve the human condition. It's not easy to do the two things together. But you have to be conscious of it. You mustn't be cynical or hypocritical because that's demoralizing and not morally sustainable. You have to be historically confident. You have to have a sense that what you are doing is somehow in tune with the mysterious unraveling of history and that you're pointing in the right direction.

What we have been trying to talk about today deals precisely with that issue. How, in the early stages of the twenty-first century, do we set a course for America that deals with the practical realities but is channeled towards this larger goal? The president said in his latest State of the Union message that the defining character of the twenty-first century is going to be the struggle against terrorism. This is an absurd statement—first of all because it's now 2008, so we still have ninety-two years to run. To define the essence of this century so early on is premature. What Brent and I are doing today is trying to grope our way towards a more complex and sophisticated definition of the challenges of the century, and to say how, in that context, an American national policy that combines power with principle is the right response.

SCOWCROFT: These labels—realist, idealist—are difficult. I don't know what I am. People write about me and say I'm a realist. During the cold war I was criticized by the left for being a realist because I was focused on the Soviet military threat rather than the existence of nuclear weapons. Now I'm criticized as a realist by the right. So these things change. I'm still the same person I was.

When I went to graduate school, Hans Morgenthau's *Politics Among Nations* was the bible for students of international politics. It is one of the founding texts of realism. At his purest, Morgenthau held that international politics is a struggle for power, and that power is the only thing that matters. States try to maximize their own power or that of their group against other groups.

Well, that's the extreme of it. To me, realism is a recognition of the limits of what can be achieved. It's not what your goals are, but what can you realistically do. The idealist starts from the other end—What do we want to be? What do we want to achieve?—and may neglect how feasible it is to try to get there and whether, in trying to get there, you do things which destroy your ability to get there and sacrifice the very ideals you were pursuing. The difference is which end of the issue you start with and, as Zbig says, how you balance ends and means. Do you try to leap for the stars? Or are you so mired in day-to-day difficulties that you don't even elevate your sights to believe that progress can be made? We need to strike some balance between the extremes of realism and idealism. The United States ought to be on the side of trying to achieve maybe a little more than it can.

But not too much. When we say we are going to make the world democratic, that's too much. And in the attempt, as we are seeing right now, we risk creating more harm than good.

BRZEZINSKI: Ultimately, we have to face the fact that we're all fallible. Striking that balance is a desirable objective, but more often than not, we'll probably err on one side or the other. That's inherent in the human condition. Therefore there will always be a debate about whether we're being too realistic or too idealistic.

IGNATIUS: We Americans are often accused of wanting to have it all, of wanting to have things that are in conflict. We want lower taxes and more services. We want freedom and protection from our adversaries. This habit of wanting it all is going to hinder us as we try to deal practically with the problems of the twenty-first century.

To take an obvious example, you both agree that climate change, global warming, is a real and growing problem for the world. To deal with it, we have to change the way we live. We're going to have to accept some limits on carbon emissions, either through a tax or some other system, and that's going to change how Americans live. How does presidential leadership get us to do the thing that's hard for any people, but I think hardest for Americans, which is to give up some of our fabulous wealth and opportunities for our long-run good and for the good of the world? Zbig, how does a president teach people to do that?

BRZEZINSKI: There's no magic prescription, but it does start with what you have just raised, namely, presidential involvement. The president is uniquely positioned to be an educator of the country, a public definer of its long-range interests and of how these interests mesh into the larger global context. Only the president can do that. The issue is how we define the good life. Are the unlimited acquisition of material possessions and ever-higher use of energy the ultimate definition of the good life? How is this going to be sustainable on a global basis?

I don't think the answers will come easily. They certainly will not come within the term of any one president. This is a debate that has to start within the country that, in a sense, has set the worldwide standard for material attainments and which, in the current global era, has to ask itself whether that standard is compatible, literally, with continued global survival. We are not quickly going to make a dramatic voluntary change in how we live, but the issue has to be put onto our national agenda.

SCOWCROFT: We first have to change the mind-set. Throughout the development of the industrial age, we have generally behaved as though the pollutants we produced just disappeared in the environment, and nature has been so capacious that they seemed to. We poured them into the ocean, we put them into the air, and they just seemed to go away. Now we've begun to realize that they don't go away. And the quantities that are being produced, with the increase of population and civilization, are beginning to defeat nature's ability to absorb them. That's the fundamental thing Americans have to grasp.

IGNATIUS: In this world that we're describing, does the United States need to think about a different kind of sovereignty? We have been blessed with this unique geographical position—surrounded by two oceans. We're not just a city on a hill, we're a city on a great big hill that's very hard to attack, so we've gotten used to an extreme version of sovereignty. Should we be thinking about a more interdependent sovereignty in the twenty-first century, where we acknowledge that our existence depends on our ability to work with others to deal with global disease, climate change, and other global problems?

SCOWCROFT: We have to. Take the environment as a prime example. The United States can exercise all the discipline we have, but it does no good if the rest of the world won't go along. The Chinese and Indians, for example, might say, "It's fine for you to propose restrictions because you went through your industrial period and spewed all these pollutants and you didn't pay anything for it. Now you're saying we have to pay a price for our development. Well, we refuse."

We have to negotiate. We have to reach across national borders. These kinds of problems, whether it's how the world deals with a growing shortage of the mobile energy that petroleum provides, or whether it's climate change, they cannot be solved nationally. It has to be done cooperatively, and that brings us back to the question, what are the mechanisms for cooperation? International organizations have too seldom gone beyond issues of war and peace or the elements of trade, into the issues we're talking about now. But they're going to have to, and the sooner we do it, the less we'll have to do it in a climate of crisis.

BRZEZINSKI: You asked about national sovereignty, and that harkens back to our discussion of the complex relationship between the realist and the idealist embodied in a single individual or in a group of policymakers. I think the redefinition of national sovereignty is implicit in all of this. But at the same time, one has to be very careful not to start talking about it too soon, even if one is thinking about it, because sovereignty is one of those trigger issues that could cause a reaction in a democratic public that has lived for several hundred years in uniquely secure and isolated circumstances, and which equates that sovereignty with its own identity. Dealing with these global issues is going to demand a readjustment or redefinition of what sovereignty means. But if we start talking too early about sacrificing sovereignty in order to deal with these problems, we'll probably produce a nationalist reaction that will prevent any solution.

IGNATIUS: Zbig, isn't that why we never get around to solving problems? We know we need to raise taxes and change the structure of social security and entitlement programs, but we know the public will go nuts. We know we need carbon taxes to reduce emissions, but the public will go nuts. So nobody ever gets around to doing it. Isn't the task of leadership to say the things that are unsayable?

BRZEZINSKI: Well, that's a typical response of a rampant idealist who wants to embarrass the realist who wishes to be idealistic but wishes also to be effective. That's the dilemma.

SCOWCROFT: But as an enlightened realist, I think the way to do it is not to start saying we have to give up some sovereignty. Instead we should be talking about the problems—

BRZEZINSKI: Exactly.

SCOWCROFT: —and how to solve them. Let the fact that we have to make some concessions on sovereignty sink in gradually. Don't put that out front.

BRZEZINSKI: Absolutely.

SCOWCROFT: Because then it's a barrier.

▶ ▶ ▶

IGNATIUS: I think you've put a good capstone on this discussion with your phrase *enlightened realism.* Or in Zbig's version, *guileful realism,* that sees that you can't do everything at once.

Let us close by exploring a question suggested by our editor, William Frucht, which arises from American exceptionalism. It sometimes seems that Americans divide the world into two categories: People are either Americans or potential Americans. We assume that everybody wants to live as we do.

BRZEZINSKI: That's the problem.

IGNATIUS: So here is the question: Is it condescending—and therefore disrespectful of people's dignity—to say that everybody wants to live as we do? Or is it more condescending to say, well, we have these freedoms, but other people don't need them. How do you walk that line? How do you respect people's differences without saying that we're entitled to things they're not necessarily entitled to, such as equality for women or democracy?

SCOWCROFT: American exceptionalism is really based on the idea of human dignity. People want to improve their lives and their position in the world. In that sense, everybody wants to be like us. They want a better life. We think the way we have devised it is the best path to that better life. That doesn't necessarily mean that others must follow the same path. American exceptionalism is frequently distorted by the notion that everyone else *ought* to be like Americans, whether they like it or not. But at its heart, it envisions a better life for everybody. Perhaps we just got a head start. That's how I think you resolve the dilemma. We have ordinarily stood for a better life around the world.

BRZEZINSKI: But it's a better life for everybody in a society that emerged and improved itself and made itself wealthier in an environment in which a relatively small number of people were blessed with very rich resources, which they were able to develop as their numbers grew gradually. When I came to America as a child, for example, the population of the United States was 120 million people. It's 300 million today. Our path to wealth cannot be duplicated in India or China or Africa, where you have hundreds of millions of people, in some places billions, already living in poverty.

So while our successful society can rightfully be viewed as relevant to others, the way we created it cannot be duplicated everywhere. Others have to do it differently. That means some significant departures from the way we have operated and have structured our system.

SCOWCROFT: No, you're right. But I think our structures and processes have created value in the world. Look at China, for example. If you compare today with fifty years ago, the average Chinese is infinitely better off.

BRZEZINSKI: Yes, but in a different way. That's my point.

SCOWCROFT: That's why I say you have to use different measures—

BRZEZINSKI: Exactly. And we have to be tolerant.

SCOWCROFT: —to develop India. And it's partly our responsibility. The means exist in the wealth of the world to do that, but it can't be done the way we did it.

BRZEZINSKI: Exactly. We cannot dogmatize our experience.

IGNATIUS: Is there a problem with this combination of American exceptionalism, a sense that we're special and uniquely blessed, and our tendency to universalize our values? We're special and everybody should be like us? One thing that I see as I travel the world is that people want to write their own history, even if they get it wrong. It goes back to this sense of dignity. It's mine; it's not yours. Even if you're right, I don't want to do it your way; I want to do it my way.

And accepting that desire of people to write their own history sometimes means accepting that sometimes they're going to write it badly.

BRZEZINSKI: Different. Differently.

IGNATIUS: Differently from the way we would.

SCOWCROFT: This is how we have evolved. A century or so ago, when the Hungarians were subordinated by the Austrians, *freedom* meant freedom from empire. That's the world Woodrow Wilson was dealing with. Today freedom means something very different.

BRZEZINSKI: The reason Wilsonianism had such an appeal was that it coincided with a particular phase of European history, in which freedom for people who aspired for it and focused their sense of identity on it was a very timely thing. The rise of independent European states and the collapse of empires was very much in keeping with what Wilson was talking about, and America became a symbol of it.

The reason I put so much emphasis on the notion of dignity in my book *Second Chance* is that it's dignity, not freedom, that people around the world—now politically awakened and aware of global disparities—really seek. People want dignity in their existence, dignity in their ability to give a meaningful opportunity for their children, dignity in the respect that others give them, including their cultures and their religions.

That thought occurred to me, as I was writing that book, in a very curious way. I was listening to a postgame discussion among football players—not all of whom, even though they all claim to have gone to college, are very well educated—and I was struck by how often they will say, whether celebrating their victory or mourning their defeat, "They didn't give us respect." And it struck me that this is a vital human emotion.

IGNATIUS: The need for respect?

BRZEZINSKI: Yes. And that is what many people in the world feel we have not been giving them.

SCOWCROFT: Yes. But our role in the world has evolved so dramatically. Go back to the Hungarian Revolution of 1848. The Hungarians raised monuments similar to the Statue of Liberty. They told us they had our ideals and asked for our help. Our response was to wish them well. We hoped they succeeded, but it was not our fight.

IGNATIUS: But Wilson made it our fight.

BRZEZINSKI: Yes. That's why Wilson was hailed in Europe. And it's precisely because we're now doing the opposite, for example in Iraq, that we're so, sad to say, despised.

SCOWCROFT: And the world's different. Wilson also created Yugoslavia and he was hailed by the Yugoslavs for doing so. And now they can't live together.

IGNATIUS: In this new world, do we have to accept that we're not exceptional; we are citizens of the world?

SCOWCROFT: No, I don't believe that.

BRZEZINSKI: We are exceptional.

SCOWCROFT: We are exceptional in offering hope, that there's a better life available for everybody.

BRZEZINSKI: We're also exceptional in the sense that no country today, in the twenty-first century, can duplicate our experience, our asymmetry between resources and population. But while we can

acknowledge that we're exceptional, I think we should also acknowledge that certain aspirations are universal, particularly the aspiration for dignity.

SCOWCROFT: And that they have to be realized in different ways.
But they should not go unrealized.

—April 3, 2008

EIGHT

THE FIRST
HUNDRED DAYS

DAVID IGNATIUS: We've talked about many of the foreign policy issues a new administration will face. Now let's turn to the practical details of how to make policy in a way that responds creatively to the world and the challenges the two of you have described. I'd like to ask you to put on your old national security advisor hats and speak, in very practical terms, about what a new president could do in the first one hundred days to enable him- or herself to respond to the world we've talked about. Brent?

BRENT SCOWCROFT: The world has changed, but the structures we employ for national security, essentially the National Security Council and its associated apparatus, were built for the cold war. The National Security Act of 1947 established the NSC, set up the

Air Force, set up the CIA and the Defense Department. All of this was constructed for the cold war, based on lessons learned from World War II. That structure hasn't changed. We have proliferated the NSC in a way: Clinton added a National Economic Council, Bush added a Homeland Security Council.

So we're beginning to proliferate structures to deal with separate subjects. What we don't have is a system to manage issues that cut across traditional boundaries, for example, partly military, partly combat, partly reconstruction, and partly civil society building. We have no way inside the government to manage those sorts of things. That's one of the first needs of a president.

IGNATIUS: Would you create a new council?

SCOWCROFT: No. But I would look at the National Security Act with a view to modifying it. We made some changes on intelligence, though it's too soon to tell whether they're adequate. The National Security Act specifies, for example, that foreign intelligence is the job of the CIA and domestic intelligence is the job of the FBI. In the cold war that was fine because most of our intelligence collection was overseas. But terrorism makes that differentiation meaningless. Part of the problem we saw with 9/11 was that we had two different agencies, with very different philosophies about how to do things, trying to pass information across a bureaucratic barrier.

Iraq is another example. Once Saddam's government had been destroyed, we set up a U.S. administrator for Iraq. Who did he work for? Well, first he worked for Defense. Then he worked for the NSC. Then he worked for—it's confusing. And in Afghanistan, there is no one in overall charge.

IGNATIUS: Certainly, in Iraq, part of the problem was that real policy-making, real strategy, somehow fell between the cracks in the interagency process.

ZBIGNIEW BRZEZINSKI: That's right.

SCOWCROFT: And even staffing. How do you staff an enterprise to try to rebuild a government? In Iraq we asked for volunteers, because there's no systematic way to do it. You need judges. You need police. You need all kinds of things that we're not organized to provide.

IGNATIUS: Zbig, what would you do in those first one hundred days to get the machinery to fit the problems?

BRZEZINSKI: Well, on the assumption that the next president wants to play an active role in shaping foreign policy, that he or she is not preoccupied primarily with domestic politics—which sometimes is the case—I would first of all urge the next president to choose as his national security advisor a person he knows reasonably well and feels comfortable with.

And with whom he has a kind of communion of mind. That's terribly important. The national security advisor is close to the president, has to see the president often. He has to be willing to exercise authority on the president's behalf, with the confidence that he reflects the president's views. So it ought to be a person with whom the new president feels comfortable, but also a person with stature in his or her own right. I think part of the problem, for example, that Condi Rice encountered throughout her tenure as national security advisor was that she really was outranked by Colin Powell and Donald Rumsfeld. She couldn't coordinate and impose presidential leadership on policy-making.

Secondly, I would tell the president that what is lacking in the U.S. government generally is some effective, centralized strategic planning mechanism. The State Department does its own thing on the assumption that foreign affairs is diplomacy. Defense Department has a myriad of planning agencies. But by and large, there isn't any effective planning organism like the one that existed under Eisenhower, who had a special planning board, I forget what it was called, under Bob Bowie. I think some deliberate effort to recreate that in the White House would be timely. Such a board would also provide a venue for informal consultations between that planning body and congressional leadership, to maintain an ongoing dialogue in the higher levels of the government regarding longer-range plans.

That planning board would, of course, be subordinated to the national security advisor. There are some aspects of that today—you probably had something like it too, Brent. I had Sam Huntington come in as a planner for a while. But I think a more deliberate effort to locate strategic planning in the center of U.S. government and not on its peripheries is essential.

My third point relates to what Brent said—and I think his diagnosis is absolutely right. There's a kind of gridlock that is inherent in functional specialization of the different departments. Part of the reason is the complexity of their structures and the fact that the current arrangements are, as Brent said, a continuation of cold war policies. But they also reflect 150 years of tradition. There's a Department of Foreign Affairs. There's a Department of War, as it used to be called, now Defense. There are other specialized departments. These divisions, I think, have outlived their usefulness.

Now, I don't think a new president can immediately undertake a huge restructuring of the bureaucracy. But if he were to do it partially, with regard to some critical issues that demand immediate attention in the first months of the administration, then he might be able to take advantage of the urgency to launch a somewhat different institutional initiative.

What I have in mind is something like this: It involves essentially three presidential task forces that are not functionally organized, like the Department of State or Defense, but are mission oriented. And each would be headed by a presidential delegate who would be the senior person—equal or even superior to cabinet members—assigned to deal with the task force's issue: global climate, environment, or what have you. If the Democrats win, obviously, Gore would be the ideal person to head a climate task force. It could draw resources from the different departments, but it would run on its own under the presidential delegate.

I would do the same—although this is more problematic and maybe Brent will shoot me down—with two other problems that require immediate attention and much more initiative than we're capable of generating from our current structure. One of the two issues would be the Middle East. I would have a presidential delegate head up a task force to deal with the complex of issues Brent and I discussed regarding the Middle East. Because that's urgent. We don't have much time.

IGNATIUS: Focusing just on the Arab-Israeli dispute? Or would this person also deal with Iran and Iraq?

BRZEZINSKI: Probably all three, because they're interrelated.

The third presidential delegate I would appoint right away would head a task force dealing with alliance relationships. How do we deal with Europe? How do we involve countries like Japan and South Korea in some of the Atlantic Alliance's undertakings? Not to suck them into NATO, but to have a partnership with them that enhances NATO's contribution to global stability. A task force could help overcome the gridlock and quickly generate action on some critical problems that require attention.

IGNATIUS: Isn't there a danger that you'd undercut the secretary of state, who's nominally responsible for those areas?

BRZEZINSKI: Well, the secretary of state is nominally responsible for the world. But as a practical matter, it's too much to handle. As a result, even urgent issues get part-time attention. Look at the Middle East. Rice has tried to give it her attention. While I fault her in part for our policies there, part of the problem is that she's really overworked. There are many other problems that can be handled in a more traditional way, where the urgency isn't so acute, or where there isn't the same need to break through bureaucratic logjams.

IGNATIUS: Certainly, where there's been one address per policy—Chris Hill in charge of North Korea and the six-party talks, Nick Burns on relations with the European allies and forming a united policy on Iran—there's been more success and effectiveness. So that argues for your approach.

Brent, the interagency system was created precisely to enable the White House to form ad hoc task forces, if you will, to deal with urgent policy matters. Under the National Security Council, you'd have representatives from State, Defense, CIA, and other relevant agencies meeting together to hammer out policies. That doesn't seem to have worked so well under this administration. And frankly, I'm not sure it worked very well during the Clinton administration either. But you had a lot of success with it under Bush I. How can this interagency process be made to work better so it's more dynamic and flexible?

SCOWCROFT: The interagency process works fundamentally the way the president wants it to work. Each administration has done essentially the same thing in a little different way, depending on how the president wanted to work. I don't think there's any magic to it. At this level, things are very heavily personality driven. As Zbig mentioned, in the first Bush term, Condi Rice was junior to Powell and Rumsfeld. In fact, national security advisors have always been junior to all of the statutory members of the NSC in rank.

IGNATIUS: In rank, but not really—

SCOWCROFT: In rank. But the national security advisor needs to be able to speak with the authority of the president. That's the key. On this convening of ad hoc groups, I don't want to overburden the national security advisor. But suppose you made all of the cabinet secretaries members of the NSC, but they would only attend meetings depending on what the subject was. Each cabinet officer would have a liaison in his department called the NSC cell. You would essentially do the same things Zbig is talking about, but you wouldn't have one group off here and another group over there, operating separately. They're still tied together, but you can have enough division of responsibility to make it work.

I don't know if that would be a better structure or not. You're absolutely right, Zbig, that there's a serious problem. The National Security Council staffs that you and I had are dwarfed by this one now.

IGNATIUS: I'm curious about numbers. How many people did you have working for you, Brent?

SCOWCROFT: I fought hard to keep the number of principals, substantive people, under 50.

IGNATIUS: What was it for you, Zbig?

BRZEZINSKI: About the same. I think we started with 35 and ended up with just about 50. Plus support staff, military, CIA. A full staff of 125 to 150, right?

SCOWCROFT: Yes. It's much bigger now. I had one deputy.

BRZEZINSKI: Same here.

SCOWCROFT: There are seven now. It has gotten unwieldy. One of the enormous advantages of the NSC for a president is its agility. If a president calls a department to ask for something, it can take forever to get it. The NSC can operate very quickly. It's important to preserve that capacity for instant response to the president. But the span of authority is getting so wide that the agency can't cover all the areas it needs to cover and still maintain that instant response.

BRZEZINSKI: Let me make another point about what the new president needs. It's something which is very hard to convey. But my experience taught me that it's very, very easy for even the most independent-minded, self-critical president to get a swelled head in no time flat. The atmosphere in the White House is so conducive to flattery, and to elbowing in order to get in the good graces of the president, that it's very easy for a president to lose a sense of reality about himself and, in the larger sense, about the world.

The president has to have, both in the domestic area and in foreign affairs, some people who are not charged with line responsibility but who are his confidants. It has to be somebody that McCain or Clinton or Obama has known well for a long time, who can be the person who says to the president privately, "That was awfully stupid, what you said," without any fear of losing their influence or their access. That's absolutely essential, especially in as complicated a world as the one we have been discussing.

SCOWCROFT: Zbig, that's called "kitchen cabinet."

BRZEZINSKI: Yeah, sort of, maybe. But not in the sense that these people offer alternative policies or make decisions. But simply keep a critical eye out and inform the president frankly, unabashedly, of problems they see on the horizon or of inadequacies and shortcomings. I don't know how to define it. But something like that.

What really strikes me when I watch the operations of Bush's two administrations, and when I think about my own, and LBJ's, is the really destructive role of flattery.

IGNATIUS: Did you feel you could be honest with President Carter?

BRZEZINSKI: Yes. But I knew him well before. I did it at first very easily and then, after a while, deliberately. It wasn't easy in that atmosphere. I had to say to myself, "My job is to tell him." But I would only do it one-on-one. And I can say this much: I really did bug him on issues. I really did. I would go back and I would argue and so forth. Only once in the entire four years did he object. I remember that vividly: His secretary appeared in front of my desk and very ceremoniously put an envelope in front of me. The envelope was the green presidential stationery, and it was addressed "Zbig." She kind of stood there. She obviously knew what was in it. And I opened it up.

And it said: "Zbig, Don't you ever know when to stop? JC." Now, let me tell you, I appreciated it. He didn't lose his temper. He wasn't yelling at me. He wasn't intimidating me. He was just saying, "Come on. Lay off after a while." I really appreciated that.

IGNATIUS: Brent, your relationship with George H. W. Bush was special. What was it like between the two of you?

SCOWCROFT: This is what I said earlier. At this level, it's all personality. I had a very close relationship with President Bush. I worked for three different presidents, and each liked to get his information, advice, and do his decision-making in different ways. And you've got to accommodate that while doing your job. Because if they don't like the way they're being served, they'll set up another system they like better. Then you've got competing voices and organizations, and that doesn't work. A new structure may be needed, but it must have the flexibility to suit any president.

IGNATIUS: Could you tell Bush I if you thought he was off base? He's such a gentleman, I would think it might be harder sometimes to confront him.

SCOWCROFT: Well, it depends how you do it. Again, it depends on the personalities. I tried a few different approaches with him. But the bottom line is, it's important that the national security advisor tell the president what you think he or she needs to know.

BRZEZINSKI: Absolutely. Absolutely.

SCOWCROFT: Not what he wants to hear. And that can be tough.

BRZEZINSKI: And you can do it in a nice way. Or you can do it in a more assertive way—I don't know how to describe it. But you can do it.

SCOWCROFT: Well, you have to tailor it to the personality.

BRZEZINSKI: Because you have to be yourself. The president chose you. Therefore he liked what you are.

IGNATIUS: One recurring problem for both Condi Rice and Steve Hadley as national security advisors has been the very strong role of the vice president, who has operated, sometimes, as his own national security advisor, and whose staff has sometimes operated as a parallel NSC staff. I wonder if you both would agree that the next vice president from either party should be very careful not to set up what is, in effect, a competing NSC staff.

BRZEZINSKI: Oh, yes. I estimate that the vice president's foreign policy staff is nearly as large as the modest staffs that Brent and I headed.

SCOWCROFT: But almost.

BRZEZINSKI: Almost. I think it's about thirty people. That's unthinkable to me. And I don't think I would have been able to do my job if Vice President Mondale had had a staff that size. He had one person. I took his principal foreign policy advisor and made him my deputy, because I liked him and I also thought it would be good for my relationship with the vice president. But to have this competing staff advocating policy, preparing papers, and injecting itself into the NSC process I think would be just chaotic.

IGNATIUS: Brent, when Bush Sr. was vice president, he was very active on foreign policy. But it didn't seem to create the same problems.

SCOWCROFT: Yet again, it's an issue of personalities.

IGNATIUS: Were you with him then?

SCOWCROFT: No, I was not. And to me, it doesn't matter how big the vice president's staff is. It's what happens to the information and with what authority it gets to the president. The president can use anybody he wants as an advisor. The vice president can be his principal advisor if the president wants him. Most presidents have not, for a variety of reasons.

But there has to be some centralized organization to make the system work. If you have competing systems, you have chaos. That's the chief problem. And it needs to be flexible enough so that the president can do the kinds of things in the manner he finds comfortable. But you also have to preserve the essentiality of a system that's able to operate quickly and efficiently to provide the president what he needs. If the president says he wants everything to go through the vice president, that's the president's prerogative. But then he needs a different system.

And it's toying around with the system that tends to destroy it.

BRZEZINSKI: There's another aspect to it, which also is worth mentioning. Most people don't realize how much paper flows to the president from the secretary of state, the secretary of defense, the CIA, in addition to what the national security advisor generates through his staff. The volume is impossible. One of the problems that has to be dealt with is that the national security advisor ultimately cannot simply become a postman. Papers come in from the secretary of state with a note on top saying "For the president." That doesn't help. You have to be able, with the president's approval, to discriminate between what should go to the president and what the national security advisor can handle on the president's behalf, in the confidence that he knows, more or less, the president's mind and sends it back, either to the department from which it originated or to other departments if the thing has to be coordinated. That's a very tricky business that also requires a great deal of the national security advisor's personal time.

IGNATIUS: In thinking about how to reshape this machinery so that it fits the world of the twenty-first century, I'm reminded of my colleague Tom Friedman's phrase, "the flat world." Our world is less hierarchical. It's horizontal—you connect across boundaries. You don't, ideally, have to communicate up through smokestacks. That's an enormous benefit, but it creates interesting challenges for foreign policy. You have a world in which people can connect in ways you can't predict or control. Can this hierarchical machinery you've been talking about be adapted so that it embraces the flat world rather than fighting it?

SCOWCROFT: President Nixon tried this. He tried clumping his cabinet officers, naming one the senior in a group. It didn't work, mostly because—this is true in my experience, too—cabinet officers will not work for each other. You cannot put a cabinet officer in charge of other cabinet officers. It just doesn't work very well as a flat system.

IGNATIUS: But does it need to? In the intelligence community, we're taking different agencies—different stovepipes—and we're insisting that they connect the dots, that they collaborate. And we're creating technologies—there's now a kind of Wikipedia for intelligence—where people are constantly interacting and creating databases and sharing them. Things the intelligence community thought it could never do in terms of information-sharing are now happening every day. But that hasn't moved generally across the government. I wonder if you think it's time to experiment with that on an issue like, say, climate change.

SCOWCROFT: But, David, it didn't happen in the intelligence community because of a flat organization. It happened because the leadership said, "You will start sharing information." They set up rules for doing that, and they then enforced the rules. That change in procedures is still not complete. I don't know whether a flat way would work. But I think we could agree that one of the first areas of focus for a new president, if he hasn't already started thinking about it during the campaign, is this organizational issue we have been discussing. It's a serious problem and addressing it ought to be one of his first areas of concentration.

BRZEZINSKI: Let me make one additional point. I think the president has to be very conscious that he has some grave problems on the agenda when he comes to office. But he also has a finite amount of time during which he is capable of mobilizing the political support of Congress and the public by virtue of his newness in office and his electoral victory.

Therefore, the new president ought to make a very conscious choice which issues require the most immediate attention. My earlier point about mission-oriented task forces is related to this. Of the geopolitical problems we discussed—and Brent may have a different list—I would say the complex issues of the Middle East are the top priority. The other issues, perhaps, can be dealt with more on a kind of a continuum and in a more traditional fashion.

SCOWCROFT: I would divide it a little differently. The Middle Eastern problems I would specifically break up. The Palestinian peace process is a separate unit which, if it's not solved in this administration, could well disintegrate rapidly. Iraq and Iran are huge ongoing problems. Afghanistan is another one. Pakistan may be a fourth one. All of these will require and get the president's attention, whether he wants to think about them or not. Even if he's a domestically oriented president, he doesn't have any choice but to start on these issues.

BRZEZINSKI: When I was national security advisor, I prepared a list of sort of global priorities for the president, with a write-up on each. I believe I had about ten, and I had some notion of what ought to be at the top. What struck me was that President Carter wanted to deal with all ten right away. That's also where the national security advisor can be useful, in helping the new president prioritize these issues.

▶ ▶ ▶

IGNATIUS: The new president will come into office in a world that is very angry at the United States. I can't remember, in my lifetime, a time when the world was more hostile to the country.

BRZEZINSKI: Historically, it never has been.

IGNATIUS: Any of us who travels around the world sees that and feels it. Maybe our biggest national security problem is that unpopularity. What could the new president do, right at the beginning, in this first hundred days, to turn that page and say to the world, "This is no longer the United States that you've become accustomed to dealing with."

BRZEZINSKI: Well, look, he could close down Guantanamo. He could outlaw torture. He could put more emphasis on civil rights. He could say, "Let's bury this culture of fear and have a sense of proportion about the threats that we face." And if America is confident and true to its principles, I think these things would happen. Of course, the larger policy issues would still need to be addressed.

IGNATIUS: Brent, what do you think?

SCOWCROFT: I think one of the first things he could do is to say, "The United States is a powerful country, but we don't have all the answers to the issues facing the world. We need help. We need the help of every straight-thinking government around the world. And we're going to seek that help. I want to reach out, to work with anybody who is trying to make this world a better place." And then implement that pledge. One of President Bush's real virtues, Bush Sr., was his use of the telephone. At first I was against it. I thought it was a very risky thing for heads of state to do. But he used it brilliantly around the world, to build a friendly climate of relationships. He didn't call just to ask his counterparts for support on issues. He called to say, "How are you? How are things going?" So when he did call on something specific, he had a receptive atmosphere. I think that's tremendously important. The United States is the only nation that can mobilize the world to take on these great global problems. But we can't do it if everybody dislikes us.

IGNATIUS: We often think of strategic communication in terms of finding effective ways for us to speak more loudly or more clearly. But strategic communication, sometimes, is strategic listening. I think that's a great gift that Bush Sr. had. I think, at his best, Jimmy Carter was a good listener.

BRZEZINSKI: And sometimes we need to speak more modestly. Reinhold Niebuhr, writing in 1937, has a wonderful passage, to the effect that the more a civilization approaches its downturn, the more fervently it proclaims its supremacy. There's a warning in that. We have tended, in recent years, to define world affairs in Manichaean terms. We are the epitome of right. Those who are not with us are against us. Those who are against us are by definition evil. I think we ought to be a little more modest about our place in the world.

▶ ▶ ▶

IGNATIUS: In that spirit of self-criticism, let me ask each of you to think back to your time in government, and recall mistakes that you or your presidents made. Because as we think about how to put the world back together, it's useful to remember things that you've learned from experience are potentially dangerous. Zbig, do you have thoughts about that?

BRZEZINSKI: Sure. You can't do too much all at once. That's one problem. Two, you can't ignore the fact that, to be effective, you have to have sustained political support. And therefore you have to be somewhat flexible about your priorities. I think that without arguing as to who was right or wrong specifically within the administration, our policy in dealing with the crisis with Iran was not sufficiently clearly defined.

IGNATIUS: You needed one policy, whichever way you went, and—

BRZEZINSKI: Yes. Implemented assertively and early. Which means either Cyrus Vance or I should have been completely overruled. Instead, in effect though not in intent, we tried to follow both strategies at the same time. I could give you another example, after which I'd be glad to give you a list of things I think we did well—and which would be longer.

IGNATIUS: Brent?

SCOWCROFT: In the early days of the Bush administration, there was an attempted coup in Panama. We didn't know who the coup plotters were or what they represented. We knew almost nothing about motivation or support. We had good communications with Panama but through parallel channels of information. The State Department had its communications; the CIA had its communications; so did Defense.

We had an NSC meeting to analyze the situation, and the participants all had different stories. We were, in effect, operating blind, because we had no coherent picture. It showed me the necessity of closer coordination within our government, so I set up a deputies' committee that would meet periodically, once a week or as often as needed, to make sure that everybody in the NSC, all the principals, had the same information. That worked immensely well. It worked, also, with the issue of the papers that everybody sends up. We let the deputies' committee look at them first. This worked, for me, very well. Again, it depends on the people involved.

But how you coordinate and keep people informed is one of the crucial jobs. For example, the secretary of state and the secretary of defense see the president maybe once a week or less. As national security advisor, I would see him perhaps a dozen times a day. They have to have faith that they're being fairly represented in your discussions with the president. And that you're telling them the things they need to know that the president tells you. If the defense secretary and secretary of state don't have confidence that you're conveying their views honestly and accurately, they'll insist on discussing everything separately with the president. The president doesn't have time for that. So you have to establish yourself as truly an honest broker. That's impossible to do perfectly. But without it, the system—at least my system—breaks down.

IGNATIUS: I think most students of this subject would say that you got that closer to right than any national security advisor in modern times. That you had a strong personality, but you managed to submerge it so that you were not seen by your cabinet secretaries as a rival for the president's attention.

SCOWCROFT: Well, I don't know about that.

BRZEZINSKI: I'll say yes.

▶ ▶ ▶

IGNATIUS: For me, one of the paradoxes of this new world is that in economic terms, globalization is a seamless and highly efficient process for making decisions. Global companies manage to react to developments in the world with astonishing speed. They draw the best and the brightest, literally from around the world. If you go into Goldman Sachs or a well-managed technology company in Silicon Valley, you'll find a remarkably diverse group of Chinese, Indians, Africans, Pakistanis, and Americans, all working together, collaborating, overcoming differences in culture and language. And the company responds very efficiently to the challenges it faces.

Yet in the world of government, we find rigid structures, often based on models that come to us from the nineteenth century or before. And none of that flexibility. I just wonder, as we think about how a new administration could make the right connections with this new world, whether there's a way it could emulate what corporations do so effectively. Is that hopeless? Is it a hopeless dream that a government agency could operate as effectively as a corporation?

SCOWCROFT: I think so, because the order of merit is much simpler in the business world. There are so many goals and interests that the government has to answer to, that the measure of efficiency is much more difficult.

BRZEZINSKI: And shareholders don't have the same leverage over corporate decisions that citizens have every two years in our political system.

IGNATIUS: It's tough to vote out the CEO, that's for sure.

BRZEZINSKI: That's a significant difference.

▶ ▶ ▶

IGNATIUS: I've got one last question for you. The last seven years have seen an increasing polarization of debate in Washington about everything, including national security. The common ground on which Republicans and Democrats once stood when they were thinking about foreign policy has shrunk and shrunk, almost disappeared. I want to ask you to talk about how some measure of consensus could be recreated by a new president and how you'd go about doing it.

BRZEZINSKI: I think it really is essential that the next president, whoever that is, make a very deliberate, symbolic effort to create bipartisanship. And that means appointments. It would be great if a Democratic president appointed a Republican—and I can think of some names—as secretary of state. Senator Hagel comes to mind, for example. But there are others.

Or in some other key position. The same is true of a Republican president: he ought to appoint a Democrat. I think the last several years have divided us substantively, because there are real differences of opinion. But we have also been driven further apart in our world views. These divisions are damaging in that they compound the uncertainty felt by the rest of the world about us, which then reinforces our anxiety, which then degenerates into fear. They reduce the sense of shared direction, of confidence on the grand issues of the day. So I think one of the tasks of the next president will be to do the few simple, obvious, not terribly difficult things to promote bipartisanship through his power of appointment.

IGNATIUS: Brent, what other ways could you rebuild this bipartisan base?

SCOWCROFT: I would agree with what Zbig has said. I think it's a Washington attitude that has been reinforced by the recent changes in the world. In past years, when we were faced with a threat, we subordinated partisan differences.

Recently we've gotten out of the habit. The Vietnam War and Watergate were terribly destructive to our sense of community. That bitterness has persisted and even grown. I think it's been accentuated by an increasing gulf between the executive and the legislative branches. Our presidents used to call congressional leaders down for a drink in the evening, just to talk. They used to bring the opposition into the cabinet room for discussions. These kinds of things are critical to establishing a sense of cooperation. Partisanship is a narrow, tactical thing. It should not be strategic and interfere with the business of government. I think the divide between Capitol Hill and the executive branch has grown ever wider. Meanwhile the Hill itself has gotten more sharply divided.

That has carried over into statecraft, where it truly is corrosive. And again, the key is the attitude of the president. Whether it's appointing people or in some other visible measure, he has to keep reaching out. And to keep emphasizing that he's making national decisions.

IGNATIUS: That we're in this together. Well, I have to say, one of the pleasures of these conversations has been to sit with a prominent Republican and a prominent Democrat—

BRZEZINSKI: Which one is which?

IGNATIUS: I often am not sure. And that's the great thing. The two of you, who are veterans of these battles, really are able to get outside of the narrow party lines and limits, and talk together to try to come up with new ideas about very tough problems. And if the two of you can do it, I hope the new president and the Congress can do it too.

—April 3, 2008

ACKNOWLEDGMENTS

T HESE CONVERSATIONS were taped at the offices of Perseus LLC in Washington, D.C. The authors would like to thank Frank Pearl, Allyson Rhodes, Libby Getzendanner, and Cynthia Taylor for their gracious hospitality.

The taping and production of recorded CDs was expertly managed by Andrew Doucette and Jamie Doligosa of Meeting Tomorrow, Inc. Transcript Associates produced the transcripts. Christine Marra of Marrathon Production Services guided the book through editing and design.

The New America Foundation provided significant support for this book. The authors wish to thank Steven Clemons and Steven Coll of NAF for their enthusiasm and help, as well as John Sherer, Michele Jacob, and Alix Sleight of Basic Books for their efforts.

The two authors would like to thank their closest associates for their assistance. For Brent, Terry Lacy, his legal advisor, led him through the legal intricacies involved, while for Zbig, Leona Schecter, his agent, did likewise. The respective secretaries, Gail Turner for Brent and Diane Reed for Zbig, managed the endless scheduling difficulties and resolved various administrative dilemmas. For Brent, Ginny Mulberger as well as Arnie Kanter and Eric Melby were critically helpful in preparing and clarifying the transcripts for publication, and Brett Edkins rendered equally important assistance in this role for Zbig.

Both authors wish to thank David Ignatius for a superb job of guiding and directing our discussions, and they acknowledge Bill Frucht's vital contribution in clarifying our intent, as well as constraining our occasional semantic excesses.

To all of the foregoing, our very sincere gratitude.

Zbigniew Brzezinski
Brent Scowcroft

INDEX

China (*continued*)
  Iran nuclear weapons and, 72,
    186
  leadership, 65, 116–117, 118,
    120–121
  lobby in U.S., 135
  nuclear weapons, 133
  Olympics, 120, 220–221
  "One China, several systems,"
    123, 125
  in open systems, 115, 116, 134, 140
  revolutionary China, 65
  as rising power, 27, 113–114,
    115–116, 121, 125–126, 133–134,
    147–148, 219
  Russia and, 133, 173, 175, 181–182,
    183–184
  six-party talks on North Korea,
    127–129
  Taiwan and, 120, 122–123, 124–125,
    135
  Tibet and, 118, 120–121, 123–124,
    125, 126, 220
  trading relationships, 135–136
  U.S. competition and, 115–116
  U.S. indebtedness to, 147–148, 150
  U.S. policy with, 119, 120–121, 122,
    131–134
  U.S. tariffs against, 150
  value system and, 114, 115
Clash of civilizations, 238–241
Climate change, 2, 28, 223, 230, 233,
  244, 245–246, 257
Clinton, Bill, 9, 254
Clinton, Hillary, 237

Cold war
  U.S. planned response to attack,
    4–5
  U.S. strategy/attitude, 2, 4, 7
Cold war end
  change in world environment, 3,
    5–6, 8–9, 13–14, 29
  end of empires, 8, 14
  end of World War I and, 8, 14
  events ending, 6–7
  international organizations and,
    29–33, 230–231
  missed opportunities with, 9–10
  U.S. in 1990s, 13, 14–15
  U.S. reaction and, 6–7, 163–164
Cold war mentality, ix, 4, 14, 29–30,
  230
Communication changes with
  globalization/Internet, 32, 65,
  227–229
Congress of Vienna (1815), 61
Cultural Revolution, 65
Czech Republic and U.S. defense
  installations, 191–195
Czechoslovakia, 158, 161, 213

Dalai Lama, 120, 123
Danish cartoons, 228
De Gaulle, Charles, 190–191
Democracy
  crackdowns against
    prodemocracy movements,
    141–143
  dividing world into "democracies/
    nondemocracies," 140

ABOUT THE AUTHORS

Zbigniew Brzezinski, formerly President Carter's National Security Advisor, is a counselor and trustee at the Center for Strategic and International Studies and professor at Johns Hopkins University. His many books include the *New York Times* best seller *Second Chance*.

Brent Scowcroft served as National Security Advisor to presidents George H.W. Bush and Gerald Ford, and as Military Assistant to President Nixon. He is president of The Scowcroft Group, an international business and financial advisory firm. He is also the co-author, with former President George H.W. Bush, of *A World Transformed*.

David Ignatius writes a twice-weekly column for *The Washington Post*. He was previously executive editor of the *International Herald Tribune*. Before joining the *Post*, Mr. Ignatius spent 10 years as a reporter for *The Wall Street Journal*. His seventh novel, *The Increment*, will be published in 2009.